TAKE ME HOME

TAKE ME HOME

An Autobiography

JOHN DENVER

WITH ARTHUR TOBIER

ISBN: 1-4959-5876-0
ISBN-13: 9781495958762

To

ZAK, ANNA KATE,

and

JESSE BELLE

CONTENTS

Contents

ACKNOWLEDGMENTS

I would like to give thanks to the following people who helped me with my recall, when memory failed, and who otherwise abetted me in the making of this book: my mother and my brother, Ron; Milt Okun; Abe Deutschendorf, who is the keeper of the family archives on my dad's side; my son, Zachary, my daughter, Anna Kate, and their mother, Annie Denver; Joe Henry, Tom Crum, Kris O'Connor, Steve Voudouris, Steve Matty, Malcolm McDonald, and Joan Candee; Kathy Mulvaney for typing voluminous transcripts; and the guys who made up the core of my band for so many years and through so many changes: James Burton, Glen D. Hardin, Jim Horn, and Jerry Scheff. Also Mike Taylor, Dick Kniss, John Sommers, Steve Weisberg, David Beecham, Doug Gentile, Ron Lemire, and Barney Wyckoff.

Special thanks to my manager, Hal Thau, who provided the initiative and the encouragement for this project; to my editor Shaye Areheart of Harmony Books, who wanted to do this book in the first place; and most of all to Arthur Tobier, without whom this book would not be between two covers.

INTRODUCTION

For close to three decades, John Denver has earned international acclaim as a songwriter, performer, actor, environmentalist, and humanitarian. He has been acknowledged for his music and his environmental work by Presidents of the United States and by heads of state in many foreign countries. He is idolized and revered by millions of people, yet when I am asked about John, my first thoughts always reflect our deep friendship; in many ways he is the brother I didn't have but always longed for.

We have been close for more than twenty years. So much has happened in that long moment of time that these days I often find myself thinking, How did it begin? How did it all come to be?

My thoughts wander back to one of his major concert tours years ago. My recollections always start with John's music . . . it's always the music.

He stands alone in jeans and a simple satin tunic loosely belted at the waist. He smiles in quiet acknowledgment of the crowd's thunderous welcome. Flashbulbs from thousands of cameras detonate and glittering stars fill the darkness. Another John Denver concert begins.

I am sitting six rows from the stage in the New Haven Coliseum with my wife Dorothy and our two children, Michael and Amy. My children, like a great many children around the country, have grown up with John Denver and his music, and I have found that John has a tremendous rapport with young people; they, more than others, sense the reality and honesty of the man, which is poignantly reflected in his songs and his singing.

It's the fifth performance in a sixty-two-day, fifty-two-city concert tour of the United States. Last night: a sellout performance in Madison Square Garden. Tomorrow: Buffalo. Then down the Eastern Seaboard and west to Los Angeles. The stage has been set up in the round, center arena, and along with everyone else, Dorothy, Michael, Amy, and I are under the luminous spell John creates at each performance.

Moments before the house lights dimmed, the Coliseum manager breathlessly informed me that eighteen thousand people were here—a new house record had been set. The audience is, as always, composed of both men and women, some old, some young, many in their thirties, forties, and fifties, all roaring their approval as the announcer booms through the darkness, "Ladies and gentlemen, John Denver!" And then John's voice soars above the din, soothing us and unifying us with his masterful songs, many paeans to the joys of a natural world. We listen and allow ourselves to respond; we become part of his poetry. There he is, one man holding thousands of people with the clear, pure sound of his music. Even after so many years, I am still overwhelmed by the power of his artistry.

John will sing thirty songs tonight and every night of the tour. He will sing and accompany himself on a variety of guitars, without interruption, for two hours and twenty minutes. Although this will be a grueling tour, his performances will only get stronger as the tour continues. John is very focused and will stick to a routine once started, plus he has the determination and will to keep fit to the end of a long concert tour.

As always, the music to be presented—its sequence, staging, orchestration, and arrangements—has been carefully thought through. There is no need for gimmickry or elaborate special effects. Onstage, John works with some of the best studio musicians in the business, people who ordinarily do not take on the rigors of a tour such as this, but who have instead welcomed the opportunity to travel and work with him.

Before John has finished the first song, it will no longer matter that the arena, like so many of its counterparts, is utilitarian and without intimacy or charm. John and the band will have created a closeness between the audience and themselves that usually exists only in a small piano bar. Throughout the evening the audience alternately sways with eyes closed, claps, taps their feet as the rhythm of the show changes as John moves from beautiful ballads to country rock and back again. I find the most treasured moments are when John is singing one of his ballads and thousands of people are so attentive and so quiet that one can almost hear the proverbial pin drop.

As any performer will tell you, some concerts are more special than others and tonight is extraordinary; the audience knows it and responds unabashedly. Yalies and townies alike stomp their pleasure, agreeing that it really *is* good to be alive.

One question that I've been asked over and over again is how John and I came to work together. It's a story I love to tell when I have time to remember all the details. We were both pretty young and hungry for what life had to offer.

◆   ◆   ◆

The spring of 1965 was a time of protest and upheaval. I was an accountant from the Bronx, just beginning to establish myself as a business manager for some promising young comedians and jazz artists. Through the latter, I met Milt Okun. A major folk music figure, Milt produced records for, among others, Peter, Paul and Mary, who were then at the height of their careers, and for the Chad Mitchell Trio, which was also enjoying substantial success. From time to time, Milt and I would meet at his studio and discuss the music business. We were both enjoying the rewards of folk's immense popularity, but were also aware that it would only be a matter of time before folk would be edged out in popularity by other musical styles.

Milt is a little older and has always been a strong, settling father figure for me and others to lean on. Although financially successful as a leading music publisher and record producer, Milt is a devoted family man whose life-style is the antithesis of what people might call "life in the fast lane."

I've always liked Milt's style, his quiet, thoughtful approach to his work, and have always welcomed opportunities to drop by the studio. It was during one of these cracker-barrel sessions that Milt first mentioned John Denver. He had been searching for a lead singer to replace Chad Mitchell, who was leaving the trio to do a Broadway show. Milt had received over 250 demo tapes from hopefuls, including one from John, who was trying to establish himself on the West Coast. What is extraordinary is that John's demo wasn't particularly good and had it been any-one other than Milt listening to it, the tape probably would have been relegated to the reject pile.

Instead, Milt invited John to New York for an audition. As

luck would have it, John had a terrible cold and the audition was anything but impressive. In addition, he tried to perform in a style that he thought would be what Milt Okun was looking for rather than singing like himself. He left New York for a singing engagement in Phoenix, Arizona, with Milt's quietly modulated "Don't call us, we'll call you" lodged in his mind. John told me later that he refused to leave the hotel room during the day lest he miss Okun's call. He wanted the job so badly, he didn't allow himself to consider the possibility that Milt might not contact him. John says he stared at the telephone for hours on end, leaving his hotel room only in the evening to play at the Lumbermill. The anticipation was driving him crazy; he couldn't eat, couldn't sleep, and was unwilling to leave that tiny room until he heard from Milt Okun. Ten days later, John received a call from Milt informing him he was the new lead singer.

At about the same time, Milt asked me to drop by to discuss the Mitchell Trio's future. Bob Chartoff and Irwin Winkler, who had been handling the group's management, had decided to shift the focus of their business toward what would prove to be a distinguished career in film. Milt suggested that I take over, along with Artie Mogull, who would act as personal manager. Artie Mogull has had a varied career in the entertainment industry. His greatest expertise is in music publishing and as a record company executive, but during the early period of John's career, Artie was trying his hand at personal management. So we were all drawn together as part of the Mitchell Trio's management team. Even though I was well aware that the trio's popularity had already begun to wane, Milt's enthusiasm for the young new lead singer was contagious.

Milt is not prone to hyperbole in describing any artist. He made it clear that he didn't think Denver's voice, at that point, was as developed as Chad's, but by the same token, he felt there was something unique and well worth nurturing in the talented young singer. Most people who choose to work in the entertainment business love to chase dreams, and I'm no different. I knew the group was good and I hoped, of course, they'd be very successful. It was more than enough to get me to agree to take on their financial management in what would prove to be one of folk music's most tenuous periods. Even though audiences were fairly erudite and it was still the predrug era, folk's popularity was on the eve of sinking to a nadir that not even an avowed pessimist could have predicted.

Milt, Artie, and I were convinced that the public would respond to Denver's talent as wholeheartedly as we had, and that in time, he would evolve into a major artist. Artie immediately began booking concert dates.

At best, a concert tour is grueling. Much has been written about the loneliness of the road and the hardships of one-night stands, possibly because many a performer has been made or broken during this time-honored show business apprenticeship. Even today most singers and groups slog their way to stardom playing coffeehouses and college campuses. College dates are more debilitating than most, because campuses are often far-flung, even remote. The routine consists of endless hamburgers in countless Holiday Inns; exhausting, bone-crunching bus trips; plane hops with landings that are best forgotten. The trio was to withstand the rigors of this discipline for three years, from 1965 to 1968. In fact, it was in those often secluded venues that John would perfect his music and meet the woman he would marry.

Our enthusiasm in New York was undaunted until we began

to realize that the more dates the trio played, the more in debt they became. They were, in fact, in serious financial straits. I was particularly disturbed because the concerts the group was giving were terrific. Denver's effect on the audience was real, and his harmonies with Mike Kobluk and Joe Frazier were superb. Yet there was no denying the trio was inexorably heading toward bankruptcy. They were learning that teamwork and good concert performances do not always translate into financial success.

It was a painful moment for me when I had to tell John that the only practical solution to their financial problems would be to disband the group. I also did something I had never done before: I told John that I wanted to continue as his financial manager, even though, as John ironically pointed out, there were no finances to manage. Even so, I felt strongly about his future and was willing to make a commitment to it then and there. John indicated that he felt strongly about our relationship as well, and in later years we have both looked back at our blind commitment to each other as a golden moment in our friendship. Our getting together at that time could be explained as karma, blind faith, even something metaphysical, but as John has said to me, "I knew it was right, and it just had to be."

My respect for John increased constantly during the hard years that followed. During that period, the most important event in John's early life occurred when the trio was playing an engagement in Minneapolis. After the performance, the group visited a fraternity party at a Minnesota college, and John was struck by the beauty of the dark-haired girl who held the signs that read ACT ONE and THE END in a frat-house review that was in progress.

When the trio returned a year later, John sought out Ann Martell and began courting her seriously, spending more than a few evenings in front of a fireplace singing to an audience of one while the snow gathered on the cold Minnesota streets. Whenever John was playing reasonably close, he would visit Ann, sometimes driving one hundred miles a night to take her to the show and back to her campus at Gustavus Adolphus College in St. Peter, Minnesota. Six months later they were married and settled in Minneapolis while Annie finished college and John continued on the road as a single performer. He had insisted on being personally responsible for the Mitchell Trio's debts and refused to let the group file for bankruptcy. It was a staggering load for a young man to bring to a marriage. Moreover, we were all living hand-to-mouth, and my job was to keep the creditors at bay, while John continued to chip away at a debt that wasn't really his. His sense of honor was impressive and he never wavered in his resolve.

I grew to genuinely love John and Annie during those years. They were so honest, and they trusted me to handle everything for them. To this day, if John believes you have the expertise to handle something, he simply lets you do your job. That trust is returned by everyone, and people give more of themselves to him than they would ordinarily. There's no question that those were exceedingly difficult times for all of us, but they were the cement that bonded our remarkable friendship.

During this time Milt continued to lend his support and counsel. In contrast to most so-called creative people in the music industry, who tend to wait until a talent is established before making a commitment, Milt was a positive artistic force from the beginning. Both Milt and I believed that there was a charisma about John that was undeniable and that he was headed for success. Even then his songs had freshness, simplicity, and beauty. Milt and I believed early in the game that everyone would catch the John Denver fever just as we had.

In these early years, John frequently turned to Milt for direction in his music. Okun encouraged John to continue developing his own sound. The dynamics were there and Denver had already begun to develop into one of the best vocal technicians in pop music. Then, as now, John's music related to events and experiences that were relevant to his life. His music has grown as he has grown.

Ironically, John's first big hit, "Leaving on a Jet Plane," was on his first album, *Rhymes and Reasons,* but it was not a big seller until it was recorded as a single by Peter, Paul and Mary. His first million seller came three albums later with "Take Me Home, Country Roads" from the LP *Poems, Prayers and Promises.* "Rocky Mountain High" was released in 1972 and was one of John's biggest successes.

In the fall of 1973, John recorded his first *Greatest Hits* album, and it became the largest-selling album ever released by the RCA Company.

No sooner did we digest that success than the single recording of "Sunshine on My Shoulders" rose to number one on the charts, followed soon by the success of "Annie's Song," and then by "Back Home Again." Wherever you turned, John's work was being played. And, in fact, the music had transcended itself to become true anthems for more than one generation. His songs were being sung at weddings, at funerals, at bar mitzvahs, at church fellowships, at bridge openings, at ship launchings. It was a cultural phenomenon. Unofficially, and unselfconsciously, John became spokesman for an age.

I found the English the most perceptive about John's work. In the April 30, 1975, issue of *Melody Maker,* Ray Coleman began his review of John's British debut at the Palladium (2,300 seats on each of eight nights sold out in ten hours) with unabashed approval:

> *An American friend, the great and tragically neglected singer John Stewart, said to me four years ago: "Watch John Denver. He's a genius. He'll defeat all the cynicism in the world because he's so real. You don't have to think too much about him—just lie back and let his sunshine wash all over you. And you know you'll feel real."*

John Stewart had been lead singer with the Kingston Trio and for a brief time he and John had teamed up and performed together.

By 1975, John was the country's biggest-selling recording artist and had more hit records that year than anyone. He placed number one on *Billboard*'s year-end listing in the categories Top Singles Artist, Overall Pop Artist, Easy Listening Artist, and Country Album. And in *Newsday,* December 10, 1975, one observer of the pop life said, "What Sinatra was to the forties, Presley to the fifties, and the Beatles to the sixties, Denver is to the seventies—a phenomenon." An uncommon phenomenon, I would have added. And uncommon phenomena are intrinsically interesting.

It would have been easy enough for John to settle into a comfortable niche and continue to cut new albums, tape TV specials, write songs, and tour from time to time. Instead, his curious mind kept seeking new endeavors and led him to further broaden his career.

John began to write and work tirelessly on projects that interested him, whether the focus was putting an end to hunger in the world or environmental concerns. In 1976 John formed a charitable organization called the Windstar Foundation, and through his generous financial support, the foundation produced a full-length motion picture about the state of hunger in the world. John's efforts in this field got him appointed to the President's Commission on World Hunger. John took that appointment seriously and still works tirelessly to inform and educate the public about hunger in the world today.

Most recently, John created Plant-It 2000, a foundation that urges people all over the world to plant as many trees as possible by the year 2000. This is a reforestation project aimed at encouraging citizens everywhere to recognize the necessity of replenishing what the world has wantonly destroyed. Plant-It 2000 has met with enthusiasm from people everywhere in all walks of life, including major foundations, businesses, and institutions. Nearly one hundred thousand were planted in its first year.

In the summer of 1993, John was the recipient of the prestigious Albert Schweitzer Music Award, "for a life's work dedicated to music and devoted to humanity." It was the first time a nonclassical music artist had been so honored.

John Denver is an extraordinary man—warm, caring, sure of himself. I feel very lucky to have shared the first part of his journey as chronicled in the pages of *Take Me Home.* He is an uncommon friend and a rare human being.

HAROLD A. THAU
APRIL 1994

When you climb a mountain, you put forth effort with every step, not resting until you reach the summit. When you cross a river you take care with every step, not relaxing your attention until you reach the other shore. Even if you have climbed a mountain nearly to the summit, if you leave off that last step to rest your feet, you are still on the way, not yet there. Even if you have crossed a river nearly to the other shore, if you take a single careless step, there is still danger.

—"AWAKENING TO THE TAO,"
LIU-I-MING
(translated by Thomas Cleary)

You can hitch your wagon to the stars, but you can't haul corn or hay in it if its wheels aren't on the ground.

—MORDECAI PINKNEY HORTON

The superior man stakes his life on following his will.

—CHINESE PROVERB

TAKE ME HOME

ONCE UPON
A TIME

They met in Tulsa. Dad was a ploughboy from western Oklahoma; Mom was a hometown girl. He was in the Army Air Corps, studying the mechanics of flight at the Spartan School of Aeronautics, and she had been first-prize winner in a jitterbug contest the year before. It was 1942: She was just turning eighteen, a high-school senior; and he was twenty-one. Her folks, Peter and Mattie Swope, had a nightclub out near the airport, where Dad's barracks were, and he came in one night for a sandwich and a beer. She and her sister worked there as waitresses, and danced with the boys who came by.

He wasn't much of a dancer, Mom said, and that should have killed it for her right there. If they didn't dance, she didn't want to know them. But she liked his smile—and you can see from the photographs in her album that he was a handsome guy. Very much the clean-cut all-American. She liked the way he was always bubbling with laughter; she liked to laugh, too.

They had known each other for six months and had been going steady for the last two weeks of that time when he finished his training at Spartan. He was to be sent back to Will Rogers Field in Oklahoma City immediately, but a bad tooth kept him in Tulsa an extra couple of weeks. It was enough time: My parents married and just sailed into the wind. Later Dad told Mom that when he met her he had been going with a girl from Southern Baptist College in Texas. A week before their wedding he drove down there to break up with her. What characters they must have been.

At first, her father was going to have none of it. But he thought it over and changed his mind. Mom *had* been a responsible child and she *was* eighteen. Also, we had gotten into the war and everybody was feeling patriotic. So he gave them his blessing, however reluctantly, and that's how it began.

I try to see them objectively, but it doesn't work. In many ways, they're still icons to me. I have to really step back to get a good look at them, and I never seem to get back far enough. The fact that I'm analytical doesn't help. My parents come out of another time, one that was intertwined with older values, different needs—especially my dad. You'd have to steep yourself in the culture to get the full flavor.

Grandpa and Grandma Deutschendorf's families were Germans from the Volga River. In the nineteenth century, at Catherine the Great's invitation, they and other families had gone to Holy Russia to farm some land that needed looking after and to get away from the war that plagued Germany. Just before World War I began, many of the Deutschendorfs uprooted themselves again; that's when some of my relatives came to Oklahoma. There was going to be terrible fighting in Europe soon, and the Oklahoma territory seemed benign by comparison.

According to family legend, Grandpa Deutschendorf immigrated with his mother's sister and her family; he was to serve as their bodyguard. He was eighteen at the time and he was planning to go back to Germany as soon as the family was settled. He knew only one word of English then and that was the name of the town that was their destination: Bessie, Oklahoma. Fate has a way of altering plans; he met my grandmother in that small German community and things were never the same. He fell in love and stayed in America. Looking back on their lives now, I see theirs as such an innocent time.

When the United States got into the First World War, my grandfather, who had not become a citizen, was considered an enemy alien. He got his American citizenship in 1941, a year before he bought the Deutschendorf farm east of Cordell and two years before he died; but in 1917, when we got into the war, he was still pretty much the same person he had been when he came over—a conscientious objector. Four years on American soil hadn't been enough time to give him a new world veneer. Federal agents wanted to take his guns away, and that left hard feelings that probably stayed with him to his dying days, as his livelihood was dependent on hunting. Rather than submit, he hiked to Canada, where that government had a looser policy, and waited out the war.

My grandparents had eleven children. My aunt Anne was the oldest; then came Dad, who they called Henry John—Grandpa was John Henry and I am Henry John, Jr.—and nine more boys, enough to field a baseball team. They took their baseball seriously, too, let me tell you. Dad was one of their pitchers, a big broad-shouldered guy like Dizzy Dean. One of my uncles who admired his pitching thought Dad would have played professional baseball if he hadn't joined the Army when he did.

They lived in Corn, Oklahoma, just above a Cheyenne Indian reservation, on rented farms. The first one, which was 155 acres, was really Grandma Deutschendorf's father's farm, the old Koop homestead, which they rented from the family after Great-Grandfather Koop died. But in 1936 the farm had to be sold and they moved onto an Indian lease, a farm managed by the Bureau of Indian Affairs. It was only thirty acres, so in order to meet their needs, they had to rent another field. They were poor, but they knew how to live poor.

They grew cotton, wheat, and peanuts; had a big garden; kept some cows for milking; went fishing in the Washita River; butchered their own hogs; and hunted for squirrels and rabbits. The hunting dogs Grandpa kept were known throughout the state. What my grandparents didn't grow or catch or make themselves, they'd get at the crossroads store. They always had a year's credit. That might not amount to more than one hundred dollars during the course of a year, but some years in the 1930s they didn't have even that much. They felt bad about not being able to pay their debts. Some of that fear of not having enough and the pride that wouldn't let them admit it was still around when I was growing up. I probably ingested it from the air I breathed at Deutschendorf family get-togethers. The important thing is they never gave up hoping.

My dad's family was a pretty impressive band of people. They worked for themselves the entire four seasons and they worked hard, but they still found time to play and entertain themselves. At night Grandpa Deutschendorf would display his skills as a champion storyteller. When he tired, his musical family picked up the slack. Dad played mandolin, my aunt Anne played guitar, and everybody sang. Old songs they were, about railroads, about mountain life, about the river, about the sky, about living and dying. They were songs that, as far as anyone knew, had been there always.

At the end of the week, which was Saturday afternoon, Grandpa would take the wagon into Cordell and mosey around the town square. He'd find out what was going on in the world, and then he'd come back and share what he thought was worth sharing. I don't think anybody ever questioned his judgment when it came to valuing news and gossip.

Another family legend has it that Grandpa was the strongest man anybody ever knew. One of Mom's sisters called him Bear. He was six feet tall, like Dad, but he weighed three hundred and fifty pounds. Once he was supposed to have lifted a car off a man who was pinned underneath, so that the others could pull him free. He was the giver of all law in my father's family, which was not uncommon in those days, but difficult for us to imagine now. I think Dad really had to earn his stripes as his father's oldest boy. According to Dad, the family would be sitting around the table having lunch and Grandpa would say, "Well, kids, this afternoon why don't we go down to the river and have a swim?" And Dad would say, "Does that include me, Pop?" Grandpa would say, "No, you've got to plow the south forty."

Dad always had responsibilities, a great many of them. His sister and brothers had them too, but his dad expected him, as the oldest son, to bear the brunt of it. When Dad came home on his first Army furlough, he had to wrestle Grandpa in the living room to prove he was a man. It was the discipline of the Old Country. Sometimes I feel like Dad tried to visit that past on me. There were times around the dinner table when I'm certain Dad was taking on the role of his father and casting me as himself as a boy, and that old, formative story was reenacted in ways neither of us could understand or prevent.

At the same time, I think that the values shaped in my grandparents' household were fundamentally democratic ones. Common decency was respected above all else. Grandma's family, the Koops, were Mennonites and Grandpa was brought up in the Evangelical Church, and they both had the open values of the frontier: You didn't judge a man by the color of his skin. My father's upbringing wasn't particularly religious, but he and his sister and brothers were expected to respect their elders, to say grace before meals, and to think good thoughts. As a child I really appreciated what I saw of them. The second youngest, my uncle Dean, wasn't that much older than me, and it was he who gave me the first sense I had of the kind of man I could be.

My mother's family, on the other hand, were Catholics and therefore more formally religious. They were Scotch-Irish and German—hardy stock—but their Catholicism used to bother the Deutschendorfs. There was someone in my father's family who was always sending us literature aimed at converting Catholics to a more—in their eyes—home-grown fundamentalism.

Grandpa Swope had a motorcycle agency in Tulsa where he sold and serviced Indians and Harley-Davidsons until the Depression wiped him out in the mid-thirties and sent him scrambling for things to do to keep afloat. He used to take Mom riding in the sidecar, to motorcycle rallies up in the hill country across the state line, when she was just a little girl.

I think my mother's family experienced the Depression differently than the Deutschendorfs. It wasn't just hard times for them; their business, their livelihood had been taken from them, and it was an intensely felt loss. I'd pick up on this mixture of pride and defensiveness when I went to Tulsa to stay with my mother's sisters. Have you ever heard anybody say, "Well, they're no better than we are"? Mom used to say that all the time. I only have to hear the words to feel again the sense of insecurity that expression evoked in me.

There was a lot of insecurity on Mom's side of the family, with one exception, my uncle Jack, who was my mother's brother-in-law and a big influence in my life. He drove a laundry truck in Tulsa, and I used to ride with him while he did his rounds. He was always up, always smiling; he always had a good word to say. There was a time when a big part of his route went through what white Tulsa called Niggertown, where most of the black families lived. Sometimes we'd stop at a little store there, and there'd be a bunch of black kids around, and he would buy us all ice cream cones. I just thought it was great that he had the time, and the few extra coins, and the interest to do that.

The way he acted was different from the rest of the Swopes, and it registered with me. Where I saw generosity, they saw irresponsibility. I'd overhear them talking: I don't know why he does that; he doesn't take care of his own family. His own kids need this, his own kids need that. They were so insecure about their place in the world that they couldn't see giving anyone else a hand up. They were full of doubts. For instance, Grandpa Swope gave up hoping I'd amount to anything because all he ever saw me doing was playing the guitar. But, ironically, it was Grandma Swope who gave me my first guitar and encouraged me and doted on me. In her eyes, I could do no wrong. She was my number-one fan from the beginning.

The Deutschendorfs and the Swopes: Two more different families would be hard to come by, particularly since they were basically from the same place and should have shared more similarities. It was a lot for a young kid to absorb and sort out. Still, I didn't dwell on these observations, I simply enjoyed myself with the Deutschendorf clan in ways that were special. When we gathered—say at Thanksgiving—all the aunts would have fixed a dish and we'd have a feast. After the meal we'd play softball and visit. The festivities would go on all day. For me it was a supercharged experience of family that would help define who I am.

After my parents were married, Dad went off to Savannah, where his outfit was transferred, and Mom made about seven trips back and forth to Tulsa. You couldn't keep her away from home *or* my father, but it was hard for them to get used to being together all the time. Mom was high-strung and Dad wasn't always the most considerate soul when it came to responding to another person's feelings. He had a way of laughing that could get under Mom's skin. She'd get homesick and hightail it back to Tulsa, and then she'd miss Dad and be off again. Wartime Savannah must have been a maelstrom, but she helped support them by waitressing. I think they were both getting used to it, when suddenly, they were sent to California.

After America had been in the war for about a year, the Army Air Forces (it later became the U.S. Air Force) announced it needed pilots and Dad applied. He was too big to be a fighter pilot, but they wanted him to become an instructor. The Air Forces sent him out to cadet school in Santa Ana, and Mom, throwing caution to the wind, went with him.

By the time I was born at the end of that year—December 31, 1943—we were in Roswell, New Mexico. Dad had started to come into his own; as fate would have it, he was a fantastic pilot, and the problem of his height was never mentioned again. It was the beginning of a dazzling career, with all the tensions that went with it. Mom and I traveled back and forth to Tulsa a lot, mostly for short periods, but once, when I was two, we stayed for a whole year. Mom worked, and when she was gone I was looked after by one of my aunts. The war had already ended and Dad was assigned to a command on Quadjalein Island in the

Pacific to carry out aerial reconnaisance missions. America was testing atom bombs and Dad would fly over the site a few hours after an explosion to photograph the effects. The only word we had from him was by mail and I think that was tough on Mom. In fact, one time she picked up a local paper and read an account of a plane crash that listed Dad as a casualty. She hadn't even been informed. As it turned out, the report was misleading. His plane had crashed, but he hadn't sustained serious injury. You can imagine how something like that, at a time of such limited communication, could tear at your heart.

Dad's next career move took us to Japan, a country of which I have little memory. There are photographs of me there. I started my school life there when I entered kindergarten. Ron, my brother, was born there; I was five. But I carry no vivid images of being in a different country, a different culture. Ron's birth—and all the excitement that follows the birth of a new child—I experienced like an angel falling from grace: "Okay, I'll go; but you'll be sorry."

I was just five years old, and five-year-olds feel things fiercely, but that line became a continuing refrain in my life. It still feels like it is from time to time.

SALAD DAYS

The formal itinerary was Tucson, Arizona; Montgomery, Alabama; Fort Worth, Texas. I'd get to see other places before I set off on my own—Tulsa with Mom and Ron; the summer wheat harvest in western Oklahoma; working one summer as part of a logging crew in the Northwest; and a brief, passionate trip to L.A. when I tried to run away from home. But the main shape of the geography I knew between ages six and eighteen—locations in which I often thought of myself as hiding out—were the places Dad was posted for military duty: a town on the edge of the desert, just a few years after the end of World War II; a town in the Deep South, the year that Rosa Parks sparked the bus boycott that electrified the civil rights movement; and a town in central Texas, the biggest city I'd ever been in, in the years leading up to the Vietnam War. Provincial places all, but complicated environments for a boy to navigate, particularly one like me. I had to go from newcomer to some form of acceptance in each of these communities. I had a tremendous sense of it all—those places, in that time—but I kept my thoughts to myself, folded away. Mostly I felt I was living in a bubble. Very little from outside got through. Busting out of that isolation was a great preoccupation. That was always an undertone of my salad days.

Not that my family lived so badly. We were a part of suburban America—we were Middle Americans. But somehow I thought a mistake had been made. I wasn't supposed to be *there;* I was supposed to be somewhere else. Someone somewhere had given me the wrong itinerary and I was lost in America. I was sure if I thought about it long enough, I'd figure it out.

In Tucson I was the painfully shy Deutschendorf son. Photographs of me at age six, freshly arrived from Japan to become part of yet another new place, show the glazed look of the precociously self-conscious. I practically disappeared behind my shyness. I don't think I felt I had too much to lay on the table in terms of personal identity; I was just Dutch's boy. Of course, I was Mom's boy, too; she was the one who managed all the difficult emotional moments, but Dad's very presence and reputation defined why we were there. He was a captain and cut a very impressive figure: He was loved and respected by his men. I realized this very early and loved and respected him, too. He liked being respected. The love, I think, made him a little uneasy. It used to puzzle him that Mom liked to spend as much time as she did playing with her children. Dad's focus was elsewhere. I always thought of him as a heroic character, and some of that heroic feeling I took onto myself—at least in my daydreams.

From six to thirteen, I was pretty much a loner. I developed only two real friendships in all the time we were in Tucson. They weren't really solid friendships, but I remember these two guys who lived on the same block—George Nuttycomb and Skipper

Gherky—very well. You know how kids are—always wanting to horse around, to fight. I wasn't like that, I didn't like to fight. Maybe I was a physical coward, I don't know, but I always tried to talk my way out of fights by putting myself on a higher moral plane in order to shame my antagonist. I'd say, "Hey, this doesn't solve anything. So you beat me up! Is that going to change how I think, or how you think? Or whether or not we agree with each other?"

I tended to strike a very solemn, very moral tone in all of this. I'd still get picked on because the kids knew I didn't want to fight, but at least I avoided the blows. Naturally, all of this made me more of a loner. I'd get on my bike and go out to the desert. We lived only three blocks from the desert. Sadly, as Tucson has grown, that part of the desert where I spent so much time has become a housing tract. But then it was *desert,* and to a grade-school kid, spending the afternoon there was a journey to a different world. I could play, explore, build forts, relive history—I was dazzled by all of those stories of antiquity we were told about in school. These adventures were a true escape.

When Dad could, he'd take me and one of my two friends out west of Tucson, where there were mountains for us to climb. I could climb anything. In fact, down the street from where we lived, there were three huge eucalyptus trees that I used to scale regularly, especially when Dad wasn't around and I couldn't get to the mountains. I loved to sit in them, so removed from the world below, thinking about the things I wanted to do someday, the kind of person I wanted to be. I would make the trees sway back and forth and suddenly I'd be a member of the crew of a manned spacecraft. It was in those trees that I first fantasized about Windstar, about having a place up in the mountains where people could come together and talk and not feel alone.

Sometimes Dad would take me quail-shooting; sometimes we'd go out through the sagebrush hunting for quail. On the whole, though, Dad didn't have a lot of time for playing. He was an officer and a gentleman and those titles carried with them a real load of social obligation. The military was a very political environment, fraught with conflict and difficulty. And I think my folks were caught up in the classic struggle for professional respectability. They worked hard at it. There were numerous occasions that required Dad's presence, and often Mom needed to be at his side. If you meant to get anywhere in the squadron, you didn't dare miss a commander's call. You had to demonstrate unwavering loyalty at all times. You put in an appearance and you left your calling card to prove you had been in the right place at the right time. It showed that you were disciplined and organized.

When we went to war again, this time in Korea, Dad was busier than ever, alternating between training pilots and flying temporary duty (TDY) for the Strategic Air Command. On TDY, he'd be gone for clips of two and three months at a time and Mom would be left to fend for herself. Ron and I depended on her for everything, which sometimes drove her to distraction—not that she would admit it. There was one year, when Dad was on TDY somewhere up near Newfoundland, when I broke the same arm twice within a period of two months. I broke it the first time rolling around with another kid whose dad was also on TDY. We were over at his family's house, when this boy and I slipped outside with one of his dad's golf clubs. We were taking turns swinging it, and the boy lost his grip. The club knocked me against a tree, I fell, and the fall broke my arm. Two months later, after the arm had healed, I broke it again, jumping off a neighbor's roof. No one remembers what I was doing up there, or how I got up there in the first place, but instead of climbing down, I jumped and crashed on my arm. Mom was beside herself. After I got the arm out of the cast again, she wouldn't let me go outside to play after school unless she was sitting out there watching me, making "darn sure" I wasn't going to break it a third time.

Mom was always eagle-eyed when it came to making sure her boys were well-scrubbed, well-mannered, well-dressed—and well-prepared to meet all contingencies, whatever they might be. I remember she wouldn't let me wear white socks, even though it was the thing to do: The colors I wore had to match. She didn't like the way I rolled my dungarees; she rolled them over, and I rolled them under. She thought I was simply trying to put something over on her. She drove me to school so that I wouldn't have to take the bus. It was she who asked my grandmother to give me her guitar, and it was she who enrolled me in guitar lessons. I was eleven.

She enrolled me in the Tucson Boys' Choir and in the little social functions the Junior League held on Saturdays to help the girls and boys with their social graces. We were taught dancing, and the etiquette of the receiving line: what you said, how you said it, and to whom it was said. Mom was determined that I should be a social success, even as I resisted.

We attended the Presbyterian Church of the Covenant. I should say Ron and I went. Dad and Mom stayed home. Many, many years later, Mom would tell me they stayed home and made love. I always wondered when they did it. Or if they did it. I studied the catechism; I sang in the choir—I loved church music. But around the time I turned twelve, I started to become uncomfortable with going to church. There were probably many reasons, but a couple of incidents suddenly turned me off to organized religion.

Our catechism teacher did something one day that really

broke faith with me. We had done something in class—this group of twelve-year-old innocents—and he was reprimanding us. He was "weeping" for us "sinners" because we weren't taking him seriously enough. He made a big show of it. Except that I saw he really wasn't weeping for us, just trying to make everyone feel uncomfortable, which he succeeded in doing. As a result, we all sort of withdrew into ourselves.

Then later someone raised what I thought was a perfectly legitimate question about one of the parables we were studying, and the teacher refused to respond. The meaning of the parable, he said, had to be accepted as a matter of faith: We couldn't question it. I wouldn't buy that. Twelve-year-old kids have built-in radar for the sanctimonious. It didn't make sense to me that there would be anything that you couldn't question. During that class, I think, I expelled him from my moral universe. I continued going to church, however, for some things I experienced there fed me spiritually.

One time around Easter our minister, a young guy named Dana Prom Smith, gave a sermon in which he tried to explain Judas, and because what he had to say came from a sense of man not from God, he couldn't give the speech from the pulpit. I liked the way he came down into the congregation and talked; I found that small act inspiring. But I had lost connection with the feeling that religion was all about a higher being who understands us and hears our prayers and answers them.

For that matter, I don't think religious feeling occupied much time at home. Neither of my folks was particularly religious in my early childhood. Their families were, but they weren't. In fact, in my house, religion was a prayer at breakfast or at dinner, and it was Dad who led it. It was always the same prayer: Bless this food to our use and us to thy service, and keep us ever mindful of the many who are needy. Grandpa Swope also always said the same prayer.

Keep us ever mindful of the many who are needy. Around the fifth grade, I started to become the social activist I am today. I developed a very special attachment to underdogs. There was a kid I knew named Laurence, who was very big for his age and very slow. For some strange reason he evoked such compassion in me that it almost hurt. One day, up on the court where we played basketball, which sat on a hill away from the classrooms, Laurence and I and a bunch of other kids were playing a game. Among us there was a Mexican kid who was a bully. In the middle of the game, he suddenly started hitting Laurence and throwing the basketball at him, calling him a dummy. It sent Laurence off. He ran off crying and I ran after him. I calmed him down and brought him back to school, which meant a great deal to me. I was very angry with that kid, but I couldn't articulate how I felt. The sense of injustice hit me deeply. Fighting back felt good.

Mom has this memory of me in sixth or seventh grade spending a lot of time with a black kid in my class. Apparently I could never figure out why or how this kid always outraced me. I have no memory of it, but I treasure the story, because it reminds me that even though I was shy, I was competitive; I wanted to win. And the boy? Mom tells me that we played together but I never brought him home. Nothing was said, but at that time blacks and whites didn't live together in Tucson, or anywhere else for that matter, and, while I felt the injustice of it, I didn't raise my voice against it. In fact I was really dismayed to learn in 1957 that we were moving to Montgomery. It was a city of discrimination and hate and the last place I wanted to be. The Montgomery bus boycott was in the news and the place was full of racial tension. But Dad was being transferred to the War College at Maxwell Air Force Base, in order to qualify for greater responsibilities. My concerns were not to be taken seriously in the face of such opportunity. I had just started a new school in Tucson and, as always, this move meant another traumatic start in a strange place. I always got good grades and since that's what Dad and Mom figured school was about, they were unconcerned.

That year—thirteen years old, going on fourteen—was a real divide in my life, geographically and every other way. It might have been, whether I had gone to Montgomery or not, but at least in Tucson I went to school with a racially varied bunch of kids. In Montgomery the schools were segregated, and so were the rest rooms and the drinking fountains—you name it. Segregation went against everything in my education that meant something to me. Living in the thick of it was a grim prospect.

I tried to put a good face on the move. When we drove out of Tucson, I promised myself that I would start life all over again in Montgomery. I kept thinking of my uncle Dean, who wasn't that much older than I was, and of what a positive guy he was. I was going to go there and be positive and happy. But almost immediately after getting to Montgomery, I lost it.

I know it didn't help my frame of mind that on the first day of school my homeroom teacher, who taught civics, interestingly enough, asked if I was an American citizen. Obviously, Deutschendorf didn't sound the right note to her. Oh God, was I embarrassed. And angry, too, that I had to explain the situation. She started to apologize, but I didn't let her finish the sentence. I knew it was a common enough misunderstanding. I knew the school was used to itinerants coming through. But I was still offended. Offended, embarrassed, and intimidated all at the same time.

I signed up for the boys' chorus just to get out of going to this teacher's study hall. I could study on my own time and I knew I didn't need the discipline she could provide. Besides, I liked to sing. I'd show *her* what a Deutschendorf could do. Unfortunately, as it turned out, the boys' chorus had been created for all the school's troublemakers, the guys who teachers didn't want lazing around while other people worked. My simple act of resistance just put me in deeper trouble.

Still, one day in that very class the world turned. I mentioned playing guitar and writing songs and my music teacher asked if I would bring my guitar in and play for the class. She asked me on Tuesday, and on Friday I brought my guitar in and sang for everybody. The decision to "come out of hiding" with my music had been a difficult one. I had written two songs at that point. One was called "Oh My Darling" and the other was called "Lazy Little Stream." I sang one of those. And I also sang Paul Anka's "Diana," with its popular refrain, "I'm so young and you're so old." I probably sang two or three more songs like that—and bang! I was no longer just another Air Force kid living in town for a while. People started to say hello to me in the halls. Suddenly I had friends. I joined a little band. Occasionally we'd travel to neighboring towns to play. I moved up in the world.

But I think I was still basically a loner and an individualist. I know I was still bent on being my own man, still apprehensive about befriending "crackers." I liked the sudden attention, but I wasn't ready to sell out for love and recognition. It hurt me to see how mean-spirited the kids I knew could be. Kids in my class would boast of going to "Niggertown" and throwing eggs at people as part of the weekend's entertainment. I felt ashamed of what was going on.

I don't think the school concerned itself much with these dilemmas or with how the kids related to one another. There was no exploration, that I can recall, of what it took to become a caring, concerned human being. The ethic was us against them, and don't forget it. Those were the only rules that were silently reinforced. *Us against them.* Nothing about us joining with them to make the world a better place.

I became even more sensitive to other people's feelings during that time. It became hard for me to argue with someone when the discussion got really heated. I had such a strong urge not to fight that I became skillful at putting myself in the other person's shoes and seeing his side of the story, even when I disagreed.

To my surprise, I was also becoming very emotional. I think I got that from my mother. You could always see and feel her emotions. They were close to the surface and she was quick to cry. Dad, on the other hand, was raised not to show his feelings. But, despite her highly charged emotions, Mom wasn't able to talk about her feelings, and I think this left its mark on me. I feel things very deeply, but for most of my life, it has been easier for me to talk casually to a thousand people than to talk openly to just one.

I began to experience this in my relations with my father. We started to not get along. I thought he was pretty hard on me about a lot of things. He would hassle me about things that he wanted done, and ridicule me if I didn't come up to snuff. I resented all this. I particularly resented his making me share a room with Ron. Here I was fourteen and we were not only sharing a room, but I had to go to bed when he did, at eight-thirty. It was a gross infringement on my freedom and changed only when I left for college.

Dad was doing a major paper on communism at the War College, and he and I would have moderately strong battles about totalitarianism. I didn't buy his concerns about communism. It seemed Christian enough to me in its social program and I thought there was more totalitarianism in our family than there was in Russia. At least I couldn't see how there could be more restrictions on freedom there. As I grew older, there weren't a whole lot of things Dad and I could talk about without the conversation becoming uncomfortable. To be fair to him, though, Mom wasn't that different. I found it hard to talk to either of them.

We got a boat that year; there were some nice lakes around Montgomery, and I learned to water-ski. I got better as a fisherman. I swam. I got interested in the stars. I loved being outdoors. I spent a lot of time by myself, with my music, trying to express what I felt. It was a difficult year in many ways and I was glad when it was over, particularly since it meant we could leave Montgomery. In some ways, the experiences I had there tempered me and allowed me to grow; but in growing, I passed from the frying pan into the fire.

Fort Worth, about five hundred miles west, was a bigger town, but as far as I could tell, I was trapped in the same bubble. High school was about cars and football and dating. And it was about class, same as it was in Montgomery. Only now I saw the situation more clearly because we moved into Western Hills, which was one of the nicest sections of town, and I went to school with the wealthiest kids in the city. You could tell who they were: They had the nice cars, the best-stocked parties, and the good-looking girls.

They were also just as petty as anyone else, maybe more so. They had the same fears as the kids they derided—the ones I hung out with—only they worked harder at disguising it. They wanted to seem superior. They were the most popular kids in school, and I admit I was a little intimidated by them. I had tiny antennae for registering hurts, and I bristled at their snobbish ways.

For one thing, I had neither a car nor a license to drive one because I was a year younger than most of the kids in my grade. Secondly, I wasn't much of a football player, and in Texas football is everything. I had the desire, I went out for the team, I could catch anything, but I didn't like the physical hammering. I still had an aversion to getting beat up, and that's what it felt like scrimmaging with those guys. I got hit hard and became less and less inclined to let that happen—and it showed. After that I got to play in one game.

Lastly, I wasn't much of a lady's man, although I had plenty of desire to be. There were three dances a year and finally I actually got up the courage to ask a girl in one of my classes to go with me to one. It was bad enough that the girl was older than me, but I had to have my mother drive us there, which was truly embarrassing. I bought the girl a corsage and I wore my first suit. We knew no one at the dance; we hardly knew each other. It turned into a cold, misty night. When I called Mom to come pick us up at the end of the dance, she was afraid to come out on the road: It was too foggy. Dad was off somewhere on TDY, so I had to call my date's parents. Her father and brother came for us—blue-collar workers, both of them—and they made fun of my incapacities all the way home. I never saw the girl again. I had never imagined such misery could exist.

But Dad, on the other hand—with Mom's backing—came into his own as a military man in Fort Worth. He got transferred to the B58 Hustler program and became a big wheel. He was flying the top-of-the-line aircraft, he was squadron commander, and later he was the head of pilot instruction. He won recognition as a master of his profession and broke several speed records, some of which still stand. To this day, I notice when a plane in the sky is flying particularly fast. We all were excited by Dad's feats. He was in his heyday. But I didn't feel any of that power. In fact, I felt quite ordinary, except for my music, which I never allowed to go to my head.

Western Hills looked good, but it was an argumentative and bigoted place: The moral fiber of the community wasn't in good condition, as far as I could see. I wasn't exactly going around championing the underdogs myself, but they had my active sympathies. With all the moving around we had done, I had developed a need for acceptance and I rarely rocked the boat.

My friends were mostly the high-school kids who belonged to the church we joined—and, specifically, kids in the senior fellowship. The fellowship was a Sunday-evening gathering of kids at different people's homes. We'd sing and dance and just socialize. Al and Lois Wagner, a couple without kids of their own, looked after the program and us. I also sang in the choir. Because of these activities I didn't feel as isolated as I had when I first arrived in Montgomery. Through my music, I won acceptance, even at school, by my sophomore year. The kids who had their noses up in the air when I first arrived came around. I moved up through the social strata, but it still felt unreal. We were well-to-do and we were isolated from the hard times others experienced. We had our little place there and it was blissful. The problems that confronted us, we were told, were only those of our own making. We created the problems for ourselves by the way we looked at things! For a short time we worried about going to war with Cuba: Were they going to launch an atomic bomb on us? But on average, the biggest problem kids had was whether or not they were going to get to use the car on Saturday night.

The first summer we lived in Fort Worth I went out to western

Oklahoma and worked on the farm of a friend of Dad's. I was paid a dollar an hour to drive a tractor, and I lived with a family of Mennonites down the road. I didn't have a car and couldn't get around much, but I enjoyed having that work to do: I enjoyed getting out of the bubble. Dad encouraged me to go there because he wanted me to have a sense of what he had experienced at my age. A kid growing up in Bessie, Oklahoma, in the 1930s did what I was doing. Despite Dad's accomplishments in the world, he still wanted me to get a feel for those people. It meant something to him, too, that I enjoyed it as much as I did. For me it was actually exciting because working the harvest had always been what you did when you were a big kid. I spent most of the time by myself on a tractor, going around and around and around the fields in a pretty blissful state, daydreaming and writing songs and thinking of the things that were going to happen in the future. I loved the way the wheat moved across the fields. And even though the wind sometimes churned up choking dust, I loved the smell of it. I reluctantly went back to school after the summer and looked forward all year to returning to the wheat fields.

My relationship with my father continued to decline. I suppose he was under his own kinds of pressures, but I found that to be little consolation. We'd still go out to the lake together and go boating, and we'd have a pretty good time, but I would rarely invite any of my friends. Dad wouldn't let anybody but me drive the boat when he was on skis. I had to do it and I had to do it his way. He was teaching the oldest son and I suffered his instruction badly. Deep below the surface, my complex feelings of rage were all muted.

In those days I retreated into a shell when someone or something rubbed me the wrong way. Once, when a girlfriend hurt me terribly, I went for months without really talking to any-body—not that I had that many bosom pals to talk to. I haunted my room and played guitar; I'd get up in the morning and play songs until my ride to school came, and after school I'd pick up the guitar and begin again. Had I been asked, I would have described myself as a dot: round and flat, without edges or depth. That's how I felt and that's what I thought others saw, too. Only my music could redeem me.

In the summer after my junior year, however, I had an experience which changed my life. I'd gone on a wheat harvest and was staying with my mother's family in Tulsa, prepared for a dispirited couple of weeks before my last year of high school started, when my uncle Dean called to ask if I'd be interested in joining his work crew. They needed someone to drive a truck and I'd gotten my driver's license during the past year. I jumped at the chance. I had always admired Dean: Everybody looked up to him, but we'd never spent much time together. He was the leader of the crew and he sort of took me under his wing, like I was his kid brother. The crew couldn't have cared less about me. They thought of me simply as some privileged kid from Fort Worth. I wasn't into the manly arts of boozing and smoking and putting people down. But with Dean around, I was protected from criticism. I stretched out. I grew. The world looked great when I was around Dean. I started to get a picture of who I would like to be, a picture of who I thought was hiding there inside yearning to come out, and that person was optimistic and positive and upbeat, a happy person who made other people feel good.

I came back revved up to do well in my senior year, but I couldn't sustain the summer's high. Circumstances never really allowed the inner me to come through with any sense of strength or character. The most devastating example was when the yearbook came out, always a big deal. I wanted to have a yearbook-signing party at home: I had never given a party, other than having the fellowship over a couple of times. Mom helped me organize it, but when the day came, nobody showed up. It was pretty sad. Mom just ached for me; we never talked about it, but I could see how badly she felt. While I was still sitting there in the mounting gloom, a call came from one of my friends. All the kids were over at Stormy Taylor's house and why didn't I come over. Believe it or not, that kind of eased the pain some, but I wouldn't go; I couldn't.

I tried to join a couple of bands, but Dad didn't approve of that very much. He and Mom were more interested in my being a good student; they had their hopes pinned on my going to college. Their thinking about my future moved straight ahead along formal lines. It was all choreographed. Dad was caught up in his world of flying, which he had worked all his life to attain. Mom was a part of that and had all of these social activities that women are obligated to be a part of on military bases. My brother was in junior high school and didn't know or want to know about anything.

That winter Uncle Dean died in a car crash and I was devastated. I got very depressed and withdrawn. I wouldn't talk to anybody. I kept to my room and went out only to go to school or my job at the five-and-dime or to church on Sunday. It wasn't going to take much to blow me away.

Finally, one Friday, I pulled myself together enough to ask a girl out, which even in the best of times was an uncommon event for me. Friday night was also beer call at the Officers' Club. Dad went and after a few beers lost track of time, as he sometimes did. Only this time he had the '50 Mercury, which was the car I was given to use on dates. His absence screwed everything up so that the date had to be called off at the last moment.

He came in very late that night and was drunk and a little obnoxious to boot. From my room, I could hear Mom go after him as soon as he got in the door. I assumed it was over what had just happened to me: I had never heard them fight before. But in fact it always sent Mom up the wall when Dad walked in late like that. In her fury, she said she was going to leave him, and Dad just laughed. Good, go, he said. He wasn't going to miss her. That was all I needed to hear because I imagined they were fighting over me. I wasn't going to be a party to their breakup. I wasn't going to be the source of trouble; I'd leave. They didn't care about me, anyway. If Dad wasn't going to miss Mom, he certainly wasn't going to miss me.

That night after Mom and Dad had gone to bed, I packed: one suitcase, some school papers, my drawing board, my guitar. Saturday morning I got up at seven as if I was going to work. I called the store and I told them we were going to Oklahoma because someone in the family was sick. I didn't want anyone calling later looking for me. I wanted to give myself a good day's start.

Mom and Dad were still asleep. I put my things in the car and drove down to the corner. But instead of turning left and going into town, I turned right and headed west to Los Angeles.

My plan, which I put together on the way, was to drive to where Carl and Nina Hart, old friends of my folks, lived, somewhere in Greater L.A. We had visited them and their children when I was a kid. I'd look them up and they'd help me out until I could get a job on a boat and become a sailor, or something. I had a little money. I was going to start life all over again.

Driving across Texas, I was preoccupied with how my folks were going to feel and with what I was going to do in L.A. But after a few hours I became filled with the glories of being halfway grown up and out in the world on my own, driving across the West, which I loved so dearly. I basked in this great feeling of freedom.

I went to Tucson, and out to where we used to live, where I looked up some old friends. I told everyone that I was out of school and heading off to do some serious work. I spent the night at the home of one of our old neighbors and took off again in the early morning. I must have left there about an hour before my parents started calling, trying to track me down. They were on to me.

In fact, Dad and an Air Force friend had flown along the highway from Fort Worth to Oklahoma in an F-102 looking for me. They even flew along a highway to California, but not the one I was traveling on.

Somehow I made it to Los Angeles, but I couldn't find the Harts listed in the phone book. L.A. was bigger than I thought it would be—it was a bit overwhelming—and I'd forgotten that the Harts lived not in L.A. but in Long Beach, and Long Beach was another area code.

I was pretty broke by that point. I spent the night in the car, parked in the lot of a supermarket, and Monday morning I called home. I didn't mention anything about running away. I just said I had gone off to look for work. If I couldn't get a job, I'd come back—and would they give me directions to where the Harts lived.

Dad was very civil; I could hear his concern. He gave me the directions and the Harts' telephone number. He asked no questions. He just asked me to call him when I got there. When I went back to the Mercury, it wouldn't start, so Carl actually had to come get me. When he called Texas to say I was safe and sound, Dad offered to fly out to get me if I'd come back. My resolve crumbled and I agreed. We stayed in L.A. together for two or three days. Dad took me to Sea World and a couple of other places. He was very solicitous.

Driving back across the country, he tried to talk to me, to put things straight and air out all the hard feelings, but I don't think he knew how to have that conversation, and I didn't help him much. He was very defensive, and never actually said he was sorry about anything. Just that Mom was sorry about what had happened, as if she alone were to blame. He couldn't help either of us as long as all the things that mattered were left unsaid.

But of course, beyond my resentments, I knew he cared. We all cared. East of Tucson, where there are hilly rocks, he stopped the car and waited for a couple of hours while I climbed to my heart's content, just as I had when I was a kid. That was our coded way in which he spoke to me.

At home all was forgiven. In fact, I had gained considerable credibility in the community because of the week I was away. I was thinking of my escapade as yet another thing I ultimately couldn't face up to, and instead it had established new ground for me. Some kids were actually in awe of what I had done. They wanted to know how I could just get up and go like that. They couldn't imagine running away from home. For a while, I was given a lot of attention and I ate it up, even though at the same time there was an inner voice saying, Okay. Here you are. Back again. That didn't work. Now what?

It was a question I didn't try to answer, but it kept haunting me.

I remember graduation being a very grand time for me. I got

invited to parties that I had wanted to go to—*the places to be*—
and I had a wonderful time. My stock was rising. But I never got
to take full advantage of it. The morning after graduation I went
off on another wheat harvest, which was a grind that summer
without Dean to look forward to seeing. And then after that, I
was off to college. My salad days were dwindling. The time was
ticking away.

College was a shaky proposition to begin with. None of us
knew anything about it; my parents had never gone to college.
We had never really talked about what it was going to be like. To
Mom and Dad, college meant access to the larger world, something they wanted their kids to have. (Mom would shed more
tears when I dropped out of school a couple of years later than
she had when I ran off to California.)

All I knew about college was that you went there after high
school. In fact, I first thought of going into the Air Force Academy to become a pilot, like Dad. That would have simplified my
choice of study. But there was a problem with my vision. They
said I could study at the Academy but I couldn't fly. In the end,
I decided to go to Texas Tech, three hundred miles away, and
enroll in their architecture program.

Mom and Dad drove me there and Dad, recognizing the special moment, said something to me, in his inimitable way, that I
never forgot: "You know, you've got a talent. You can play guitar
and you can sing. Not everybody can do that, but that doesn't
make you any better than anybody else. Just remember that."

That statement summed up Dad's democratic, egalitarian
credo. He was acknowledging my ability, but he didn't want me
to get too big for my britches. I think that stuck with me because
it was such a clear communication—he was telling me the thing
he most wanted me to know. It was one of the few pieces of

advice he ever gave me, and one of the most meaningful things I ever learned.

Frankly, college itself was a trial, although a manageable one—at least for a couple of years. I wasn't a scholar, but I got through. What made me happy—and what kept me at school—was the music I was making, and sometimes getting paid for. My gigs provided just about the only money I had; but it was enough. My folks paid most of the bills and Texas Tech was a state school, money didn't matter there as long as you had *some* in your pocket. Actually, it was a great environment for an artist. I sang with a group called the Alpine Trio and sometimes I sang by myself. Even in the dorm, I was the troubadour. You could always find me in my room at the head of the stairs. My dorm mates liked to share their stories of conquest and plunder, and I liked to listen while playing the guitar. I think during that period I was trying to lighten up a little.

But school was not what I was interested in. Architecture was not what I was interested in. And in the third year I started out really distracted, and I cannot remember why: Life? The future? I don't know. It was another adolescent crisis with no voice. That November John Kennedy was assassinated and I, like the rest of the world, was inconsolable.

That Christmas I went home to Florida, where my folks were now living. I drove down hoping to be open with them, hoping they'd help me figure out what I wanted to do, but we had a terrible time. I was very tense—it was what you feel before you make a break—and Dad and I were at each other's throats.

When I went back to school I gave myself an ultimatum: Either do better than average in the marking period coming up, or leave school. The time had come to either get music out of my system, so that I could take school seriously, or to see how far I could go with my music. At the end of the month, I had the answer. Like a throw of the *I Ching.*

Everybody I knew, from my professors to my friends, told me I was making the biggest mistake of my life. And Dad expressed his displeasure in a letter. He wrote me three times in my life, and each was a letter of such condemnation that afterward all you could do was look for an oven to put your head in and end it all. But this was the best of them; it had a silver lining.

He chewed me out pretty good for what I was doing. But then he said: If that's what you want to do, what you have to do, then you should do it; see where it goes. If you get into trouble, we're here. And when you get tired of fucking around and want to go back to school, we're here for that, too. The envelope contained a check for $250, which was a lot of money to me.

The letter was more moving than I've described it and I knew the love it contained. I may never have experienced a more profound expression of my father's love and concern. Here I was writing off everything that my parents believed in, everything they hoped for me, and they let me go—with their blessing.

I had just turned twenty; I was still Mr. Serious.

CITY OF ANGELS

When you are in a place, you never think of it as generating a particular kind of energy, and therefore affecting your own energies. But then you don't have to understand things for them to be the way they are. That is a lesson that came home to me with great intensity one year when I was at Lake Powell, doing a fast. Even though I'm crossing wires here, it's what I think of when I remember returning to L.A. in 1964. Lake Powell is an incredible place—a huge canyon carved out by the Colorado River that the U.S. Army Corps of Engineers dammed up in the middle of the desert—and doing a fast is a pretty magical experience. I had gone there with Ron Lemire, this fellow I had hired to cook for me on the road once upon a time. Ron had introduced me to macrobiotics and changed the way I thought about the food I ate, and fasting was a way to explore another side of this interest we shared.

We were going to leave Lake Powell on Easter Sunday, and on Good Friday, which happened to be a full moon, we went out to a place on the lake called Rainbow Natural Bridge, which is a two hundred-foot arch of stone, to test the magic. The Indians say that if you walk under the bridge to the other side, you can leave your troubles behind. So when the moon was up, we went out there in our speedboat and walked through, then sat for a while in the shadow of the moonlight, light-headed and purified from the fast, talking about plans and dreams, and where life was going for us. When we were all talked out, we went back out into the moonlight, said a prayer, and left our troubles, cares, guilts, all of that, left them, walked back under the bridge, got in our boat, and went back to camp. We were as spiritually pure as we were going to get.

When Ron and I got up the next morning—the lake was as still as glass—without warning we were at each other's throats. Out of nowhere, a whole different field of energy was working on us, and we weren't prepared for it. Our instinct was to push back against it, and that meant push at each other. I said, "There's no need to try to stay another day; I'm ready to go home now. If we stay, we're going to get into trouble." And we were out of there.

When we started back in the boat, it was a glorious peaceful Saturday morning: not a cloud in the sky. But by the time we reached Bullfrog Basin—about a three-hour ride—the wind was blowing hard and the clouds were coming up. The people at the basin had to come out in powerboats to guide our houseboat in. We got everything unloaded, paid our bills, and went up to this little airstrip, about a mile and a half away, where we'd flown in. I got the plane I was flying ready, taxied down the runway, and took off into the wind coming off the lake just as this wall of water, an intense rain that took away all the light, passed through. We beat it by less than thirty seconds. It turned out to be the biggest storm in Lake Powell history: highest winds, most rain, huge drop in barometric pressure. We had felt it coming that morning. We had felt that storm coming in some primitive part of ourselves, and we had reacted with aggression and fear. Instead of staying detached and letting it go through us like the Buddhists say you should, we took it out on each other.

I think of that story because it is emblematic for me of the things that act on us and that we do not understand, and rarely accept. Yet these things have a powerful impact, and we respond to them psychically. L.A. was like that when I arrived in 1964: It had an energy environment all its own. It was a lot different from what it is today, but full of the same tensions. Things you couldn't see or touch would either overwhelm you or you'd learn to accept them.

I drove from Phoenix on in through San Bernardino to Pasadena and then to Los Angeles and was amazed at how it had all grown together: It was all city. And though I'd been there before, it was like seeing it for the first time.

That first day I drove down Sunset Boulevard and saw the RCA building. I thought about Elvis Presley and Paul Anka, and said to myself, "Maybe someday I'll sing for RCA." Wishes sweeter than wine; I had a lot of those daydreams in my first freewheeling days.

I can still conjure up the physical sensation of driving over I-5 in Hollywood, and going under the bridge at Mulholland and down into the San Fernando Valley. When the smog settled in, you could not see the mountains, which are only thirteen miles away, but on a clear day they appeared amazingly close. I couldn't believe how beautiful they were. When I didn't have enough money for gas, I'd get to the top of Mulholland, put the car in neutral, and coast all the way down, just to save a little extra gas for the straightaways.

And then when I lived at Randy Sparks's place in Bel Air, I used to love to drive up Stone Canyon Road with the top down. In Los Angeles the gladiolus and honeysuckle permeate the canyons in the spring, or after a rain, and it's intoxicating; a wonderful smell. Every once in a while, when I'm back in L.A., I can step out my door and catch that smell, and I'm transported back through time.

The first few weeks I stayed in Long Beach again with Carl and Nina Hart, my parents' friends. Mr. Hart was a civil engineer, and he gave me a job working for him as a draftsman. In the evenings, I cruised around and sang at every place I could; I drove through a million intersections, just following the music.

The Harts' eldest daughter was dating a fellow named Paul Laughlin, and Paul, who was going to Long Beach State, introduced me to a guy named Denny Brooks, a fraternity brother who was already an established performer. He was singing at a couple of clubs in Orange County, the Mecca and the Bon Amie, and he showed me around. He also had an album out, which had the practical effect of adding to my confidence and making me feel that mine wasn't so wild a dream. I added one of his songs, "The Far Side of the Hill," to my repertoire.

About the same time, I got hold of Ken Ballard, a fraternity brother of mine with whom I had performed in Texas, and who was now making the scene as part of a group called the Cherry Hill Singers: Ken, Niles Brown, Dave Fractman, who was the banjo player in the group, and a couple of other guys whose names I can't remember anymore. They were performing at a place in Pasadena called the Ice House and suggested that I just come along. It was that kind of free and easy.

The only L.A. club I'd heard of before then was the Trouba-dour—the Christy Minstrels' first hit album was called *Live! At the Troubadour*—so I was mildly surprised to learn about all these other places; it really opened my eyes. Of course, the city itself was a revelation to me. People didn't live in houses; they lived in apartment buildings, especially just off the freeway, and it seemed that all the apartments were full of young people just beginning to make their way in the world.

I think it fed my ego when I realized that people my age were still in college. Being a college dropout in that place and time was no disadvantage. All of these clubs had folk music and hootenannies, and a night when the stage was open to people who walked in from the street. Although I had planned for my open stage debut to be at the hip and trendy Troubadour, de-buting at the Ice House turned out to be just as inspiring.

The next week I performed at Ledbetter's, Randy Sparks's place in Westwood, where all the UCLA kids hung out. At their hootenanny on Sunday, I sang four songs, and Randy was knocked out by my voice. He was having a great deal of success with the Christy Minstrels at the time and said he'd be inter-ested in recording me. If I remember correctly, I took Dave Fractman with me to Gold Star Studios and taped four songs for Randy and Jack Daley, who was Randy's manager (and soon to be mine), to take around. I cast my creative seed upon the water and waited for something to happen. It didn't take long.

In fact, I found myself needing a new place to stay almost immediately. The Harts were having a hard time with their daughter Diane, who was a good kid but a very rebellious ado-lescent, always getting into trouble. I guess due to our closeness in age, I was brushed with the same coat of reprimand. Nina Hart, who was almost like a sister to my mom, and had lived with Mom and her family for a while, was a very feisty and emotional woman. I came into the house one day, just after giving Randy the tape I'd made, and Nina and Diane were having a fight. Nina was throwing dishes around and I said something to calm her down, and she said I'd better move out.

Having to phase into a new situation so suddenly took my breath away, but it was also exciting to contemplate going off and getting an apartment—exciting *and* scary, actually. I looked for places around UCLA and found nothing I could afford, but then I learned another energy-related lesson—namely that receptive fields attract what they need. When I went by Ledbetter's to check on my tape, Jack Daley not only offered me a job for a hundred dollars a week as opening act for the Backporch Majority, which was like a farm club for the Christy Minstrels, but also a room at another place of Randy's, the quaintly named Folk House, in Encino, where most of the members of the Backporch Majority lived.

Encino reminded me of Fort Worth; it was suburbia, and the Folk House, on the floor of the Valley, was a three-bedroom bungalow a couple of houses from the Ventura Freeway. The inhabitants were Karen Brian; George McKelvey; Mike Crowley, a banjo player from Kansas City; Danny Dalton, who had been the leader of a group called the Dalton Brothers and later had a brief career doing commercials as the Marlboro Man; and a beautiful blonde whose first name was Louise and whose last name I can't remember, who went on to sing with the Christy Minstrels and later married Danny.

The Folk House had been the scene of some pretty wild parties, but about a week or two before I moved in somebody had gotten really drunk at one and wound up getting killed on the freeway. So Randy was making an effort to tone things down just as I arrived. He'd come by only once in a while, to direct a rehearsal, but everyone joked that he'd bugged the plants in the house to make sure we were behaving. With me that was no problem. I was just so polite and careful about everything. Most of all, I didn't want to say the wrong thing. I didn't want anyone to think I wasn't a worthy aspirant to what they were doing. I was only a few years younger than everyone, but I felt very junior; just this naive kid who was excited about having a chance to be onstage regularly and sing.

Living there was, on some level, a reenactment of my college dorm life. Except for working at the club, I spent all my time in the house—shy and reclusive as always—learning songs. Mike Crowley, who was the real musician of the group, kind of took me under his wing; he loved my voice. He was really my first mentor on the guitar. He taught me to play "The Bells of Rhymney," on a twelve-string guitar, which became one of my staples.

Meanwhile, Danny Dalton, who was the front man for the Backporch Majority, was teaching me about stage presence. It was he who got me to think about what I wore on stage, about my patter with the audience, and even whether my hair was combed or not. Knowing how to be a front man—introducing songs, setting up a good rapport with the audience, using humor to make them comfortable—meant a great deal to me. It had an influence on where my career went.

If I say I was timid back then, I should mention that I was also very much the person people came to know as John Denver, a guy they easily accepted into their homes via television. That quality was always there for me.

Once Dad came out to see me. It was a couple of months into my new life. He happened to be in Southern California on a military junket and he came by Ledbetter's to see where I worked. Afterward I took him out to the Folk House to show him where I lived. He didn't have much to say, but I had the sense he was forming a report for Mom. It wasn't just the money-earning part of it that I think impressed him but the fact that here I was, still a straight-laced kid, taking care of myself, not doing anything stupid: I wasn't hanging out with crazy people, drinking and smoking marijuana. To tell you the truth, I didn't even know marijuana was around. I think Dad was quietly trying to take in whatever signs of transformation there were, watching like a spectator and accepting what he saw at face value. At least that was my fantasy. I guessed he was going to go home and tell Mom that she didn't have to worry about John.

Ledbetter's was on Westwood Boulevard, between Wilshire and Santa Monica. You walked in the door, went through a little passageway where you bought your ticket, and then through the swinging doors. It was a typical folk club of that time: a stage against a brick wall, a main aisle, some seats against the oppo-site wall, a tiny dressing room. The room held maybe a hundred and twenty people. Then, in the back through another set of swinging doors, there was an area called the Backporch, and that was where I worked: a bar that served nothing but beer, a floor strewn with peanut shells, and red-checkered tablecloths on all the tables. Monday was dark, Tuesdays through Thurs-days you could come and stay for the night, but on Fridays and Saturdays there were two and three shows and you only got to see one for the price of your ticket.

My act ran about twenty minutes. I think the first week or so I sang the same four songs over and over; I didn't know any others that were appropriate. But before long my repertoire was expanding. I developed my own small following who joined the growing lines of people waiting to get in on the weekends, and

I started running the Sunday-night hootenanny, signing up the performers and introducing the acts.

On Monday nights, I would go to the Troubadour.

What's irreplaceable about this time for me isn't so much the individual places or the groups but the whole scene: the community of spirit we shared. In many ways I regret that I didn't embrace it as I might have. It was like being part of a small republic where we were all happy citizens. I also remember it as an incredibly fluid time, with one group emerging from another and then re-forming yet again—and then again, forming and re-forming. No sooner had the four Cherry Hill Singers been absorbed into a group called the Men (thirteen voices), for example, than this group broke up into a couple of other entirely different smaller groups, including one called the Association, which had some pretty big records. Another was the Modern Folk Quartet, which I thought was one of the best performing ensembles I'd ever seen. But the center didn't hold. What was there one day, was gone the next.

It was around this time that folk was evolving into folk rock. The Beatles had already made a beachhead in America with their performance on "The Ed Sullivan Show," and in 1965 Bob Dylan would appear at the Newport Folk Festival playing an electric guitar—very different events, but both catalysts for change. The folk groups, like Peter, Paul and Mary and the Kingston Trio, still used acoustic instruments, while folk rock had a harder edge, with electric instruments, drums, and songs that tended to be commentaries on what was going on in the world, not just ones with conventional love lyrics. I can't say I wasn't tempted to grow in that direction.

I'd met a kid from Chicago at the Troubadour named Roy Marinell, who was also trying to make his way in L.A. as a musician. He had some interesting thoughts about what was hip about the Beatles, which he readily shared; I was persuaded. In fact, I was greatly influenced by the whole scene at the Troubadour. It was a big deal for me when Elton John came there. I had bohemian leanings, too, appearances to the contrary (my uniform at Ledbetter's, which Danny Dalton had suggested, included this funny blue lapelless jacket and a nice pair of slacks).

Hanging out with Roy, I started listening to musicians other than those with the Backporch Majority, who were tutoring me. It was through Roy that I met Roger McGuinn, then known as Jim, who was so taken with the Beatles that he wanted to form an equivalent American band. This was before bands were a thing. Oddly enough, Roger had worked as an accompanist for the Chad Mitchell Trio not too long before. He came with Roy to hear me sing at Ledbetter's one night. He was even more of an introvert than I was, which was difficult for me to imagine. I was one of the few solos on the L.A. folk scene; everyone else was grouping up.

After my performance, I joined Roger, Guy Clark, and David Crosby to talk about forming a group. I sang a couple of songs with them, to test the water. The problem is I felt so square in their presence; they seemed so hip. I let myself be intimidated. As much as I enjoyed singing with them, I wasn't in their class.

Still, I pursued it and sang with them a couple of times, and attended a few more meetings, until finally one night I went to some little club across the freeway from Westwood to hear David Crosby sing. It seems to me we began to argue about something—all words, but real combat nevertheless. He was the most arrogant, obnoxious person I'd ever met and totally disdainful of my cultural naiveté. I think that, as much as anything, put me off the scent of this group we were forming.

Ledbetter's was a place apart from all of that, a pocket of folk tradition, and few of the musical changes taking place elsewhere touched the club. Because of that, I think it was the perfect place for me. Given who I was and what my inclinations were, I don't think I would have survived out there in that other scene. I couldn't have sustained a job for that long a time, gotten used to being onstage, built a repertoire, started being a performer.

The war in Vietnam had been escalating and I was no longer in school, so when my draft notice arrived in the summer of 1964 it scared me to death. I couldn't conceive of trying to evade the draft in any way, but the prospect of going to war appealed to me even less. I had heard of a doctor in town who helped kids get out of the draft, even to the point of concocting ailments, and I went to see him. I am missing two toes from an accident with a lawnmower—a terrible thing that happened when I was eighteen—and he concocted a bit of medical history, without having to fabricate much. Those records plus a letter suggesting deferment were all I needed; my 1-Y classification was granted. I think the anti-draft movement had yet to gain momentum, but discontent was rumbling up from the ground.

Around this time, at Randy's urging, I acquired a stage name. I had no problem with Deutschendorf, but he and Jack Daley were convinced that I needed a more mellifluous-sounding tag if a career in recording was to be in my future. They suggested I call myself John Sommerville (after a musician they knew who had taken on yet another name); I chose Denver, which I associated with the Rocky Mountains, and I identified with those mountains. A name isn't easy to give up, but on the other hand I wasn't going to let anything stop me from pursuing every chance I got to be in the music business. If these guys thought Deutschendorf wouldn't fit on the record label, then Denver it would be.

In the fall of 1964 I bought myself a brand-new Ford Mustang convertible, using a bank loan that Randy cosigned. With a salary of a hundred dollars a week, no rent to pay, a twenty-minute show and good encores, I figured I must be a success in the world, and I wanted to show it. The transformation was complete.

I had even acquired a band of acolytes, a group of fraternity boys from UCLA who came to all the hootenannies at Ledbetter's. They had musical goals of their own and called themselves Somebody, Anybody, Everybody, and once, when they were playing down in San Diego, I helped them with sound and lights. Afterward they looked on me as their mentor, a relationship which Randy just hated. Although they patterned themselves after the Backporch Majority, they pointedly didn't do any of Randy's songs, which he must have taken as a rebuke.

I did have one girlfriend that first year in L.A.—a real sweetheart—who was a student at UCLA and living away from home for the first time. It breaks my heart to remember how puritanical I was with her, and there she was pining for me to love her. She told me once that she was the kind of girl who would trip me and beat me to the floor. Where I came from, you just didn't sleep with someone before the two of you were married. I never even allowed the thought to seriously pass through my mind, sober soul that I was. I was *much* too serious for my own good.

However, that Christmas I underwent a metamorphosis. I

knew I was developing my musical talents at Ledbetter's, but that's about all. It seemed as if nothing was coming from Randy's overtures to Capitol Records on my behalf. My twenty-first birthday was approaching. Suddenly, with the force of a wind rising, I felt the urge to take matters in hand. Don't ask me what my specific thoughts were, but nature wasn't going to be denied. Randy gave me some time off and, antsy for travel, I left town for a month. It was one of the most eventful months of my young life.

Christmas with the folks in Florida was a disaster. It started out fine, but during the last half of the holidays Dad and I were at each other's throats the whole time. We simply didn't know how to stop. Really bad stuff. Later I discovered how upset he was with his place in the military at the time. So going home was not a success. On the other hand, the club date I got myself on the way back in Houston, at Max Webster's club, The Jester, where I performed just after Christmas, was a bit of a triumph.

I was originally engaged to play there for two weeks, but due to popular demand, it was extended to four. The Kingston Trio, performing at another club in Houston, came by to hear me one night, and when I returned the visit, they introduced me from the floor and praised my show. One night the audience included Alan Lomax, whose songbook had become one of my bibles.

Most significantly to me, I lost my virginity on that trip. She was a young girl working at the club. We went to dinner one night and I came on about wanting to sleep with her. Where I got the courage for that I don't know; it must have come in the wake of feeling successful about my gig. I remember being ready to backpedal if I had misjudged the situation. Oh, the rapture of a girl's body! What had I been so afraid of finding there?

But when I got back to Los Angeles with my newfound knowledge, I discovered that my old girlfriend had moved on to someone else—someone more ardent in pressing his claims, I suppose. She didn't have time for me anymore. I kicked myself sixteen ways from Sunday. After my set at Ledbetter's, I'd go over to the Rusty Nail—now that I was twenty-one—and drink my broken heart away. Was there no justice in the world?

In addition, even though I'd been gone from L.A. for little more than a month, the music scene had gone through a serious transition. What everybody around the Troubadour was anticipating had come to pass. The Men, for example, had added a drummer in the interval and were now using electric instruments. More important, Roger McGuinn's efforts had borne fruit. The Backporch Majority had gone on the road, split up, regrouped, and reappeared in various guises. One faction reinvented themselves as MC Square; another returned to Ledbetter's as the Green Grass Group. Moreover, Randy had arranged a big showcase for them—invited agents and everything—without including me in the show. He had hired David Crosby to be the opening act (and that was the cruelest cut of all). As the spring progressed, I felt left behind.

When the Christy Minstrels broke up, I knew that was it; the folk music movement of the Sixties had passed into the history books. Kenny Rogers, who had been one of the Minstrels, started a group called the First Edition (which included Kenny Vance of the Backporch Majority). He had a hit with a song that included that wonderful line "I just dropped in to see what condition my condition was in." The lyrics captured precisely how I was feeling.

The Byrds, L.A.'s first rock band, with McGuinn, Crosby, and Guy Clark, had taken flight. Before then what was new in folk music in this country was already happening in England: the

Beatles, Herman's Hermits, the Rolling Stones, the Animals, Gerry and the Pacemakers. All of a sudden, it was happening here, too. In particular, it was happening right where I lived.

The Byrds' big hit was Bob Dylan's "Mr. Tambourine Man"—I sang a folksy version of the same song but without any idea of what it was really about. And when I looked the other way, here came Jimi Hendrix, redefining the music in another direction. My consciousness reeled. To make matters worse, Randy was no longer interested in me. The record deal he and I had talked about was definitely *kaput.* My relationship with him was coming undone. What with one thing and the other, as my mother might say, I felt if not exactly a tragic figure, then certainly a roundly rejected one. It was one more thing that I had messed up. The Sixties were moving on and I was missing them.

Ledbetter's eventually burned to the ground and Randy lost all of his instruments, including some I coveted myself. When the building was rebuilt, it became Comedy Club West. All but a few of the folk clubs disappeared. Monday night at the Troubadour became the place to hear new rock bands instead of folksingers. I remember going there one Monday night after I had just seen the Rolling Stones in Long Beach. Frankly, I just didn't get it. I didn't get Mick Jagger or his onstage gyrations. It just did not compute for me. Anyway, here was this young kid with his band at the Troubadour trying to imitate Mick Jagger. Every time he caught someone looking at him, I swear he'd redden with embarrassment. Then he'd concentrate and do Jagger again, trying to get it down before he caught someone else's eye. Singing folk for a living was dying right before my eyes.

But while it was upsetting to feel left behind, I had deep reserves of self-esteem. I wasn't Dutch's boy for nothing. After a month of nursing rejection, I drove down to Scottsdale, Arizona, and performed at a place called the Lumber Mill. Mike Kirkland of the Brothers Four came in and saw the show and told Milt Okun about me.

Milt was one of the leading lights of the folk music industry, and his name was about as much as I knew of the commercial end of the business. He was the music producer for the Brothers Four, Peter, Paul and Mary, and the Chad Mitchell Trio, among others. He had asked everybody in all of the groups that he was working with to let him know if they heard anybody on the college campus trail who was worth listening to. Milt was auditioning singers to replace Chad Mitchell, who was going into a Broadway show. He suggested I send in tapes, which I did, though, I don't think I held my breath hoping for it. I heard there were hundred of singers applying. It was late spring. The Vietnam War was getting bigger, and everyone and his brother seemed to be restless to go on the road. I certainly was.

I had this big eighteen-string guitar and lots of ego that I was trying to keep under wraps, though in the privacy of my own thoughts it was screaming for attention. It had been pretty noticeable to me on that trip back home over Christmas. In Houston, I had sensed a real edge to my feelings. Every night there had been a different audience who liked what they heard. I wanted badly to make real plans. Randy's sudden lack of interest in me was at odds with this growing sense I had of my talents. I was feeling eager to get away from L.A. again.

A month later—by then it was summer—I was back in Scottsdale working at the Lumber Mill, when I got a call from Milt asking me to go to New York to meet the other members of the Mitchell Trio, as they had been renamed. He had enjoyed the tapes and said he liked the quality of my voice. I hadn't thought the tapes were that good, so his enthusiasm put Milt in a very special place in my eyes even before I met him. He wanted me to audition. Could I make it? With uncharacteristic bravado, I said I was already packed: I'd come on Sunday. It was going to cost me a fortune, more than I really could afford, but his call sent me into orbit.

Actually, it wasn't bravado as much as it was me trying to be professional and lighthearted at the same time. How else to deal with New York, a place I'd never been. I figured it couldn't be much different from or more complicated than L.A. In fact, when I landed at Kennedy Airport I rented a car instead of going into Manhattan by cab, thinking I was going to enjoy this to the hilt, and wound up looking for East Thirty-fourth Street on Staten Island. I thought it looked too much like a fishing village to be Manhattan, but I figured I was just new at this and if I kept going I'd see some skyscrapers.

That night, when I finally had myself ensconsed at the Hotel Lexington, down the block from the Waldorf-Astoria, I decided to go out looking for some action and got lost again. *And* got myself into an embarrassing situation.

I walked over to Madison Avenue, which is barren on Sunday nights, feeling dumbstruck by the magnificent architecture, the likes of which I'd never seen before. I was feeling very lonely and vulnerable—worried about the next day—and filled with desire. Suddenly my desire took wing. Down the street, there was a woman window-shopping. I'd probably seen too many movies, and I just got carried away with myself—after all, there I was in sandals, bright-eyed and natural: *the natural man.*

As we kept getting closer, I could see she was a very attractive, well-put-together woman, who in retrospect I realize probably lived in the neighborhood and was just having a leisurely stroll around her block after dinner. But I was in a different frame of mind: I'm in a big city, and I'm fantasizing about boy meets girl. It's clear to me that I was already invested in the romance of road life. Pretty soon she and I are at the same window, I see that she is a beautiful woman, and I say, "Are you a model?" "No," she says, nonplussed, "I'm full-scale," and she walks on. I lost it all, right there. I don't think I've fully recovered from that embarrassment to this day. The blush still comes to my cheeks whenever I think about it.

Anyway, after a false start, the audition worked out well. I'd gone over to Milt's studio on that first day, after finding my way to Manhattan from Staten Island. I met Milt and, as it turned out, Joe Frazier. Mike Kobluk and Joe were the other two-thirds of the Mitchell Trio. Joe was one of the "free" people, a wild spirit who lived on Manhattan's Upper West Side, and Mike was very conservative and lived in Chicago. The audition was set for Monday, but Joe had come by a day early just to see who this kid Denver was. Milt had been very excited about my tapes: He said he had heard a life and a personality in them. But when I sang a couple of songs for him in the studio, I tried to sing like Chad—a high lyrical tenor, which I could not do well—and it disappointed him. I could see it. He sent me off with Joe to learn a couple of songs, and called Mike in Chicago to tell him not to worry about coming to New York: He didn't think I was the guy they were looking for.

With Joe's help, though, I not only loosened up, I learned a couple of really tough songs—I had a great feeling for music— and I learned the difficult parts just like that, which impressed even me. I sang them for Milt after he returned from a meeting, and he was knocked out by it. Talk about a reversal of fortune. He called Mike back and told him to come in on Monday as planned. That day we got together and sang, but when the audition was over, they said: Good, but don't call us, we'll call you.

I flew back to Arizona, with all kinds of unused energies. I must have known I was coming to the end of my tenure in Los

Angeles. At least the vibrations I was carrying back with me weren't in synch anymore with what was happening there. I'd no sooner arrived in Phoenix and driven to Scottsdale than I got myself into a drag race, something I had never done before. I had gone by the Lumber Mill for a bit and was heading to my hotel, where I was supposed to wait for the Mitchell Trio people to call, and I spotted this car in the middle of Scottsdale Boulevard. The driver was revving and revving his motor like mad, desperate to prove himself, just like me, and I took the challenge. After our quick start, though, I decided I really didn't want to speed, so I stopped and let him go on. Well, a cop was right there, fuming at my audacity, and he gave me a ticket. Which should have been the end of it, but when fields of energy clash, it's hard to account for the results.

A couple of days pass, and I'm at the hotel, still waiting for Milt's call out by the swimming pool, when I decide to go down the road to the A&W Root Beer stand to get some lunch. I'm in my bathing suit and a shirt. Way down the road, just as I'm pulling out, I can see a police car coming, but I go along to A&W unconcerned. Just as I start to turn in, the police car pulls up real close behind me, its lights flashing. Before I know it, there are a couple of cops standing by my car, asking for my license. I think to myself: What has this got to do with waiting for a call about my future? And as they go off to check things out over their radio, another police car arrives, lights flashing, and then another, and then two unmarked cars with plainclothesmen, and I'm surrounded.

A crowd starts to collect. They want to know what's happening and so do I. I'm a poor, innocent guy, I protest. Pretty soon the guy with my license returns and starts giving me the third degree. Where am I from? What am I doing here? How long have I been in town? Where are the rest of my clothes?

Another guy wants to see the trunk, and when I open it for him, there are empty shotgun shells all over the place. They were left over from a hunting trip. What are these for? the guy wants to know. What are they doing here? Do you have a gun?

By now I am pretty nervous. I protest, saying again that I don't believe I've broken the law here and that I don't know why I've been stopped. What are all these questions for? "Well, son," the officer says, trying to calm me down, "I'll tell you. Yesterday a bank was robbed in downtown Phoenix and the suspect was described as a man in his early twenties, driving a dark blue Mustang convertible with California license plates."

That was me, of course.

They questioned me for about an hour, and then told me not to leave town until I heard from them!

That night I watched an old John Derek movie, one of those films he made when he was with Ursula Andress. He's traveling across Arizona and she picks him up. She's married to some old rich fat cat she's not into, so she and Derek have an affair. When he leaves, she murders the old man, then tells the police that John Derek did it. Now the police are after him. And as if that isn't bad enough, he's also being chased all over Arizona by some crazed motorcyclist with a chainsaw. I mean, how bad can it get? And, of course, later that night when I'm asleep, these thoughts invade my dreams: It's me they are after. Can my life be over already? I was just getting started.

The next day, Milt Okun called; I had been hired. And the police called: They had arrested the suspect, driving a tan Mustang fastback, with Arizona license plates. I was free to go. So what if life was incongruous? Suddenly it didn't matter.

OH, BABE,
I HATE TO GO

All my bags are packed
I'm ready to go
I'm standing here outside your door
I hate to wake you up to say goodbye
But the dawn is breakin'
It's early morn
The taxi's waitin'
He's blowin' his horn
Already I'm so lonesome
I could die
So kiss me and smile for me
Tell me that you'll wait for me
Hold me like you'll never let me go
'Cause I'm leavin' on a jet plane
Don't know when I'll be back again
Oh babe, I hate to go

There's so many times I've let you down
So many times I've played around
I tell you now they don't mean a thing
Ev'ry place I go I'll think of you
Ev'ry song I sing I'll sing for you
When I come back I'll bring your wedding ring
So kiss me and smile for me
Tell me that you'll wait for me
Hold me like you'll never let me go
'Cause I'm leavin' on a jet plane
Don't know when I'll be back again
Oh babe, I hate to go

Now the time has come to leave you
One more time
Let me kiss you
Then close your eyes
And I'll be on my way
Dream about the days to come
When I won't have to leave alone
About the times I won't have to say
Kiss me and smile for me
Tell me that you'll wait for me
Hold me like you'll never let me go
'Cause I'm leavin' on a jet plane
Don't know when I'll be back again
Oh babe, I hate to go
I'm leavin' on a jet plane

Don't know when I'll be back again
Oh babe, I hate to go

I left L.A. the way some people leave a good movie, lost a bit in the stars—and in the story—but easily putting it behind me. I figured I'd be back soon enough, if not to convince the right parties I was Orpheus reincarnated—and get to sleep at the Bel Air in one of the suites set aside for the gods—then at least to reclaim my electric guitar and priceless record collection (which was only the first of many misguided notions I've had in my life as John Denver).

Back in Texas, my dream of being a vagabond troubadour never went beyond getting to Los Angeles. I was so intent on learning to be a performer that I hadn't thought ahead to the next part: of heading off again, bound for glory. I knew there were other places I'd want to go once my career was under way; it just hadn't hit me yet where those places might be.

Actually, if I was bound anywhere, in the sense of having a destination, it was just to the future. Maybe I thought the idea was simply to be true to myself. Or to know my true self, anyway, and stand revealed. I think that was probably the big picture for me. If someone had come along then and shown me how far I had to travel to fully apprehend who I was, I would have been knocked off my feet. What was I—twenty-one, going on twenty-two? What did I know? I certainly didn't know I was going to have to live another thirty years before I could claim to have some real insight into this business of living. But I was convinced of two things then. I was going to find out about my country, the U.S. of A., which was what had been marked on all the stuff I grew up with—especially the ideas. And I was going to find out about the time in which we were living. No one could have invented a better vessel for me in which to chase after those chimeras than the Mitchell Trio. Their music expanded the spaces of my life.

Initially the group had consisted of Chad, Mike Kobluk, and another guy, whose name escapes me now; he was with the trio for only a short while. Chad had, perhaps, the most distinctive personality of the three and he had a beautiful Irish tenor, so when they were looking for a name that would distinguish them from the other folk groups around, they chose his. It was a good choice; "the Chad Mitchell Trio" had a ring of authenticity. But I don't think the group clicked until that third fellow left and they auditioned to replace him. One of the musicians who auditioned was Tom Paxton—which gives you an idea of the quality of the talent they had available to them—but the fellow they brought into the group was Joe Frazier. Joe's personality more than the others' began to define and shape the Mitchell Trio—he was politically very, very liberal, and outspoken. Milt Okun's penchant for political and social satire was a big influence on the trio's work, and that influence was strengthened by Joe's presence. The satirical material, which we fashioned from Broadway theater and night club lyricists, from the Weavers' repertoire, from Jacques Brel, made the trio unique on the folk scene. In replacing Chad, I literally stepped into their limelight. And in so doing, I stepped beyond the charted territory of what I had known before.

We had a week of rehearsals in New York before opening at the Cellar Door in Washington, D.C., which was one of the better-known and classier folk/jazz clubs in the country. They gave the new Mitchell Trio a real coming-out. The country was immersed in an unpopular war, and we were the musical accompaniment to the dissident faction that was starting to swell. When we waxed satirical about President Johnson's daughter,

Luci Baines. She is no Jackie,
But then who complains?
She may be tacky, but she is the brains
behind the foreign policy.

or sang the "I Vuz Not a Nazi Polka":

Each and every German dances to the strain
of the I Vuz Not a Nazi Polka.
All without exception, join in the refrain
of the I Vuz Not a Nazi Polka.
Goering vuz a crazy ve vanted to report,
sing the I Vuz Not a Nazi Polka.
We all thought that Dachau vuz just a nice resort,
sing the I Vuz Not a Nazi Polka.

our audiences roared their approval. We were more fun than a barrel of monkeys. (In fact, a little later on, during a swing through California, we would be auditioned for parts in a group called the Monkees that was being "created" for a new TV show. As it turned out, the producers didn't think we seemed juvenile enough for the job—although in certain respects I was more juvenile than I like to remember.)

In recognition of the potentially subversive nature of some of our material, we got ourselves photographed outside the offices of the House Committee on Un-American Activities. With our verbal slings, we pictured ourselves as Davids slaying Goliath. Aside from the pleasures of performing and learning to thumb my nose at the establishment, I made friendships in those two weeks, on that first professional date in Washington, that are still an important part of my life. If this was what it meant to be gainfully employed, I was more than ready.

Of course, the transition from obscurity to recognition took place so quickly that it hadn't dawned on me to sit down, as a grown-up would, and figure out how all of this was going to work out in practical terms. The salary was $250 a week, which in L.A. or Phoenix would have been fine, but Washington is and was then a pretty expensive city. We were staying at the Holiday Inn in Virginia, just across the bridge from Georgetown—this is 1965—and my hotel bill came to something like $250 for the week, or about as much as my paycheck before taxes. I had a brief surge of feeling absolutely stupid and of wondering *how* to make things better.

But that puzzlement was nothing compared to my uncertainty about expressing a political consciousness. Aside from arguments I'd had with my dad, I had no experience articulating the opinions that I had kept to myself previously. Now I was just charging ahead without looking—a quality of mind I've broken with only recently. Characteristically, when I had a mind to do something, I'd do whatever it took.

Eventually, those things got sorted out and, more significantly, my career took a big step forward. I was no longer just another folksinger. I had become part of a nationally known group that had a recording contract. We were doing college concerts and playing club dates like the Cellar Door. The trio's musical repertory gave me the language I needed, and our performances together gave me the push to use it. I was like a child discovering how far he could run. Sophisticated as the satire was, I felt right at home with it. I liked the dark humor of the songs we sang, as well as the darker centers that the humor framed. A favorite of mine was Tom Paxton's profound commentary on our time:

We didn't know, said the burgermeister,
about those camps on the edge of town.

We didn't know, said the Southern gentleman,
about the Ku Klux Klan.

We didn't know, said the puzzled voter,
about dropping bombs on Vietnam.

Another song I liked singing was Phil Ochs's droll "Draft Dodger Rag":

Oh, I'm just a typical American boy
from a typical American town.
I believe in God and Senator Dodd
and in keeping old Castro down.
And when it came my time to serve
I knew better dead than red.
But when I got to my old draft board,
buddy, this is what I said:
Sarge, I'm only 18,
I got a ruptured spleen,
I always carry a purse.
I got eyes like a bat,
and my feet are flat;
my asthma is getting worse.

The songs were wiser than I was at that point.

When we went up to Madison, Wisconsin, to play a campus date, Joe got me to go with him to a student demonstration against Dow Chemical, one of the big corporations that was supporting the war in Vietnam. We sang a couple of songs and suddenly I was off into something that had not been a part of my life before. I did it willingly, but it still made me nervous. I wasn't used to seeing myself as a rabble-rouser. It felt right to buck the establishment, but what bothered me was the potential for violence.

One night while we were performing at the Cellar Door—I can't remember if it was on our first visit there or the next—a Marine threw a glass at us from the balcony. It could have hurt any one of us if his aim had been better; it could have easily broken an instrument. The guy was drunk, he missed, and the club's security guards got him out of there, but that shook me up a little. At a couple of the college homecoming dates we played, you could cut the tension with a knife.

We worked with Dick Gregory a couple of times during those years. He was becoming more and more committed to ending the war, and each time we performed with him he inspired us to get more involved in protest ourselves. We went with him to Washington to participate in that city's first big demonstration against the war. Would I have gone if I hadn't been part of the Mitchell Trio? I doubt that I would ever have been as involved. Being in a new circle of friends was good for me; I soaked up the truth like a sponge.

At homecoming concerts, parents would come up after the show full of anger, sometimes livid with rage, about what we had done onstage. I think I was confronted more often than the others; maybe what I did on the stage—talking directly to the audience—made me more approachable. These were people who had had a son killed or injured in the war or they had a boy there now: How could I say that what their son was doing was wrong? How could I say he wasn't doing the right thing defending this country? What did *I* mean that their son's death was without meaning? And, of course, I was a draft dodger myself. Why wasn't I fighting? Where did I get off being so judgmental?

The fathers were *really* angry, and not far from throwing punches. I didn't know how to talk to these people. I didn't know how to tell them that I thought war was wrong, that it wasn't furthering our goals as a society, that killing someone was not my idea of acceptable behavior. I became victim to a whole lot of feelings I didn't necessarily understand at the time. I didn't want to say their sons were wrong and I didn't want to say my country was wrong, but the war *was* wrong. I knew that with all my heart. We, as a people, had to take a step forward and learn something different. I felt that singing those songs was part of that process. Facing up to these emotions left me deeply conflicted—I still wasn't accustomed to being so forthright, and, as I've mentioned, I was a little tender about confrontations. It took some real soul-searching to continue on the path I had chosen. My dad, of course, abhorred the things that the Mitchell Trio did. I don't think he honored me for the success I was having, although eventually he felt differently.

And some of the parents at these concerts eventually came around, too. In fact, the tide turned just a few weeks later. When I was marching in Washington against the war, I ran into some of the families who had confronted me on campus and they said, "We're with you." That's how quickly it turned. Suddenly the brutality of the war had come home and people were saying that they saw it differently now. What gives meaning to the life of my son, they said, is what I'm doing here today. I felt their torment.

One night at the airport in Columbus, Ohio, getting ready to go on the road again, I happened on some families who were obviously seeing their sons off to Vietnam. Moms sending their boys off to war; how unfair life could be: the loss, the loneliness. I went through all those emotions standing there, watching those families, watching what I couldn't bear to see. I felt such sorrow and compassion.

The war was profoundly changing the country.

In the midst of all this ferment, though, I was growing as a musician and that seemed to give me the energy to continue traveling around the country, which I loved doing. Not only did we do the first serious recordings of my career, but I was given an opportunity to bring some of what I had done before—the songs that were part of my repertoire—into the group. Those songs, like Bob Gibson's "That's the Way It's Going to Be," and Bob Dylan's "Mr. Tambourine Man," and "The Bells of Rhymney," which was a solo I did on the twelve-string guitar, were the ones I was up front on. If the songs we sang were my own compositions, that added to the pleasure I was having. It was a very exciting time for me.

I wasn't getting a whole lot of feedback about my own music, but, nonetheless, I started to feel comfortable about bringing in new material. I had a girlfriend named Bobbie at the time, whom I had met in Scottsdale while performing at the Lumber Mill. "For Baby (for Bobbie)" was an early attempt to order my romantic thoughts. Our romance, if I can call it that, began after she came to a show and lied about her age to get in. Later she told me that she had locked her key in her car and asked me to help retrieve it. For a year, I tried to coordinate my trips with her schedule so that we could see each other, even after she went off to Stevens College. Looking back on our relationship, I remember her as my confidante more than anything else. In the first flush of being a sexually active creature, I found that she was the one with whom I'd carry on endless conversations. But a point came when we both realized we weren't going to change into different people, and when I saw her again years later, I sensed that we both knew we had made the right decision when we discontinued our relationship. Not that we ever sat down and discussed it. Still, "For Bobbie" became one of the songs we did and we included it on the trio's next-to-last album. That small achievement gave me the confidence to bring the trio in closer contact with the audience. The other guys had always been aloof and standoffish when we performed. I broke down the barrier that stood between us and the people to whom we were playing. The satisfaction of doing that fed my growth even more.

By the time we came back to the Cellar Door for our second engagement, in 1966, a year after we started out there, there were lines around the block. David Steinberg, the comedian, was our opening act. Everybody was coming to see us. I was still a shy, introverted fellow, living a financially spare kind of existence, but onstage, I really opened up.

The money continued to be a problem in those days and I spent a lot of nights in airports. In Chicago one night, I couldn't afford the twenty-dollar cab ride in from O'Hare *and* the hotel, so I occupied a chair in the terminal. I remember it being such a long, cold night. It seems to me I had similar moments at Newark and Kennedy airports: short on funds, sleeping in chairs instead of beds. If ever I felt needy, it was during this period.

The worst time was when I had tonsillitis during a three- or four-day layover in Manhattan. There was no one around to rescue me, and I was down to my last thirty-five cents. I had been staying at the Great Northern Hotel, thinking that I simply had a terrible cold. Finally on Sunday, I had to go to the emergency room at Roosevelt Hospital to get something for the pain. The resident on duty wanted to admit me for a tonsillectomy, but I refused; it didn't feel right. I wanted to wait to talk with Milt in the morning. About two A.M. I spent the thirty-five cents on a milk shake; I couldn't take the pain any longer. That was the only thing that got me through the night.

♦   ♦   ♦

We had a couple of weeks to kill after that second engagement at the Cellar Door and, having no place in particular to go, I stayed around Washington. I had a lot of friends in the area and one of them, Jim Cunningham, invited me to stay with him and his roommate at their place in Virginia. I was beginning to forget what it felt like to have a settled life. In Chicago that summer, finding myself with some money in the bank, I'd bought a Triumph 500 motorcycle—if Dad wasn't going to honor me for my success, I'd do it myself—which I drove back to Washington. I felt it lent me an air of being a man in control of his own destiny. I was recording, I was performing, I was on my own, and I had wheels again.

I kept busy those two weeks doing things with friends, letting certain feelings work their way to the surface. One night, when Jim and his roommate went to a party, I decided to stay put and started out the evening working on an oil painting. I'd gotten interested in painting while studying architecture in college. I was playing around with an idea. I had a six-pack of beer and a couple of sandwiches. And then I picked up my guitar and wrote a song with my soul wide open and my mind picturing the scene as if it stood before me, real enough to touch. I called it "Oh, Babe, I Hate to Go."

I wrote the song not so much out of the experience of feeling that way for someone, as out of the longing to have someone to love. When I got through, I knew I'd written my best song yet. It was so exciting that, late as it was, I called Andy Poole, a friend who lived in the District, roused her from her sleep, and rode the Triumph over to her place to sing it for her. She was really knocked out by it, as were a few other people I sang it for.

A few days later, I rode up the turnpike to the Philadelphia Folk Festival and sang the song for Milt, who had come down to hear the trio perform, and he was blown away. He saw the possibilities right away, and there were so many.

Actually, the entire festival was an auspicious occasion for me. I got to meet people who were my heroes and heroines, like Tom Paxton, Judy Collins, Joan Baez, and Phil Ochs, and that was very exciting. Just being there reassured me that I was part of what was happening. And to be there making music on the same stage with all of these people whom I admired so much put the frosting on it.

For a while, during this period, I tried to get back into the role of the older brother. Ron had gotten into a bad automobile accident. His best friend was killed and he and two girls in the car had been badly injured. Dad had recently retired from the Air Force and he and Mom had left Florida, looking for work. They had let Ron stay behind with a family friend in Fort Walton Beach so he could finish his senior year of high school with his friends. By the time he got out of the hospital, though, he'd missed so much of the school year, there seemed no point in his going back, and I suggested he travel with me for a month or so.

Ours had always been a distant relationship, and it is still not what it should be, but at that moment we were both happy to be together. I think I wanted to share who I was and what I was doing with Ron, and I think he was open to finding out. Time was short, though, and all the traveling around kept us from really connecting on the level I had hoped we would. Soon Ron went into the Army and off to Vietnam, and that moment sadly passed.

♦   ♦   ♦

During my off-hours in D.C., I hung out at the Cellar Door, where all of my friends worked, and sometimes I'd get up on the stage and sing the songs that I had written; they were always well received. People would say, "Johnny, you ought to record those." So that fall, when we were out in L.A., I went back to Gold Star Studios, with Paul Prestopino and Bob Hefferan accompanying me on guitars, and cut this little album of about thirteen songs. I never gave it a name, but I made two hundred and fifty copies, which cost me all the money I had in the bank, and sent them out as Christmas presents to people I had met around the country. One of them went to Peter, Paul and Mary, and they so loved the song "Leaving on a Jet Plane" (Milt had made me drop the title "Oh Babe, I Hate to Go" when he published it) that they featured it on their new album, and that felt real good. They were at the top of their game at the time. "Leaving on a Jet Plane" was going to become their first and only number-one hit. So my sails started to fill.

I won't tell Annie's story here—it needs its own space, its own fretwork, but this was the period she came into my life: Ann Martell of St. Peter, Minnesota.

What she saw in me, I don't know. Maybe she was attracted to the vagabond I was, although I have to say I was also well-mannered, and, on the stage at least, I could be sparkly and cute (unlike those wild boys you'd hesitate to bring home to Mom and Dad). Milt says I was courtly. If so, it was probably to hide the fact that I was so repressed. Still, I bubbled over with high spirits; how could Annie resist such wide-eyed innocence? We met at a concert that the trio gave at Annie's school in Minnesota, although *met* might be too inaccurate a word to describe our first encounter. I think she thought me a bit crass for coming on to her. But something about her stayed in my mind for months and months, and when the trio came back through the area, on the way to another college date, I looked her up. Apparently her resistance had softened. Anyway, she saw something she liked and we fell in love, got married, and at the end of that summer went off to Europe together on the second part of our honeymoon, which we were taking at the same time as the Mitchell Trio's first European tour. Unfortunately, the tour never really got off the ground. We played only one date and that was in Stockholm. Most of the rest of the time we sat around broke.

The debt that tour incurred dogged me for years, but I have only myself to blame. You can take the measure of my seriousness during this period from the way I dealt with the situation. That autumn the trio's financial adviser, Hal Thau, let us know that every time we went out to perform we were losing money and that it made more sense to disband rather than to keep digging ourselves in deeper. It would take several months before we actually did disband, and at that time I insisted on personally honoring our obligations. Even though we were all going to go in different directions and the debt was the trio's, not mine individually, and even though Hal suggested we walk away from it, I felt strongly that since Mike and Joe were retiring from the business and I was staying in it, honoring our debt was the right—the only—thing to do. Hal disagreed, but he respected my determination, however naive, and he helped me to see it through—in installments. Most of the debt was with one of the airlines, which eventually they turned over to a collection agency. Hal kept the agency bounty hunter at bay until, fifty and seventy-five dollars at a time, the obligation was met.

After that aborted tour, the trio never regained its momentum as a performing unit. Sometime that fall, Joe Frazier got increasingly difficult to work with. He started wearing his hair like Prince Valiant and being gratuitously flamboyant, if not outright provocative. He began showing up later and later for concerts. At first, to fill in the time, I'd go out and do my little solo set, and then once Joe arrived, we'd do our show. But it got increasingly frustrating to Mike and me, and we ended up parting company with Joe and replacing him with David Boise, a singer from Texas. This was yet another edition of the Mitchell Trio, with me assuming de facto leadership of the group, taking on more and more of the basic housekeeping.

We kept working as a trio, and we did a third album, *Mitchell Trio Alive,* which included our version of "Leaving on a Jet Plane," as well as another song I had written, "I Like to Deal with the Ladies (as sung in the shower with a 27-piece orchestra)." As a viable commercial entity, though, we kept losing altitude. When Warner Brothers Reprise, the label we were on, held its sales meeting that fall to show off who they were excited about in the upcoming sales season, we were not included. They were excited about Jimi Hendrix, the Beatles, and, interestingly, Peter, Paul and Mary's version of "Leaving on a Jet Plane," arrangement by Milt Okun. The music out there was changing, and at least on an individual basis, it seems I was changing with it.

We tried to breathe new life into the group by signing with a booking agency called Variety Theater International. Originally the trio had been managed by Frank Fried, but when Chad Mitchell left to pursue his own career, Fried left with him. A fellow named Tom Mallow, who worked out of Chicago, took on the job. We stayed with him for a while, but eventually things didn't work out. Next we signed with Chartoff and Winkler— Bob Chartoff and Irwin Winkler. Theirs was a big company, but ours was a short-lived relationship because they were starting to get into movies and couldn't really look after our needs. It was through Chartoff and Winkler, though, that I had met Hal Thau, who became my accountant, then my business manager, eventually my personal manager, and always one of my closest friends. He was an accountant for Chartoff and Winkler, as well as for many of their clients; at that time he was a young guy just starting out who'd been given the trio's accounts to keep straight. When Chartoff and Winkler got out of the management end of the business, Hal found Artie Mogull, a veteran of the recording industry, to manage us. But in the fall of that year, along with everything else that was changing, Artie went off to California to work for a record company. We then signed with Variety Theater in Duluth, near where Annie and I were living. Variety Theater was run by a fellow named Len Naymark and his partner, Gordon Singer. We all liked Gordon then, but in my opinion, he turned out not to be the friend I thought he was.

Variety Theater made a niche for itself booking concerts at a string of small liberal-arts colleges, primarily in the Midwest. They took whoever was hot and got them gigs at schools, and gave them a guarantee for the run of the tour: so many weeks for so many dollars. In those early years of touring, no other management company was doing that. If a school couldn't afford its first choice—say the Fifth Dimension at ten thousand dollars a night—Variety Theater could offer them Friends of Distinction at four thousand. In folk music, Peter, Paul and Mary would be the higher-priced choice and the Mitchell Trio the lesser one. You had to pay all your own expenses, but Variety took care of the travel arrangements, making it easy for you to get around.

We were going to get $30,000 a month and it sounded fantastic; it came to $1,250 a night.

One night, when we were playing in Colorado Springs at the Air Force Academy, the guy who Variety Theater intended to send along to take care of our needs didn't make it out of the Duluth office because of a late-fall snowstorm, so at the end of our two concerts I picked up the check and was quite surprised: It was for $3,500, not $1,250. That was a bit of a shock. If I'm going to be exploited like that, at least let me know about it. All that Gordon could say on his behalf, when I asked him about it, was that they were taking all the risks by giving us a guarantee. That was the end of that relationship as far as I was concerned.

We had a night or two off between the date in Colorado Springs and some other engagements, so I took off for Aspen. An old girlfriend was living there and knew the clubs. At that point I thought I could get some work in a ski resort. Annie and I had been to Aspen once before when I was courting her, and we were in love with the Rockies: It was our fantasy to go back there. I went to the Leather Jug in Snowmass, where I knew Chad Mitchell had worked the year before, and the owner, Jack Caswell, gave me a job for two weeks over Christmas. The two weeks became six. For the first time in its brief history, Snowmass had people coming from Aspen to hear someone sing. I was packing the place every night. Caswell had me come back the last few weeks of the season. Then the owner of the Refectory in Snowmass hired me to perform for a month at his place in San Francisco and invited Annie and me to stay at his house.

In the meantime, the days of the Mitchell Trio dwindled to a precious few. In fact, we had lost the right to use the name. Under the terms of the original agreement that had set up the group as a business entity, we could keep the name as long as some member of the original group remained. When Mike Kobluk finally retired, he was replaced by Michael Johnson, and the trio was renamed Denver, Boise and Johnson. But I knew I had to start making moves of my own if I intended to stay in the business, so that's why I started booking my own engagements. A couple of times I teamed with John Stewart, whom I admired greatly and who was going through the same kind of shift with the Kingston Trio that I was with my group. He was a songwriter and, like me, he wanted to do some things a little more modern than what the Kingston Trio was doing. Our voices had a distinctive sound together.

That spring, I hooked up with a concert bureau that booked coffeehouse acts into colleges. As "the writer of 'Leaving on a Jet Plane,' formerly of the Mitchell Trio," I could earn about five hundred dollars a week, which was top dollar on their circuit. The circumstances were humble—you slept and ate in the dorm of the school where you were playing, and you carried your own setup from place to place—but the interest was there; I could see that what I was doing was working. I got only four gigs that spring, but in each place, there'd be fifteen or twenty people on the first night; on the second night those people would come back with their friends; on the third night it would be packed; and then it would stay packed for the rest of the week.

And then that summer—1969, the summer of Woodstock—a minor miracle occurred. Milt Okun landed me a recording contract—I think he'd already been turned down by sixteen record companies. RCA liked my tapes, and when I came in and auditioned for them, they liked me—*they* being a courtly gentleman named Harry Jenkins, who was the man responsible for Elvis Presley going to RCA. It was a standard record deal: two albums a year for two years. I was elated. Of course,

I was also disappointed not to be a part of Woodstock, even hurt not to have been invited to perform, but it wasn't as if it was a surprise—I simply didn't occupy that niche—and not being a part of it at least showed me who I was and where I was at that time.

My first album, *Rhymes and Reasons,* came out that fall, about the time Crosby, Stills and Nash had their first big hit, "Marrakesh Express," and two more divergent paths by folksingers couldn't have been clearer. There, on one hand, were the representatives of the flower-power generation, and here was I, still a Midwesterner singing folk songs. Instead of regretting the divergence, I went with it. My response to Woodstock was to record a couple of songs that reflected the social and political bent I'd developed with the Mitchell Trio, songs that I'd include on my second album. One was Tom Paxton's antiwar protest "Jimmy Newman," which starts out low and builds, enabling me to use my voice passionately, and the other an early song of mine, "Take Me to Tomorrow":

> *Hey, everybody, tell me how do you feel?*
> *Are you satisfied with your life, do you think*
> *   it's real?*
> *Tell me, how is your head, what are your dreams?*
> *Do you have any plans, do you have any schemes?*
> *Do you care about anybody?*
> *I'd like to know is the answer "No"?*
> *Take me to tomorrow, take me there today,*
> *I've had my fill of sorrow, and livin' this way.*
> *Take me to tomorrow, that's where I'd*
> *   like to be,*
> *The day after tomorrow is waitin' for me.*

By my third album, which RCA issued in the fall of 1970, my social and political leanings were defined even more clearly, if only for myself. On that album I recorded Tom Paxton's "Whose Garden Was This?" which was the first song I did about the environment. The album, which went by the same name, bored everybody to death, and sold fewer copies than any record I've done, but it was pivotal in freeing my tongue.

On my first promotional tour, I sang "Follow Me," which is still one of my big songs:

> *It's by far the hardest thing I've ever done,*
> *To be so in love with you and so alone.*
> *Follow me where I go, what I do and who I know*
> *Make it part of you to be a part of me.*

At press receptions, I'd also do "Leaving on a Jet Plane" and "The Ballad of Spiro Agnew," which made everyone laugh and take notes. It didn't always get played on the radio, but I was making advances; people were getting to know John Denver. My price for performing went up and I started to make a little money. I put a small band behind me, just a few instruments that kind of melded together. After that third album, the Cellar Door booked me as a headliner for the first time. It was one of those sweet moments when life takes on a deeper note—a synergistic moment, when the whole is greater than the sum of its parts.

The Mitchell Trio was fast becoming history for me, but the basic lessons I'd learned while working with them hadn't been lost. I'd learned that powerful songs are powerful not because they're pretty or bouncy or funny, but because they're about the human condition and what we all aspire to; I'd learned those were the songs I loved.

I'd learned also that one of the things that moves people is someone saying musically or otherwise what they don't know how to say, or are afraid to say, or don't expect to hear said, and certainly not from someone on the stage; I'd learned that I love to be the bearer of that gift.

And I'd learned to recognize songs that allowed me to sing with my whole self, songs that started quietly and then built up until I was singing from my toes, reaching for that high note to put my feelings into. These were songs that had been all around us, but experience had made the stories they told seem more acute. It surprised people when I'd sing "I Wish I Knew How It Would Feel to Be Free"—this young white kid, with the granny glasses, who didn't seem like anyone who would worry about that.

I had started learning how to find those songs in myself.

A N N I E ' S   S O N G

You fill up my senses
like a night in a forest,
Like the mountains in springtime,
like a walk in the rain,
Like a storm in the desert,
like a sleepy blue ocean,
You fill up my senses,
come fill me again.

There are days now when Annie would just as soon sprinkle me with disappearing powder and forget she ever knew me, but I say that with rue. Our marriage fell apart, but we're parents together and that tie binds. We're fated to be in each other's lives. We still have differences. We might get prickly with each other from time to time. And for a long while, there was bitterness between us. Now I'd say we've become good friends again.

Like the day when Annie called to commiserate about our then eighteen-year-old son, Zachary, who had just gone back East after a school holiday. He was off to do his last semester of high school. The message Annie left on my answering machine was full of feeling: "Hello, John. This is your first wife! What about that Zak? He's out the door. He's gone. Call me when you can."

So the lines of communication are still open. We're still learning about each other, and she's still trying to educate me. I'm one of Annie's continuing subjects of psychological study. I know she feels she knows me better than anyone on Earth. Good friends get to know one another whatever games they play. I'm sure I still love her. "Annie's Song" still has meaning for me.

We met in the spring of 1966. The Mitchell Trio had performed a concert at Gustavus Adolphus College in St. Peter, Minnesota, and afterward we were invited over to the Student Union, where there was a charity drive going on. All the fraternities and sororities were doing things to raise money, and I got drawn over to a group of students in one of the lounges who were doing a show. I couldn't figure out what the show was about, but this one gal in jeans and a flannel shirt, with the tails hanging out, filled me with wonder. She'd come out onstage every so often carrying the signboards announcing the passing scenes. Deep inside I could feel love on the wing. Isn't love at twenty-two meant to be fearless? Fearless is certainly what I was trying to be.

The show ended and someone who'd been to our concert came over with a guitar and asked if I'd sing some songs. I agreed and Annie sat right down in front. Her friends told me later it was the first time that they had seen her quiet for that long. And of course I sang every song just for her. I wanted her to know how I felt, even if I didn't know how to say it. The attentiveness of my audience ended up giving me courage, though, and as we were leaving, I boldly asked this girl her name and where she was from, hoping it might be someplace where we'd be performing; I knew we weren't planning to be back at Adolphus for a while.

"This is where I'm from," she said. "I'm a hometown girl." And lightheartedly I parried something like "Oh, that's too bad," which she misconstrued. She thought I was being a jerk—and that was the end of the conversation. I stood rebuffed.

But in the fall, the trio came back to Minnesota to do a show in Mankato, and while we were driving through St. Peter, my thoughts flashed on this girl, Annie something. That pitiful attempt of mine to make conversation was forgotten, but I remembered the girl. What mystery made me want to call her? In Mankato, during the sound check, some people from Annie's college happened by, and one of them knew Annie Martell and told me how to get in touch with her.

No, she hadn't forgotten me. Yes, she'd like to come to our concert. Yes, I'd pick her up—even though I didn't have much time before the show. No, she wasn't quite ready when I got there. Her friends had given Annie such a teasing about going out with me that she had lost track of what she had to do to get ready.

While I waited for her in the dorm lounge, a bevy of girls came through eyeing me surreptitiously as they signed out for the evening; I had no inkling who they were. I think some of them hid behind the bushes to watch Annie and me come out.

The girl who her friends said you couldn't keep still had been to Europe since I last saw her. Florence was the most beautiful city in the world, she said. Her hair was cut short; it had been long when I first met her. She'd filled in; she looked great. She came to the concert and then a couple of nights later she came to another one nearby. Our courtship began to flourish.

That second concert fell on a Saturday night. Annie came to it with her father's front-wheel-drive Oldsmobile Toronado. Her folks were up in Minneapolis for the big football weekend: the Gophers of the University of Minnesota that Saturday and the Vikings of the NFL on Sunday. Her dad was a serious football fan. I was staying in Minneapolis, so we decided to drive up together. I had Sunday off and Annie wanted me to meet her parents, whom I liked immediately.

By the time we got there, Jim and Norma Martell had been to the University of Minnesota game and out to dinner, and they were really loose and very funny. Annie's dad owned a restaurant in St. Peter. He told me later that as much as we laughed together that Saturday night, he woke on Sunday with a start, realizing that Annie had let me, a perfect stranger, go off with his car.

The next afternoon, while Annie's folks were at the NFL game, we spent a chaste middle-American afternoon in their hotel room, but it worked its magic. By the time we kissed good-bye and I saw Annie off to school, I was smitten. Smitten at twenty-two. (What was Annie, nineteen?) I was ready to die for love.

That night I went to the movies to see David Lean's *Doctor Zhivago,* and all of this pent-up yearning was released. The tragedy and unfairness of human life, the waste, all flashed by in the scene where Zhivago sees Lara—the woman he has loved so passionately and lost to war—in a crowd and tries to get off the tram he is riding to get to her. When he had a heart attack and couldn't reach her, I just fell apart. Zhivago is dead and they are never to be reunited.

Afterward, I walked around downtown Minneapolis for hours weeping inconsolably, crying not only for myself, but for lovers everywhere. I felt really alone. For no reason I can put my finger on, other than youthful romanticism, I was convinced that my relationship with Annie, like Zhivago's with Lara, was doomed. There must be deaths such as his every day all over the world. I had just seen those families saying good-bye to their sons at the airport in Columbus, powerless to alter the course of fate. All of those themes played in my mind that night.

Was I in love? Someone once said that I was in love with love. Maybe that was true. Whatever it was, I was blind to it. It was happening and I was powerless in the face of it. It just hurt bad.

One weekend I got real flak from Annie's dad for taking her to Seattle, where I was performing. He was afraid I was seducing her, and those things just weren't done where we came from. Of course, we both longed to touch and be touched, and to have a loving relationship right there and then, but we were too dumb and shy to go against the grain. We didn't even sleep in the same bed, much less make love. I was simply showing Annie the delights of Seattle, which I had come to know when I worked the summer in a lumber camp there. That was my notion of how two people became lovers.

I was still very much the vagabond king, living out of suitcases, with no place to call home. I visited my folks only rarely, so I started to hang out with Annie as much as I could, and began to think of Minneapolis as home base. At one point, Annie said to her mother, "What am I going to do with him?" and her mother replied, "Don't worry, you'll think of something."

That Christmas I inveigled an invitation from Annie to spend part of the holidays with her and her family. I had such a nice time getting to know them: her parents, her sisters, her brother. I brought along a model of the Apollo spacecraft and spent most of the time working on it with Annie's brother, Ben.

Later that winter, Annie's school ski club went to Aspen and

I showed up there and surprised her. We slept together one night, after we both had had too much to drink, but again, it was all very innocent. In the morning, I went out to the drugstore to buy Annie a toothbrush, and when I came back she was gone. She didn't want her friends to know how close we had grown.

Annie, I might add here, was a person who never needed approval. She was raised in one place. She went to grade school, junior high school, high school and college all in the same town. Her father was a successful businessman and she was always really popular. The most popular girl around. On top of everything, she was really pretty. Winning approval was never something she had to contend with. In that sense we were opposites. Her involvement with me created a bit of a quandary.

Out on the road again, I found myself desperately missing her and decided I wanted to marry her. I didn't know how to take care of myself, much less another person, but I heard the ancestral voices: You're twenty-three years old! It's time you were settling down with a good woman! It's time to be thinking of having a family! Time to be putting down the foundation of your house. I didn't realize at the time that I had no idea who I really was.

When I popped the question on the phone, Annie turned me down flat. I didn't know what to do next, and the relationship might have died right there, but in those days, matters of the heart were all-or-nothing propositions. I'd give all or nothing. But before things got really bad between us, Annie's best friend, Ann Sullivan, called and played matchmaker. "You ought to call her," she told me. "She really misses you."

I swallowed my pride and proposed again. This time she said yes.

"Yes?"

"Yes, yes."

Obviously, I had no great insight into what I was setting off to do. I was completely disregarding the fact that the Mitchell Trio was going downhill and carrying with it my bank account. I just let myself be carried along by the momentum of this new fact of my life. I prepared for marriage.

In New York on some Mitchell Trio business, I went to Tiffany's and bought an engagement ring, which I carried around until I got back to Minneapolis. Ring in pocket, I took Annie to dinner at her dad's restaurant. When she went off to powder her nose, I slipped the ring into her glass of Great Northern sparkling burgundy. When she discovered it, we had a big laugh. All the good things I had hoped for were happening.

On June 9, 1967, we had a big wedding in a modern and beautiful Lutheran church in St. Peter with the venerable Reverend Millard Ahlstrom presiding. The ceremony and its trappings had a bit of the past and a bit of the present, which suited the way Annie and I saw ourselves. Mike Kobluk came and sang. My family was there, including Grandma Swope and my mother's sister from Tulsa. So were David Boise, Paul Prestopino, and Bob Hefferan, the guys I worked with who were my closest friends. After the ceremony, Annie's folks hosted a reception at their restaurant. The toast was made to Henry John Deutschendorf and his bride. It was a great party and we hated to leave. Early the next morning, we flew to L.A. to pick up my Mustang, and then we drove to Arizona.

That was the start of what was to become a fairly peripatetic life for me. More than I expected it to be, probably even more than I had experienced as a child—and more, I'm sure, than Annie bargained for. Our honeymoon (I hate that word) was spent in a trailer that Annie's grandparents kept in Tempe. It

was the height of the summer and the place was fairly uninhab-
ited, but the senior citizens who were there all took us under
their wings.

We spent our time playing together. I introduced Annie to the
desert and to old friends in Scottsdale. One night, making love,
I apparently fractured one of Annie's ribs. That next evening we
couldn't figure out why she was in pain, until a doctor diagnosed
it. Even then I was confused because the doctor was so discreet
when briefing us. Annie said just pay the bill. I had become
ardent, but I was still dumb about ordinary life.

Toward the middle of August we loaded up the Mustang with
my worldly possessions and drove across the country, first to
Philadelphia, where the trio had a concert date, and then to New
York, where we performed in Central Park. New York gives out
an energy I'm not quite comfortable with, and so perhaps that's
why we had our first falling-out there.

It happened when we were leaving a restaurant, Annie and I
and Joe and Mike. I think I was a little drunk. A newscaster from
one of the networks—a black man—was there and he said hello.
I don't know what possessed me, but I not only said hello back,
I wanted to make conversation with him. At the time, the trio sang
this beautiful song called "See the Little Brown Boy," and as part
of that we performed a skit about Lyndon Johnson being prepped
by one of his staff before meeting Martin Luther King, Jr.

In concert, as satire, the skit was funny, and in Washington it
had brought down the house. But that night, with me slightly in
the tank and forcing the skit on this poor man, it wasn't funny.
Annie got very upset with me, and I got very upset with her for
being upset. I couldn't stand being made to feel foolish, so I said
some rude things to hurt her, thereby proving myself to be
the fool.

Annie never forgot and neither did I.

We made up the next morning, and went off on our ill-fated trip to Europe with the trio. In retrospect, I realize it was a voyage that was misconceived from the start.

I still recall one incident in Italy with a pang of guilt. We were traveling around the countryside and accepted a ride from a couple of strangers, two guys who turned out to be wiseguys. Annie sat up front with the driver and I sat in back, and there was a point when the driver surreptitiously started to fondle her leg. I could see the guy's expression in the rearview mirror. It was a scene out of a Grade B Italian gangster movie, but no fun while it was happening. I finally said something confrontational and they let us out in the middle of nowhere, but not before I felt totally diminished by the situation. I felt guilty that I hadn't been more masterful in avoiding the whole experience. I still had little capacity for handling trouble.

Why were we in Italy, anyway?

To see the beautiful Michelangelos, and also because Annie had loved Florence when she visited it the year before—with a boyfriend—on a school trip. I was jealous. I wanted to take her back to the city where she'd had "the best time" and show her an even better one.

And we did have a good time. We visited friends, we toured, and I took lots of photographs. One day, while crossing the Ponte Vecchio, we bumped into an American girl handing out fliers advertising an American bar in Florence, and I wound up singing there. To strangers, we must have seemed like delightful youngsters, making hay while the sun shone. And the sun shone all the time.

And then we arrived in England to begin the trio's tour, and none of what we had hoped would happen did. All but one of the bookings that had drawn us there in the first place fell through. We were staying at the posh Park Court Hotel, and initially we were put up in the honeymoon suite, but then we had to vacate because we could no longer afford the rates. In fact, most of that week we couldn't afford to eat out; we had to bring food back to the hotel room. It was an aimless time. We didn't use it to get to know each other better. Annie's face got longer and longer.

When Mike, Joe, and I decided to take our act to Sweden, Annie decided to go home. I didn't know if she was discouraged about our lack of bookings, or just truly homesick. Either way, I took it as a kind of abandonment; I still hit myself for letting her go off. I couldn't tell her how much I needed her. I should have talked with her about it and maybe we could have figured something out. Instead it just became an unspoken source of grief for me, and my immature reaction was to think: If Annie chooses not to come with me, and be with me on the road, she shouldn't expect me after a two-and-a-half-hour concert, giving heart and soul to an audience, to go back to my room alone.

I didn't start thinking about being with other women right away, but as our separations became a regular feature of our lives, I found infidelity the only solace for my disappointment with Annie. I don't think I ever forgave her for leaving me, or forgave myself for my reaction.

What a time bomb I had created! And defusing it, finding a more amiable perspective from which to see things, was beyond my capacities at that point. I was still so young. All I could manage with any consistency was fending off the infernal demands of financial obligation that so quickly came to be part of our lives. The wounds were tucked away out of sight, but I still nursed them.

◆　◆　◆

During the first few years of marriage, we tried living in the Midwest, first in Chicago and then in Minneapolis. In Chicago, Mike Kobluk passed on an apartment he and his wife had occupied in the Marina City complex—forty-seven stories up. We were living there, in fact, when the Mitchell Trio disbanded, and for a while it was financially touch-and-go. Some months we'd even be overdrawn at the bank and seriously late meeting the rent. Fortunately, neither the bank manager nor the rental agent ever harassed us about it. Both, in fact, went out of their way to be kind to us, holding on to the paperwork until we could get some payment to them.

Most everything from this time is now a blur. What I remember mostly is being on the road continuously and trying to pay bills. I'm sure that's exaggerated by the passing of time. I must have been around home more than I remember. Either that or else Annie came on the road with me more than she would later.

When I try to think about our marriage during this time, I always come back to this one grim memory of a meal Annie fixed for our next-door neighbor. It might have been the day after we moved in. This apartment was home now, and Annie wanted to do the neighborly thing, so she invited our neighbor over for a pot roast dinner, except she didn't know how to cook it. It was terribly underdone and unchewable. And I wasn't very sympathetic. I even became angry about it, angry beyond cause—which is a theme that has run deep in my life. Moreover, I couldn't admit my anger. In those days, I created so much tension for myself around the business of living! No matter how hard I tried, I couldn't help taking it all so seriously. I think I inherited a worrying nature from my mother, probably from all those middle-of-the-night bus rides to Tulsa, coddled in her arms, while she cried about yet another blowup with Dad.

(When I was four and five, my family spent a couple of years in Japan, during the Occupation after World War II. Photos in my mother's album show me looking a little warily at the camera. It is the look in the eyes, I think, that's the telltale sign. My own children don't have it—never had it. What was on that boy's mind?)

Anyway, Chicago just proved too expensive for Annie and me, and after a year we moved to Minneapolis, where we found a nicer place for less money. I think it says a lot about who we were then that we moved into a staid suburban development rather than a place near the university and its Sixties countercultural haunts. Someone coming from a folk group might have been expected to do otherwise.

Nonetheless we resonated to the notion of being flower children. We particularly liked the idea of loving each other, even if we were having difficulty in that regard, and within that notion of loving, importantly, there was the notion of standing up for what you believed. We were still down-to-earth, conservative Midwesterners, the boy and girl next door, attached to the values of our childhoods. If we sinned, it was with guilt.

I remember the time Annie experimented with marijuana. We had friends over, which seemed always to be the case. Ann Sullivan, Annie's best friend, was there, and also a guy we knew who made jewelry and leather goods. He was the reincarnation of a Yankee peddler, traveling the West selling his wares and coming back to Minneapolis with all the latest herbal remedies. After dinner, he offered us a smoke from his little stash. Not that any of us were regular users. I'm not sure I hadn't smoked once in Washington during my last days with the Mitchell Trio.

Ann Sullivan said she had done it a number of times, so we all lit up and Annie Deutschendorf tried it. Almost immediately she gave up her dinner.

I also remember being very strident in conversations with Annie's friends, who were still mostly students. This was most obvious when the discussion came around to what was going on in the world. At that point I saw myself as a Worldly Figure, and I liked being thought of as one by my captive audience. I *was* out there in the world, after all! I had a lot of information about how people were living, information about things that were going on, and images in my mind of where I thought the world was going, given current trends (none of it was very pretty). I wanted things to change, and I wasn't afraid to speak out: I liked being listened to.

I think my strident tone, along with some of my more fanciful formulations, drove Annie a bit crazy. Most of the time she thought I was indulging my ego by making pronouncements, but I was really trying to reach the point where I could say those things musically. One day, in the shower, I started to write the song "Rhymes and Reasons":

So you speak to me of sadness and the coming of the winter
Fear that is within you now that seems to never end
And the dreams that have escaped you and a hope that you've
* forgotten*
You tell me that you need me now and you want to be my
* friend*

And you wonder where we're going, where's the rhyme
and where's the reason

I was trying to define my beliefs as a man, what I thought life was about and for. Where's the rhyme and where's the reason?

And it's you who cannot accept it is here we must begin
To seek the wisdom of the children
And the graceful way of flowers in the wind
For the children and the flowers are my sisters and my
*   brothers*
Their laughter and their loveliness would clear a
*   cloudy day*
Like the music of the mountains and the colors of the
*   rainbow*
They're a promise of the future and a blessing for
*   today.*

Where those particular lyrics came from, I don't know. I can only guess. The biblical resonances are hard to miss. And as much as I thought of myself as lacking in religious feelings by then, I can't think of a song that better defines me at that time, and maybe still:

Though the cities start to crumble and the towers fall
*   around us*
The sun is slowly fading and it's colder than the sea
It is written: From the desert to the mountain they
*   shall lead us*
By the hand and by the heart and they will comfort you
*   and me*
In their innocence and trusting, they will teach us to be
*   free.*

I was convinced that one day we were going to live in the mountains. People were going to want to listen to what I had to say, and what I had to say to people would be meaningful; I would lead "by the hand and by the heart." Annie took it all with a grain of salt, as well she might.

By that summer I landed my contract with RCA. My job back at Ledbetter's in the early days had paid less than seven thousand dollars a year, and now I was going to get seven thousand dollars an album guaranteed. A modest advance, but it looked good; in fact, it looked great. Suddenly a solution had arisen for our money problems. After that things kind of built, and they built for both Annie and me, really.

The first two albums had modest sales, but with the release of my third album, *Whose Garden Was This?*, the current seemed to surge dramatically. So many possibilities emerged then that I could hardly think them through. Our lives were never going to be the same.

For one thing, Hal Thau thought I needed a personal manager again, someone who would be able to look after my career on more of a regular basis than he or Milt. And so in 1970 Jerry Weintraub and his wife, Jane Morgan, came into our lives. Jerry used to boast about being able to sell bathing suits in Alaska—he was Mr. Charm himself. Jane was, of course, one of the great cabaret singers of her generation, and we were all—Annie, me, my mom, my dad—great fans of hers. With seeming suddenness, here were Annie and I, little Midwestern kids really, spending time with an international glamour girl and her handsome consort from the Bronx. Holy moly!

Late that summer, when we attended the annual RCA trade convention in Mexico City, Jerry invited Annie and me to join him and Jane at their beach house in Acupulco. We were charmed out of our socks.

One weekend that fall, Annie and I went to New York and used the Weintraubs' very posh apartment on West Fifty-sixth

Street, high above the city's cares and woes. It went far beyond any idea either of us had at the time of what constituted elegance. My star might have been on the rise, but we were nowhere near this class. We both felt the allure.

When Jane opened at the Plaza, Annie and I had a ringside table and Jerry had Jane make a big deal of me. It seemed as if everybody in show business and politics was there, including the mayor of New York, John Lindsey. And the famous designer of Jane's gowns was there, with five models on his arms. Holy moly again.

When Jane sang "Leaving on a Jet Plane" and introduced me, I was overwhelmed. This was decidedly a step up from the Golliwog Lounge at the Ritz Sheraton in Minneapolis. Being there was exciting and challenging, and I could feel enormous new vistas opening before me. Annie felt it, too. Some of it, I think, might have happened too fast for her. She liked Jerry and Jane; they were among the most interesting people we knew. I began to realize, however, that under these circumstances Annie disliked being "Mrs. John Denver." Understandably, the hullabaloo that was attached to that buildup didn't mesh with her sense of self. Out on the road, I think she felt very much in my shadow. She didn't have a chance to be herself very easily. She was interested in sounding out her own depths, and there weren't many people out there to acknowledge that.

Vivacious as Annie was, in my opinion, her best day was Sunday. This was her time for drawing into herself, quietly reading or reflecting, and I loved that about her. It was wonderful to be around her when that was happening. She had an amazing capacity for bringing all of herself forward into everything she did, including those times when she would draw away into her own space. Unfortunately, my songs seemed to have only a small place in those depths.

In Minnesota she had a job for a while, but mostly she stayed home, involved with her friends. And that pattern continued when we moved to Aspen. The more we were apart, the more we invited people and things that weren't part of our relationship into our lives.

When I think about what I was doing with the Mitchell Trio and for the first few years after we disbanded—how serious I was about matters of self—I conjure up a little scene from childhood. We are up in the mountains and some of Mom's family is with us. We have stopped on the side of the road, where there is a little bit of a hill and some beautiful views of the land off in the distance. Dad is getting ready to snap our picture and I run out of the frame and up the hill, with one of my aunts in pursuit. When I look back, I see all these looks of reproach, which the Scotch-Irish part of my family excelled in. Their mouths are not moving, but their look is saying: "Come on back, where it is safe. Here's where you belong." And I'm frozen between the two impulses—to stay reined in or to run off, out of the frame. Out of control.

Onstage, fortunately, I could be myself without having to go out of the frame, and I could put all that I had into what I was doing. I was always scared when we went out there—there wasn't a single night that my hands weren't shaking—but I could mask it with my granny glasses and bangs, and hide behind a sparkly and cute facade. Still, deep down I was involved in this terrible struggle about whether to stay reined in or let myself go.

In New York in the fall of 1970, I started to cut my fourth album for RCA, *Poems, Prayers and Promises*. We put off doing the mix until after the holidays. As I said earlier, the Cellar Door in Washington had booked me as a headliner for the first time, and I was opening the day after Christmas. Annie came with me, and our old friends Bill and Taffy Danoff—the Fat City band—were the opening act. It was like a family reunion. On a previous visit to the Cellar Door, I'd heard a song of theirs, called "I Guess He'd Rather Be in Colorado," which I wound up including on the album I was recording. So we were feeling very good about seeing one another and about working together in the days ahead.

The first night, the audience was very responsive. After the show, full of ourselves, Annie and I took off for a late-night get-together at the Danoffs'. We rode along with Kris O'Connor—otherwise known as K.O., who managed the Cellar Door and would soon join my show as road manager—and his wife, Bonnie. Along the way Kris's car banged fenders with another car when the driver ran a red light. There wasn't much damage to the cars, but when we braked, I reached out for Annie, was thrown forward, and broke a thumb. We had to stop for a while at the hospital, where my thumb was taped so that I could still play the guitar. By the time we got to Bill and Taffy's house, we were wired and wide awake, and we ended up sitting around, amid fifteen sleepy-eyed cats, singing songs to one another.

We were still singing as the stars began to fade. At one point, Bill brought out a song he had been working on, which he said he didn't seem to be able to go anywhere with; he hoped I might have some thoughts on what to do with it. He and Taffy played it through while I followed along, and we kept at it. I wrote a bridge finally, and maybe the second verse. When we finished, Annie and I went off to sleep for the rest of the day.

That night, Taffy and Bill did their show; I did mine; and afterward, when I got an encore, I brought them back onstage with me and we did the new song, "Take Me Home, Country Roads." The place went crazy.

Almost heaven, West Virginia,
Blue Ridge Mountains
Shenandoah River.
Life is old there,
Older than the trees,
Younger than the mountains
Growin' like a breeze.

Country roads, take me home
To the place I belong:
West Virginia, mountain momma,
Take me home, country roads.

All my memories gathered 'round her,
Miner's lady, stranger to blue water.
Dark and dusty, painted on the sky,
Misty taste of moonshine,
Teardrop in my eye.

Country roads, take me home
To the place I belong:
West Virginia, mountain momma,
Take me home, country roads.

I hear her voice, in the mornin'
   hour she calls,
The radio reminds me of my home
   far away,

And driving down the road I get
a feelin'
That I should have been home
yesterday, yesterday.

I think I'm most myself when I'm writing a song because I'm trying to be honest with what's happening. I'm open. I'm really listening. You're in touch with a whole spectrum of moods, you really are. You listen to this thing that's going on in your head and the thoughts take direction. Suddenly there is a line of words on your tongue, and that one line brings with it hundreds of others. And then it depends on the day, and on the season, and on where you are—late winter, early spring in Minnesota, for example. One year I was inspired by early spring in Minnesota to write four great songs in one day. The moods came on.

The first draft of a song is in my head when I sit down to learn it on the guitar. Sometimes the melody has to be changed, but once you get it started, once you sit down and learn it with the instrument, the learning of it—actually being able to sing it—leads you someplace. It's the discovery of your song that's so wonderful. In fact, if I start out thinking I'm in control of it, it doesn't work.

There were times when I'd be struggling with a song, and then when I'd get out of the way, the song would be there. In neon lights. Right in front of me. It's a way of looking, I think. What you need to see comes forward once you stop trying to see it.

I wrote "Annie's Song" riding up in a ski lift one day early in 1974. It was soon after our first serious separation, and we'd just come back together. There was nobody on the mountain when I started out that day. No lines. I skied down this very tough run, all out of breath, my heart pounding, my thighs burning, and I skied right onto the lift. I'm riding up again, sitting there catching my breath, looking down at where I'd just been a few moments ago, all this physical stuff going on, when suddenly I'm hypersensitive to how beautiful everything is; the sky is a blue you only see from mountaintops. Then I became aware of the other people skiing, the colors of their clothes, the birds singing, the sound of the lift, the sibilant sound of the skiers going down the mountain. All of these things filled up my senses, and when I said this to myself, unbidden images came one after the other. The night in the forest, a walk in the rain. The mountains in springtime. All of the pictures merged and then what I was left with was Annie. That song was the embodiment of the love that I felt at the time. The embodiment of that emotion was this person, my wife. So the song got to be about her and about all of my complex feelings in regard to her. In the ten minutes it took to reach the top of the mountain, the song was there. I skied back down, drove home, went up to my office, and learned the song on the guitar.

In my songs, I could say things that I didn't seem able to say directly to Annie. I needed the form and the music to help me communicate. And even with the music, what was frustrating was the feeling of never seeming to complete the communication. When I started recording, I'd come home from the studio with the song I was working on finally sounding like what I had heard in my head and I'd play it for Annie, and she would turn professional on me.

"Isn't there too much echo?" "Aren't the drums too loud?" "Isn't the guitar out of tune?" It was as if she was indifferent to the song itself. She claimed, in fact, to have fallen in love with me despite my songs, not because of them.

She didn't want to be in my shadow. She wanted to be responsible for herself and to do her own thing.

Whatever meaning "Annie's Song" had for me on a personal level, there was also a larger context. I wrote it to speak to what is universal in the human experience, to transcend a couple of lovers. It could just as easily have been about love for a brother. Or a father. Or a friend. It could just as easily have been a prayer.

POEMS, PRAYERS, AND PROMISES

Meeting Jerry Weintraub in the cosmic flow was like *aspiration* meeting *inspiration*. We were braves from two different tribes, two streams of experience, but with a common language. It was synergy in play. Our friendship was going to defy gravity.

Unless you are a movie star and an agent is doing your bidding, your personal manager is your most important professional relationship. It's all a big case of trust, and if you're lucky, this person becomes your best friend. If he's good and smart, he's going to put you in situations that give you a chance to grow. With Jerry that was true in spades. It also seems true that as professional relationships lengthen they tend to meander. Certainly my experience bore that out, too.

It was Hal Thau who knew Jerry and got the two of us together, though both Hal and Milt Okun said later that they were surprised that it worked out between us. Temperamentally we were dead opposites. When I got older and more experienced, the moral ambiguities of working with Jerry became clearer. I think Hal and Milt probably understood him better than I ever did, but professionally it was a brilliant matchup, and that's how I approached it.

By way of explaining his thinking, Jerry would often say— sometimes more than once in a conversation—that he was a street kid from New York. When I first met him, this meant nothing to me, but in retrospect, I think he was proudly pointing to his wiseguy invincibility.

He wasn't one to harbor doubts; what he harbored was schemes. He was full of schemes—schemes for promotions, schemes for everything. Even as we shook hands at that first meeting, his mind was sizing up the situation—and me. When I think about my days with Jerry now, I think of it as my experience of selling my soul to the devil.

Jerry was large of stature, so when he came on, he came on *very* strong, whether it was in his charming mode or that darker side, when he let himself be overcome with anger. I witnessed this only rarely, though, because it was important to Jerry not to be seen losing control.

He was about thirty-one then—not a great deal older than I was, although he seemed older because of his experience—and he reminded me a little of a fleshy young Elvis Presley, his mouth especially. He curled his lip and smiled the way Elvis did, and had the hair and the profile to go with it. Frankly, he looked lethal. In the entertainment industry, he was just the kind of guy you wanted on your side. He was very smart about people, very sharp, always a bit ahead of whoever he was dealing with, working out the angles, as if he were still the pool shark of his youth. I was twenty-six at the time and he read me like a book.

When I signed with RCA, there were a slew of people offering me management deals and wanting to sign me on the spot.

Jerry, because he seemed so laid-back, was the only one who inspired my confidence. It struck the right note for me when he flashed that Elvis smile and said, "I don't need to sign another artist just to sign another artist. If there is something we can do together that would be exciting, then there's reason to pursue this."

What he wanted to do was put me to work in television. Remember this was at a relatively early stage in the development of television programming; not many popular singers were being welcomed by the medium. Elton John, to cite just one example, couldn't find work on American television at that point; he was too much of an exotic. That was true of almost everybody in rock music, and folksingers fared no better. Neither the Mitchell Trio as a group nor I as a solo performer could have bought our way onto a show. Jerry, from the very beginning, touted my down-to-earth unpretentiousness as a quality that people would welcome into their living rooms. Late in the fall of 1970, I made my first appearance on "The Merv Griffin Show." And not, as I said earlier, just to sing a song but to banter with the host.

What made for the synergy was that I delivered on Jerry's opening. John Denver—this creature of mine—came across on the TV screen and came across very well. Even though I was still one uncertain person, I have to admit there was something in what I was projecting that held together: the granny glasses, the long hair, the slightly Western twang, the slightly self-deprecating sense of humor. Jerry thought I might even get to work in the movies. Fantastic, I thought. He seemed at that moment to epitomize the worldly experience I lacked.

In the midst of this inspiring beginning with Jerry, we recorded "Take Me Home, Country Roads" and it turned into a phenomenon. The song came out as a single before the album and for the first time Jerry was truly excited about what we were doing. One of the jokes that went around was that he had bought up a hundred thousand copies of the record and was warehousing them in New Jersey to give the impression of a runaway hit.

Actually, it took a long time for that record to happen, and while we all had a hand in making it go, Jerry worked at it indefatigably, leveraging all the promotional possibilities, making RCA work hard to straighten out all the production kinks that surfaced, and following up on the shipping of the record. He promoted me with ingenious schemes, too. The photo in the two-page ad he took out in *Variety* to announce my appearance at the Troubadour was doctored to make the crowds standing outside the door to see John Denver and the Fat City band look larger than life. And so they proved to be. It was a smash week for us, for Jerry as much as for me. With hindsight I can see that he was already planning his assault on Hollywood.

When I first started working with him he had, I'd say, only a modicum of clout at RCA. He had a couple of acts with them, including his wife, Jane Morgan, and the team called Zaeger and Evans, who had just given RCA a hit recording called "In the Year 2525." With the success of "Country Roads" he started to wield his power like a sacker of cities. He was almost imperial with RCA when the first pressing of the single of "Country Roads" was distributed with a noticeable distortion, much to my dismay. I would have hated to confront RCA myself; Jerry made RCA do a second pressing immediately. That was in March, and in May the album was issued.

Through the summer the song got into the national bloodstream. It first aired in Minneapolis, where Annie and I were still living. I had taken the record around to a very hot disc jockey named Johnny Canton at station WDGY, who liked the song and gave it tremendous play. After that, word of mouth moved it. The same thing happened from city to city.

In fact, that became the pattern for all my hits. First the disc jockeys would support my work; then RCA would notice what was happening and push to have the records played. Come September I was no longer John Denver, writer of "Leaving on a Jet Plane"; I was John Denver, the guy you heard on the radio singing that song yesterday.

On a return visit to Merv Griffin's show, a fellow guest, the boxer Rocky Graziano, initiated me in the art of mimicking myself when well-wishers recognized me in public places, like airports. I think I had a gift for it. I enjoyed making people laugh, particularly since I'd always taken myself so seriously. In fact, eventually I got to mimic myself on "The Bob Hope Show," the two of us dressed alike in granny glasses and long mops of hair: two John Denvers instead of one.

By then, of course, I'd proven that I was a performer whom American audiences *would* welcome into their living rooms at night. I'd arrived. It had been a long haul, not an overnight success. I still didn't have a settled image of the performer I wanted to be, but at least I was beginning to experience some of the recognition I had fantasized about back in L.A. when I was starting out.

I'd do twenty-five albums for RCA over the next fifteen years, but the first three were greatly influenced by Milt Okun and his song repertoire. "The Ballad of Spiro Agnew," which I recorded on the first album, says it all: There's Milt, whose music went back to the Weavers and their songs of social conscience, and me, a young white boy from a military family, trying hard to be more than a sympathetic supporter of the civil rights and anti-war movements.

But I had a dream too, which started to form way back at the top of those eucalyptus trees I'd climb in Tucson when I needed my space. I think of the parable of the five talents. I'd been given these gifts—my voice, my upbringing, my personality, my song-writing ability—and I wanted very much to do things with them; I was intrigued with the idea of continuing to develop my talents, exploring the outer limits. I wanted to go around the world utilizing these gifts. I saw something out there. By the time *Poems, Prayers and Promises* was out, I think I'd broken through to that place. Now the opportunity to do all of that was at hand.

There were two other such recessed places that success had me breaking through to, if I can continue using that image. Happily, one of them had to do with being a performer. Earlier when I referred to how seriously I had worked both in L.A. and in my days with the Mitchell Trio, focusing on my music rather than on screwing around, as my dad had worried I might, it would have been more accurate to say I was learning my trade. Whatever I was going to do, I wanted to do it well. At that time my trade was being an entertainer: I hadn't yet written any songs. As part of that training I was learning what I could do with music. Learning different songs. Even learning how to play the guitar—because I hadn't really ever worked hard at being a guitar player. But mostly learning different songs. A song on the radio would catch my ear and I'd want to know it. I'd be haunted by some image it shaped for me. I remember being obsessed for days with Donovan's song "Catch the Wind." There were many such haunting, mysteriously beautiful songs being written during that period, each one more beautiful than the last; I was their attentive listener.

A young John with his mother and father.   *John at fourteen.*

John, Ron, Erma, and Dutch.

The Mitchell Trio: Joe Frazier on the left and Mike Kobluk on the right.

Posing with a young fan after a concert.

The new Mitchell Trio—
David Boise, Michael Johnson, and John—on "The Mike Douglas Show."

LEFT: *Dating Annie.*   ABOVE: *John and Annie on their wedding day, June 1967.*

ABOVE: *Annie and John at Lake Tahoe.*

With George Burns.

With Frank Sinatra, 1976.

With Jacques Cousteau, 1974.

BELOW: *With the Muppets, 1979.*
OVERLEAF: *John with his son, Zak, who was then three.*

With the trio a whole new vein of material was made available to me and my sense of the entertainer's role broadened. I started to find out that there is a lot more you can do with music on a stage than just sing it. You can make people think. You can make them laugh at things going on in the world. Sometimes you can even make them laugh at themselves, which is the hardest thing to do—and everybody needs that. The satirical stuff we did in Washington—poking fun at the President—was a big, big thing for me to do. It was exciting to have an impact like that. It was a revelation to me when I could make a bridge to an audience's psyche.

You could also be passionate with your voice. When I sang solos, I gravitated to songs like "Mr. Tambourine Man" and "The Bells of Rhymney" because I liked the dynamic range I could give them. I could communicate a lot of feeling with my voice, which I was not able to do by just sitting down and talking with somebody. I always attracted a fugitive audience for the solos I sang while waiting for Joe Frazier to show for a concert, or after hours on club dates. There was something about the emotional registers in my voice that worked for people, that communicated to them, without my being consciously aware of it or understanding it. In fact, I feel I've begun *consciously* using those registers only in the last ten years.

And then gradually my aspirations shifted and I started writing songs of my own, trying for my own affects. This was also a revelation, particularly in what it taught me about communicating. People who listened to "Leaving on a Jet Plane" thought it was about war, and probably those identifications are what made the song a hit for Peter, Paul and Mary. We were once again a country of young soldiers going off to fight a war. Fantasies of apocalypse were resurfacing. That wonderful phrase in the song "I don't know when I'll be back again" brought all the yearnings out in the open. But for me the wistfulness had more to do with the simple facts of my life at the time. I was living in hotels, going from place to place, performer on one hand and anonymous on the other. I remember when I started to pen those words I was thinking of Gordon Lightfoot's "In the Early Morning Rain." A big old airplane on the ground, getting set to go . . .

Of course, I see all of this so clearly only in retrospect. At the time I was just living. On the stage, with my own material and all these affects at my disposal, I could really get into it. Wistfulness was just one of the emotions I was exploring.

The other place I broke through to with the success of "Country Roads," less happily in retrospect, was the true subject of life on the road. Not that I hadn't had innocent *amours* before, but now I began playing around double time. It was the old story of success playing havoc with moral inhibitions. I found myself away from Annie more and more, and the circles of our lives seldom converged. I convinced myself that what I was doing didn't matter; that it didn't affect Annie. I was just experiencing the excitement of somebody new and different. I had no sense of the pain it could cause. I hadn't developed that understanding yet; that was to come later, out of my own pain. Besides, there are a lot more things than sex that bond two people together. Sex is pretty easy. It can be pretty cold, and pretty callous, and pretty meaningless. It fills a void, but I never held it supreme. And I couldn't understand, in my naïveté, why Annie would look at it differently. If she wasn't going to be with me—if she wasn't going to include me in her life—I couldn't see how she could deny me my romantic inclinations.

You came off a show, having bared heart and soul, and the adrenaline was working. Talking with your buddies took you only so far back to so-called normality. You could admire the design of your hotel suite only up to a point. There were attractive women around. If they were available and a little challenging in their availability, and soft and warm, that spelled romance for me and I could almost not resist. At that point in the night I could be shameless. I started living a lie with Annie.

Once I got seduced by one of Jerry's secretaries, who then unwisely reported her success to Jerry. He fired her on the spot and then gave me a brotherly talk about how treacherous women can be. Given all that was about to happen to me, he said, people were going to try to take advantage of me—apparently just as his secretary had planned to do. I had to be more discriminating; not so wild. Frankly, with Jerry on board—because now he started to spend some time with me on the road—I can't recall things being any less enmeshed, but I'll let him deal with his past in *his* memoirs. I'm sworn to silence.

In the midst of this flux, Annie and I moved to Aspen. It was Christmas 1970. Mountain promontories had always been part of the equation for us, and when the numbers for "Country Roads" kept growing, I figured we could afford our dream house. If I was going to succeed as an entertainer, that was where I wanted to enjoy the rewards. So one day, taking advantage of a long-standing commitment to perform a couple of benefit concerts for the Visiting Nurses Association, Annie and I drove to Aspen together like characters out of an F. Scott Fitzgerald story and started a new phase in our lives. I was turning twenty-seven and she was maybe twenty-five; we knew we were about to experience Dame Fortune's largesse, but we didn't know quite the extent of her generosity. We were trying to be grown-ups about it. Winter had settled in and there was snow on the slopes; the whole setting went right into your soul.

After the first benefit concert, we spent the remainder of the day looking for a house, but everything was at least twice what we could afford. That night, before the second benefit—a midnight concert—we drove to a reception in North Starwood. The night was beautiful and unearthly, with a full moon and a sky so bright you could go cross-country skiing. What I wouldn't give, I thought, to see our days unfold here. My identifications with the have-nots of this world came into play right there.

But, as in a fairy tale, our kindly host, sensing our dilemma the next morning, suggested that we look just at land. So far, Starwood had been only minimally developed. He brought us up to the promontory where my house now stands and told us to take a look from there. I looked out over the valley and saw that no houses had been built yet. Even before Annie came around the car to where I was standing, I knew we'd found home. We'd stumbled on it, but I'm convinced it was preordained that we'd find this place.

Just the land alone cost all the money we had at the time. We rented a place in town and began to count the days. It was going to take another year before we could start to build. For 365 days, I fantasized about what living there was going to be like.

The day the building contractor was to break ground I came up from town to be on hand and found these two old codgers, Jim and Percy Pratt, standing around a little uncertainly. They were the foremen on the job, both of them six and a half feet tall and homely as mud fences. I almost couldn't take my eyes off them. We introduced ourselves. "Well, Mr. Denver," one of them said finally, "where do you want to aim this thing?"

A couple of hours later, there it was, the whole house laid out in pegs and string, and pointing through the hundred-year-old scrub oak to the mountains beyond.

Every day that I was not on the road, I would travel up the mountain to see how much they had done, and I'd sit up there and wait for sunset. Life didn't seem so ephemeral from a perspective where you could see the day unfold. Invariably, as my mind meandered, my thoughts dwelt on the nature of higher ground.

Appropriately enough, the album after *Poems, Prayers and Promises* was called *Aerie,* which RCA released in February 1972. It didn't perform as well as the first album and I slid a little on the charts. But then barely seven months later, before I had a chance to wonder if fame was really so fleeting, RCA released "Rocky Mountain High."

He was born in the summer of his 27th year
Comin' home to a place he'd never been before
He left yesterday behind him
You might say he was born again
You might say he found a key for every door

When he first came to the mountains his life
*   was far away*
On the road and hangin' by a song
But the string's already broken and he doesn't
*   really care*
It keeps changin' fast, and it don't last for
*   long*

But the Colorado Rocky Mountain high
I've seen it rainin' fire in the sky
The shadow from the starlight is softer than a
   lullabye
Rocky Mountain high

He climbed cathedral mountains, he saw
   silver clouds below
He saw everything as far as you can see
And they say that he got crazy once and he
   tried to touch the sun
And he lost a friend but kept his memory

Now he walks in quiet solitude, the forests
   and the streams
Seeking grace in every step he takes
His sight has turned inside himself to try and
   understand
The serenity of a clear blue mountain lake

And the Colorado Rocky Mountain high
I've seen it rainin' fire in the sky
You can talk to God and listen to the casual
   reply
Rocky Mountain high.

Now his life is full of wonder but his heart
   still knows some fear
Of a simple thing he cannot comprehend
Why they try to tear the mountains down to
   bring in a couple more
More people, more scars upon the land

And the Colorado Rocky Mountain high
I've seen it rainin' fire in the sky
I know he'd be a poorer man if he never saw
    an eagle fly
Rocky Mountain high.

It's a Colorado Rocky Mountain high
I've seen it rainin' fire in the sky
Friends around the campfire and everybody's
    high
Rocky Mountain high.

I remember, almost to the moment, when that song started to take shape in my head. We were working on the next album and it was to be called *Mother Nature's Son,* after the Beatles song, which I'd included. It was set for release in September. In mid-August, Annie and I and some friends went up to Lake Williams to watch the first Perseid meteor showers.

Imagine a moonless night in the Rockies in the dead of summer and you have it. I had insisted to everybody that it was going to be a glorious display. Spectacular, in fact.

The air was kind of hazy when we started out, but by ten p.m. it had grown clear. I had my guitar with me and a fishing rod. At some point, I went off in a raft to the middle of the lake, singing my heart out. It wasn't so much that I was singing to entertain anyone back on shore, but rather I was singing for the mountains and for the sky. Either my voice gave out or I got cold, but at any rate, I came in and found that everybody had kind of drifted off to their individual campsites to catnap. We were right below the tree line, just about ten thousand feet, and we hadn't seen too much activity in the sky yet.

There was a stand of trees over by the lake, and about a dozen aspens scattered around. Around midnight, I had to get up to pee and stepped out into this open spot. It was dark over by those trees, darker than in the clearing. I looked over there and could see the shadow from the starlight. There was so much light from the stars in the sky that there was a noticeable difference between the clearing and everywhere else. The shadow of the starlight blew me away. Maybe it was the state I was in.

I went back and lay down next to Annie in front of our tent, thinking everybody had gone to sleep, and thinking about how in nature all things, large and small, were interwoven, when *swoosh,* a meteor went smoking by.

And from all over the campground came the awed responses: "Do you see that?" It got bigger and bigger until the tail stretched out all the way across the sky and burned itself out. Everybody was awake, and it was raining fire in the sky.

I worked on the song—and the song worked on me—for a good couple of weeks. I was working one day with Mike Taylor, an acoustic guitarist who had performed with me at the Cellar Door and then had moved out to Aspen. Mike sat down and showed me this guitar lick and suddenly the whole thing came together. It was just what the piece needed. When I realized what I had—another anthem, maybe; a true expression of one's self, maybe—we changed the sequencing on the album we'd just completed, and then we changed the album title.

The first single we released from the album was "Goodbye Again," the final song of a trilogy that had begun with "Leaving on a Jet Plane" and continued with "Follow Me." The second single was "Rocky Mountain High," and it became hard not to hear it being played, the radio rotation was so heavy. If my recording of "Country Roads" made me a star, the recording of "Rocky Mountain High" gave me superstar status.

And the remarkable thing about it was that it was a long song. It was hard to do long songs even in those days; now you can't really do them at all. The music has to fit the program niche. This didn't. But we worked it, we got a response, and it flew up the charts.

That summer before the record was released must have been the freest summer I'd ever had in my life. I wasn't working all that much. I wasn't big enough to be in the big venues. I was a college concert act and there weren't any college concerts in the summer. Nor was I big enough to do fairs. I did a few concerts with Blood, Sweat and Tears as their opening act, but that was it. I was home that summer. I got to feel the mountains under me. In an attempt to redeem my untested youth—"All work and no play makes John a dull boy"—I hung out with my friends.

My friends were those I'd made the first year I'd worked in Aspen—particularly the trio of Paul Lurch, Michael Shore, and Don Straka, a wonderful guy otherwise known as Crow. They were just a bunch of guys who weren't in show business and weren't impressed with anyone who was, but they had come one night to hear me sing and loved the songs. Mountain boys love songs fiercely. Crow would listen to me sing Tom Paxton's song "Cindy's Crying," about a girl strung out on heroin, and he'd be unable to hide his tears.

Naturally, I got stoned with those guys: It was 1972. Exploring inner space had become as important to my generation as the exploration of outerspace. I tripped out on acid for the first time with Crow, and we took our motorcycles over Red Mountain, down to Lenado, and then up to this place called Periphery Peak. The line "And they say that he got crazy once and he tried to touch the sun" from "Rocky Mountain High" came out of this. What a far-out experience that was.

It was also in that summer that John Munchoff, a friend from Minnesota, came with his wife, Lana, to visit, and ended up getting killed riding my motorcycle. I marked that, too, in "Rocky Mountain High." Some people had the idea that the song was about getting stoned in the mountains, and it's true that was going on, but the song was about how exhilarating it was to *be* there, to feel free, to have come to such a place, both personally and geographically. And it was a reflection on mortality.

That was also the summer that Annie and I, all boxed in about communicating, and getting tenser with each other by the moment, first did EST training. I wish I could recall the humor of those days because it wasn't as grim as it might sound. Those were the early years of the human potential movement, of what Tom Wolfe called the Me Decade, and EST was a big part of that explosion. When Werner Erhard, the head of EST, came to town, Annie and I heard about his work and decided pretty much simultaneously that it might be of value to us.

We went to the training sessions without preconceptions— Aspen in those days, just as now, was full of cures and therapies—and we found EST deeply affecting. For me, it helped a lot. If nothing else, I found a framework that allowed me to be a bit more articulate as a person, particularly as it involved feelings that suddenly I had a handle on, feelings that I'd only been dealing with before in the most fragile way. I liked the idea that came to me through EST that I could stay centered even when I was down. And there were those days. What a relief to sort out one's inchoate self, one's silences. Werner became a close friend, as did others in the training.

EST is about being honest, about working through to an expression of your real self. Could I come clean about my sexual infidelities, and risk losing Annie? Should I bare my heavy heart? For months and months, I wrestled with my conscience. Sex was the last thing I could confront. And next to last was marriage.

After "Rocky Mountain High" did as well as it did, I kept up a hectic road schedule. It seemed as if I was on the road half my time. Jerry was not only drumming up concert dates—an exhausting schedule of one-night stands coast to coast—but was pitching me to all the networks for a series of TV specials. As part of that buildup, he set up more and more television appearances for me. I must have been a guest on "The Merv Griffin Show" alone a dozen times. I went off to London for a couple of months in the spring of 1972 and did a BBC show in Shepherds Bush Green, where there was a live audience and less pressure about succeeding than in American television. I wanted to get used to doing television before I had my own show, and the BBC had a channel on which contemporary American music was being explored. I had made one appearance on a show that Mary Travers did and another on a show that Tom Paxton did, and I liked how it felt: informal yet formative. The director, Stanley Dorfman, was really sensitive to the music. I was given a chance to do six weekly shows live on Sunday night.

The regular crew was made up of me, Bill and Taffy Danoff, and Pan's People, a group of dancers whom I danced with—if you can call what I did *dance*. It was a small family of players. Each week there was a guest artist with whom I sang. One night we'd run fifty-eight minutes, another night fifty-nine, another sixty-one. It was like doing English music hall, both intensely professional and professionally laid-back. About the only time I'd get to see anything of London was when we'd film a couple of segments outside someplace, which gave us a chance to change sets and clothes. I can't remember doing much of anything else while I was there besides the show. They worked us hard.

I'll never forget flying home that time. It was the end of May, springtime in the mountains. Friends of ours were getting married. The time in England was the longest stretch that I'd spent that far away. I flew into Chicago and missed my connection to Denver, so I had to charter a plane to take me to Aspen. When I arrived, Annie was standing there waiting for me, in a dress of deep violet, with the green mountains behind her. Her skin was tanned, she was a healthy-looking woman. Her eyes were shining. She had long wavy hair. God, she looked good. That was a wondrous moment, a frame frozen in my memory, one freeze-frame among the many. And it roiled my guilt like a wave hitting the beach.

Back when I studied architecture in college, we were given to understand that a perspective had to answer to a point of repose—what your view rested on and gave back when you looked out reflectively. Would that be true, too, for the architecture of the heart? As I reflect on the period of time recounted above, my dad suddenly comes to mind—he and the whole edifice of fatherhood that so shaped our relationship. I've been thinking about fatherhood a lot lately, and trying to prize open the reasons behind my thoughts. I'm trying to think back to my earliest view of Dad, and then ahead to this moment—in my fiftieth year—because my oldest children are now young adults and my youngest child is just getting going. A lot of personal history hinges on the father we have and the father we choose to be. I've always liked to think that we put ourselves in the circumstances in life that will support us moving through to wherever it is our spirit is going.

Annie and I had been married for quite some time—seven, eight years—when the thought of having children first came to us during those early Rocky Mountain years. But we had both been busy and involved, so we didn't press the idea. Once, when we were working with the Hunger Project, we saw some film footage of children suffering from hunger, and Annie said something to the effect that "these children are our children." However she meant that, I heard it. We hadn't been trying to have children, but neither had we been trying not to. I think that's when we created an opening in our lives for children. It became the focus of our lives together.

Time passed, though, and nothing happened. Initially it was Annie who submitted to all kinds of tests, but none of them proved positive. Medically she was just fine; she was a fertile woman. Then they checked me out, and lo and behold, we discovered that the problem was mine. Apparently, my body was producing only a minute amount of sperm, and of the sperm that was there, such a small amount had the mobility to swim upstream that it was unlikely, the doctors felt, I could ever produce my own children. There were things I could try to do to raise my sperm count and to improve my sperm's mobility, since at least there was something there to work with, but the odds were heavily stacked against any success.

Neither of us dwelt on it. Actually, it wasn't even much of a surprise, as I had always harbored a vague sense, from early youth, that I might not be able to have children. Annie and I started to weigh our feelings about adoption and decided that's what we wanted to do. We then went through the adoption process, which I remember as a time of great humility.

Once we started processing the adoption papers, whenever I found a quiet moment in the day, including just before I got out of bed in the morning, I offered a prayer to this little spirit out there: "Whoever you are, wherever you are, I don't know what you have to go through to get here and be with us, but we love you very much and can't wait to be with you."

With all of those anticipations streaming through me, we came to New York. I had four sold-out nights at Madison Square Garden and we were staying at the Sherry-Netherland. It was May 12, 1974, and that night I dreamed that three people in white robes came and gave me a little boy. We hadn't specified either sex in our communication with the adoption agency, all we wanted was that the baby be healthy enough to live with us in the mountains. We were active people, we liked to be outside, and we wanted that for our baby as well.

But in my dream, when the baby was put into my arms, I noticed that it was a boy—a dark-faced boy with round eyes and a little bit of an overbite—and as I was holding him, he looked up, grabbed my thumb, and smiled. In the morning, I recounted the dream to Annie. Eleven days later, Zak was born. We didn't see him then, but we were notified about his birth, and when he was about two months old, we went up to Minnesota, to the adoption agency, to pick him up.

I remember hearing "Annie's Song" come on the radio as we were driving there. It had become the number one song in the country that week, which struck me as an interesting coincidence. For some reason, I automatically translated that piece of information into a projected entry in Zak's baby book: On this hot day in August, the number one song in the country is a song Dad wrote for Mom.

Anyway, we arrived at the agency. Zak was being flown up from the South. There were papers to be signed. There was also a little formal procedure to go through, designed to help adoptive parents deal with the anxiety of meeting their child. They had walked us through the place when we were there before. You first went down a long hallway, and then upstairs at the end of another hall there was a little room decorated as a nursery, with a crib and a couch. This was where you were supposed to get your first glimpse of your baby. We had just been told that the young woman who was bringing Zak had been delayed, and were trying to keep from feeling disappointed, when the door at the far end of the hall opened and the woman appeared after all, with our child. Without a word, she came running down the hall and handed the baby to me. He had round eyes, and this little bit of overbite, and when I held him he smiled and grabbed my thumb. Zak was the child in my dream—exactly the same child. I recognized his face and I think he recognized mine. At least, he looked at me in the most knowing way. Right there, dream and reality came together for me.

In fact, dream and reality became entwined almost as a matter of course during this period. Jerry, as I mentioned earlier, got me on "The Bob Hope Show," which made my face and my work familiar to millions. Then he got me on as host of a get-out-the-vote midnight special in California, which was replete with satirical sketches and vetted me, at least in my mind, as an accepted TV star. Next he secured ABC's backing for a series of John Denver television specials and beat the death out of ABC to get them to promote the show. At the same time, he got RCA to release a *Greatest Hits* album of my work . . . and the promoting all dovetailed. We all saw Jerry do that, but *how* he did it was uncanny. The way he planned all of these things and took the time to set them up and to create the audience was Jerry at his best. The album sold ten million copies, which at the time only a couple of other albums had matched.

Then we were looking at movies, and I became part of Jerry's first Hollywood project, a comedy called *Oh, God!* It was a script that had been knocking around Hollywood for five years or so, with a part that I might have been born to play. Rather than either of us taking a fee, Jerry insisted we split the proceeds fifty-fifty. At the time, it was a gamble, but the film turned out to be one of Hollywood's top grossers. My percentage of the profits, which I was given in lieu of salary, must have netted me more than $1 million.

I should probably digress for a minute here and say a few words about the money, because as it started to roll in, it was interesting to see how it was discussed and moved around in different configurations. In fact, after the success of "Country Roads," there arose a kind of low-level battle between Hal and Jerry, which usually wound up with Hal and Milt against Jerry, and me more often than not siding with Jerry simply because I declined to support the others—I didn't want confrontations. Now the conflicts were continually about money: how much of it there was and who should get it. Hal was very brave in dealing with Jerry's escalating demands as our financial balloons rose higher and higher, but he developed high blood pressure from the constant battles. First Jerry wanted this, then he wanted that. For this he wanted 25 percent; for that he wanted 40. Nothing was ever settled that wasn't unsettled later.

The truth of the matter is that at the time I didn't really care about any of it; by the time we were into the second RCA recording contract, I already had more money than I had ever imagined. More important to me was the chance it presented to make a difference in the world. Jerry had said at one time that if he did his job right, I should be able to work in any field I wanted, anywhere in the world, anytime. During this period he was really living up to that boast. When conflict arose, I continually expressed my loyalty to Jerry: "Hey, this feels great to me," I'd say. "If that's what he wants, I think he deserves it." Consequently, I held out for peace among the warring factions.

LOOKING FOR
SPACE

If I said I didn't yearn for immortality, I would be lying. Attempting to play high-school football in Texas was a precocious bid for that, whatever else it was. In eleventh grade, before I'd ventured to sing in public, I viewed greatness as being a tailback. Would it be otherwise for one of Dutch's kids?

But my membership in that fraternity always seemed unlikely. All I got to play, as I've mentioned, was one game, and even then, when the coach put me in to play, the public-address announcer so garbled my name that none of the people I was trying to impress knew it was me out there. I never did acquire that aura of *jock* that set other guys apart.

Still, that desire to be a hero was ingrained; it was woven into everything I tried to do. However much I kept it down, it grew with me.

When I set out at twenty, a *career* of heroic proportions danced before my eyes, but the fact is I had a skewed view of what really was heroic. Most of what I desired would have been served just by having creative work to do. In the recording studio, I always felt like I just showed up and these other guys did all the complicated stuff. I just played guitar and sang.

Here I was, then, still in the golden spring of life, still ripening, and already, with "Country Roads" and "Rocky Mountain High," I had a career that promised to be larger than life! The possibilities had Jerry working double time. Was I ready for this, or was I headed for self-destruction? What was this going to cost me? Could I possibly keep my end up? How, under these circumstances, could I stay balanced? Dad's advice to see myself as no better than anyone else wasn't going to help. I needed a coach. In the EST workshops, Werner Erhard used to talk about finding your "space."

Now it is not unusual to hear people say, "You're invading my space," but when Werner brought his training to Aspen, "space" was still a novel concept for many of us who had moved there, like latter-day pilgrims, looking for space in the mountains. We didn't have words for what we wanted, but Werner offered a clarification. It wasn't space as geographical terrain that he referred to so much as it was a stance—how you wanted to show up in all the facets of your life.

Our focus was on space you had to find yourself, define for yourself, and take responsibility for, the result of which would be that people would respect it. The environment you created in which to live life was a place for the spirit to dwell. In that space everyday desires found fulfillment. It was about such space that Henry John Deutschendorf, Boy of the Open Plains, often wondered.

Space that was yours to make! What an amazing concept, I thought in those early EST workshops. My brother and I, and probably most of our generation, had been programmed to be reticent about making that kind of space for ourselves. We were mostly encouraged to get on with life by being outward-looking. Of course, for my folks and those of their generation, the inner man tended to be pretty much unexamined. For them, their characters were settled sometime in their thirties, their time for growing up. That was it for self-reflection. There wasn't much around to motivate them to continue to explore their inner lives.

In the Aspen community in the early 1970s self-reflection was on everybody's agenda. How to *be* self-reflective may not have been all that clear, but I knew it had less to do with my own singular comforts and more with life as it was being lived on the planet—and with developing a new consciousness about life. In the trainings that were developed there, people who had the time for it went searching for answers to things that we had never been able to question before, but that since then we question a great deal. All of us, in a manner of speaking, were emotionally bruised or abused children, and to some extent we all came from dysfunctional families.

Werner Erhard was an ideal guide on the journey out of the metaphysical woods of my parents' generation. I would find other guides as life went on, but Werner would always remain one of them. He was accused of being a huckster, and has been tarred with the same brush that some critics apply belittlingly to New Age thinking in general, but I always found that what he had to say had particular meaning for me. "Do you live at the effect of what's going on in your life," Werner would ask, "or do you take responsibility for what's going on?" When I heard that in 1971, I acted on it—not in all the areas of my life, but in those where I had let myself be a victim.

Werner was a guide without intellectual conceits, which was of real importance to me. Around intellectual conceits I'd go dumb. I was too timid to express myself, too shy to say what I thought needed saying. With the exception of my experience with the Mitchell Trio, I'd had little opportunity in the dozen years that I'd worked as an entertainer to stretch out as a thinking person. When you're a superstar, the road rewards you for exposing your vulnerability, not for the paths your thoughts take. You're stroking and being stroked. There's a lot of late-night laughing. Though I didn't feel exactly prepared to come forward as a participant in public debate on the larger subjects in life, the fact is it's something I wanted to do.

My dilemma registered with me especially after my celebrity took off. The first time I appeared as guest host of "The Tonight Show," I must have said "far out" fifty times if I said it once. Being "cute" onstage was my way of covering up a fear I had of being seen as vacuous. Every time one of my guests would say something interesting, I would say "far out" without even thinking; it was like having a nervous tic. In fact, for a lot of people, that's when "far out" came into the vernacular. I have a feeling it will be in my obituary, that and the phrase "Rocky Mountain high."

My frustration, up until that point, had always been that Dad hadn't known how to teach me. He hadn't known how to educate. He hadn't known how to open up the world over there and bring me into it with his perspective, and say what it was he wanted me to get out of life. I had always been trying to learn from him, but he hadn't readily shared his thoughts, and I'd been left wandering in a mental thicket.

He was especially mum on matters of sexuality. Once when I was just a little kid, while walking home with him from the golf course, where I'd loyally tagged along pulling the golf bag, I noticed a golf tee in his mouth and piped up, the aspiring son: "Dad, that's dirty! Why have you got it in your mouth?"

In typical enigmatic fashion, he answered, "There are lots of things dirtier than this." Now, what exactly was he talking about? I had some hazy idea that it had to do with sex, but that's as far as it went.

That was always it. He'd charge the moment and leave me hopelessly caught in it. He'd decline to elaborate, just as he would decline a couple of years later, when he found me in the bathtub exploring myself sexually: "That's not something you play with," he declared. In fact, he was telling me the opposite of the truth. But his was the voice of authority. However misguided, I was bound at that age to follow that authority, and what cemented my confusion in those few exchanges was the fact that in every other respect sexuality didn't seem to exist in our home. So through ignorance I developed a pathetic awe for what was really an inappropriate subject for a child to be made to worry about.

Werner's sensitivity training helped me begin to disengage from all that. He helped me outgrow what I should have outgrown long before. I'd never heard anyone articulate how the mind and memory work to keep your life ensnared and how ultimately you have to be responsible for changing the situation yourself.

It wasn't that I bought everything EST was about, but rather that EST—in the form of the dialogues that Werner orchestrated, whether in workshops in Aspen, or at EST board meetings in San Francisco (which I attended religiously for a while), or on the road the few times he and I traveled together—gave me the incentive and the opportunities to elaborate on my thoughts, and to take responsibility for them. In the twentieth century, what could be more heroic?

Moreover, I felt comfortable among the people he drew together. I appreciated having the chance to shine in their company. They were interesting people—CEOs, educators, the chancellor of the University of California—with interesting things on their mind, and they were interested in knowing who I was, and what I had on my mind.

I'd let a lot of my early interests lie fallow and now I was able to go back a step and pick up some of those paths again. Space was a metaphor for what needed to be internalized. It wasn't a fixed entity, but spiritual territory to be staked out and built upon. It was part of an old dream of mine, and with Werner's help I set out to apprehend it.

Those times when I stood up in workshops or at board meetings and expressed what was on my mind were moments of supreme accomplishment for me. One of the ideals in EST was being open about what you were denying in yourself, then working in your own life to move through it, taking some step in that direction and making it be an expression of yourself. For me, risking those expressions of myself, whether to sing or to speak, in that company of people had the effect of being self-empowering.

The workshops themselves were cathartic for me, as I know they were for a lot of others. They would press all your buttons until suddenly in this room full of people—strangers for the most part—you'd discharge anger, or guilt, so heated with grief that it would literally raise the temperature in the room. The emotional charge took your breath away and bonded you, in empathy, to those who were listening.

Before EST came into the picture, I was already searching for expressions of myself, beyond my music, but it was EST that gave me the confidence to follow through. In 1972 I was already thinking, "Love the earth as you would love yourself," and I was full of zeal and energy, eager to do something "good" in the world—those were homegrown values, still intact if unpacked. Having the capital to play with only cinched it; I was going to invest in "good works." There are sophisticated ways to describe such altruism, but the simple words also say it: I'm an American child, learning and yearning for what it takes to be free. I had resonated to the notion of flower children in the 1960s, to the notion of loving one another. I had resonated to the notion of putting daisies in soldiers' gun barrels. And within that notion I had resonated to standing up for what you believe.

On the heels of the success of "Country Roads," I went out to Boise, Idaho, with an ABC film crew that was making a documentary about birds of prey. The film's producer, Robert Rieger, was a fan of my music and had asked me to write a song for the sound track. Not only did I consider this a good use for my music, but it gave me the chance to see up close how a documentary was made, to learn about these birds from one of the world's great ornithologists, Morley Nelson. I had more than a casual interest in the subject. I'm fascinated by the fact that eagles have been a symbol of every civilization in the history of man.

So I went on location with the crew. Appearing in the film with Morley was Nell Newman, Joanne Woodward and Paul Newman's daughter. During filming I lent a hand as a volunteer baggage handler. When the cameraman had to move to a new vantage point, for instance, I carried the tripod or whatever else would be needed at the new location. Among the things that we had to move about was a young red-tailed hawk, whose broken wing Morley had nursed back to health, and a golden eagle that Morley had just taken in.

On the last day of shooting, it was decided that we'd release the hawk at sunset. When the time came, I was unceremoniously given the eagle to hold. Except now I'm not sure if I was its keeper or it was mine.

Eagles have an opaque nictitating membrane, which is like an inner eyelid that they can use to protect their vision when they come diving out of the sky at high speeds. It lowers and lifts when you least expect it. Poised there, with the eagle held out in front of me, I was imagining myself in eaglelike flight, when the nictitating membrane suddenly lifted and the eagle caught me in its gaze. For an instant, I thought this was it—good-bye, Mama. Held there in that gaze, I almost stopped breathing.

Twenty seconds was about all the time the eagle needed to dispose of its interest in me—a humbling experience. But for me that look stuck. That look, and the power in it, lodged itself in my heart. For an incredible twenty seconds I had the feeling of connection, as if we were seeing into each other's spirit. The eagle sparked my idealism: This is the way I'd stay grounded, by being in nature and teaching about it.

Here is the song I wrote:

Oh, I am the eagle
I live in the high country
In rocky cathedrals that reach to the sky
I am the hawk and there's blood on my feathers
But time is still turning they soon will be dry
And all those who see me and all who believe in
    me share in
        the freedom I feel when I fly

Come dance with the west wind and touch on
    the mountain tops

Sail o'er the canyons and up to the stars
And reach for the heavens and hope for the
future and all
that we can be and not what we are

That same summer, I went up to the Canadian Rockies to work on another of Rieger's projects and met Tommy Tompkins, whose life took hold of my imagination in yet another way that exercised a big influence on how I wanted to define my space. Tommy was a former Northwest Mountie who for nine months had lived in the wilderness alongside a pack of wolves. A film he had made about it had been shown on Canadian television and Rieger had gotten hold of him to do a show on bighorn sheep. He wanted me to write the music for it and to serve as host-celebrity; apparently, I'd done so well in Boise, I'd get to play myself. This is the opening lyric for "Rocky Mountain Suite," the music I wrote for the show:

Up in a meadow in Jasper, Alberta
Two men and four ponies on a long lonesome
ride
To see the high country and learn of her people
The ways that they lived there and ways that
they died

And this is the chorus:

Cold nights in Canada and icy blue winds
The man and the mountains are brothers again
Clear waters are laughing
They sing to the sky

The Rockies are living
They never will die

Being someone who thinks at times that I have the heart of a mountain lion (and even that I might have been one once), someone who in my salad days explored the great silences of the desert outside of Tucson, I saw this assignment as a kind of gift, one I gladly accepted. The question the show posed—how does one live in nature without upsetting its balance?—is one that I haven't stopped asking for the past two decades. With Tommy instructing me in the arts and crafts of survival in the wilderness, we set out, literally and metaphorically, for the territory ahead.

Annie came for the last part of that trip and we got to spend some time together in the woods west of Calgary. It was sort of a fairy-tale time, the end of summer, and I can't remember there being many times after that when the two of us came together in harmony, unburdened by the fact that we weren't dealing with our contradictions. It was a fabulous drive home, through rolling hills, and there was even a double rainbow in the sky above us at one point. I remember thinking that if we were true druids, we could go at life more slowly; enjoy this more, enjoy each other. But Starwood beckoned, and beyond Starwood, the audiences beckoned, and we kept going. I tucked the experiences with Morley and Tommy, and of making documentary statements, under my belt.

The *Greatest Hits* album released in 1973 sold more than 10 million copies eventually, and "Sunshine on My Shoulders," one of the songs on that record, which had been issued originally with "Country Roads" on the *Poems, Prayers and Promises* album two years earlier but which the deejays had largely ignored first time around, went to the top of the charts. I had written the song in a fit of melancholy one wet and dismal late-winter/early-spring day in Minnesota—the kind of day that makes every Minnesotan think about going down to Mexico. On one level, it was about the virtues of love. On another, more deeply felt level, it reached out for something the whole world could embrace:

Sunshine on my shoulders makes me happy,
sunshine in my eyes can make me cry.
Sunshine on the water looks so lovely,
sunshine almost always makes me high.

If I had a day that I could give you,
I'd give to you a day just like today.
If I had a song that I could sing you,
I'd sing a song to make you feel this way.

If I had a tale that I could tell you,
I'd tell a tale sure to make you smile.
If I had a wish that I could wish for you,
I'd make a wish for sunshine all the while.

When it was released initially, the song didn't impress the industry as anything special. Its meaning didn't sink in. But while the war in Vietnam was winding down to a disastrous finale, the song suddenly reached out to touch a deep chord of need in the country. Just when there was so much going on in the world that was costing us dearly, and things were seemingly out of control, here was a dove coming back with news of dry land. Or at least a song that soared upward, and took its audience back home.

For a time I could do little that was musically wrong; my

name, face, and voice were recognized everywhere. In fact, a Wall Street analyst, who was also a fan, professed to see a correlation between the trough of despondency that the country had fallen into and the popular response to my songs; he then proceeded to factor that curious relationship into his theories about the wavelike fluctuations of the stock market.

The flip side of all that success was the sudden pressure it put on me to live up to all of the attention. Much of the pressure was self-inflicted, I'm sure, but a fair amount of it did come from the outside. There were dozens of causes that needed support, and it was important to look at them seriously and determine which of them I felt strongly about. I tried to do this through the framework that EST provided. In other words, if I was going to help, I was going to get involved, and it was going to be an expression of myself. What were the issues that incensed me? What issues aroused positive feelings? Some days it felt as if what I was holding at bay was nothing less than the chaos of the world. The seriousness (always-so-serious John) with which I went about everyday life only aggravated the situation.

In Aspen, for example, after I did EST everyone wanted me to do their training. Even the crazies showed up wanting to get into my space, and some of it was scary. Some people came up to the house in the middle of the night when Annie was home alone and frightened her. Some came to town to claim me as their next Saviour. One man came on foot, with a team of mules, all the way from Missouri, wanting me to reveal myself as John the Baptist. A woman holed up in the Jerome Hotel for weeks, knitting an endless afghan, refusing to leave her room until I'd agree to see her. Another woman started sending me all of her belongings, beginning with her underwear, through the mail, in preparation for moving in with me; she was convinced that we had had an arranged marriage. There were days when life became surreal.

It also started to get a little scary on some of the tours, especially when we began playing before audiences of twenty thousand or more. Having been very open about my involvement with EST, I attracted a lot of New Age eccentrics, some of whom tended to be physical in ways that threatened to get out of hand. Threats were made against my life; not everybody was pleased with the "noise" I was making.

To help me try to keep it all together, Kris O'Connor, my road manager, introduced me to Tom Crum, who became my personal trainer. Tom ran the International Martial Arts Academy in town. He and I had met in passing years before, just after the two of us had arrived in Aspen, and we had friends in common. It didn't take long for us to see each other as kindred spirits.

Tom was a mathematician who had chucked the corporate life that had been laid out for him by his parents to come and live free in the Rockies. He and his young family had actually started out for Jackson Hole, Wyoming. At first he taught children at one of Aspen's alternative schools. He started coming up to the house every day to give me instruction in meditation, breathing, and sitting. Tom believed that all of man's miseries derive from his inability to sit quietly in a room alone; in me, he had the perfect specimen. Tom convinced me that while I was really high from all of my success, and fully willing to commit myself to and participate in worthy endeavors, I needed a grounding influence to bring back the spiritual impulses that I drew my music from.

By the time we were out on the road again, Tom was with us to manage our security arrangements, as well as to continue helping me keep my head clear of the chaos. Not only were Tom and I in sync philosophically, but we found ourselves given to the same idealistic impulses. In the course of one of the road trips, while philosophizing about the threat of nuclear power, we started to shape the collaboration that a couple of years later would become the Windstar Foundation, an institution that was school, meeting place, and model environment combined.

In retrospect, I see that my interest in the environment—an interest that began to surface as soon as there was space in my life for its expression—was rooted in the things I imagined back when I was swaying from the top of that eucalyptus tree. All the individual strands of activity that I was drawing around myself were focused in that one direction. Through my connection to EST, for example, I was invited to dinners at the National Space Institute, which was rocket expert Wernher Von Braun's think tank, set up to win support for the space program. Von Braun was a hero of mine, even though I knew he was a controversial figure.

Once at a Windstar symposium, the comedian and civil rights activist Dick Gregory denounced Von Braun as a supporter of the Nazis and threw the meeting into an uproar. One of the participating astronauts walked out in protest. Two days later, though, the astronaut and Gregory shook hands; the symposium had taken them to a place where they could find common ground.

Though he probably knew very little about me initially, Von Braun quickly recognized that I, like he, was a natural dreamer. At times he seemed to take advantage of me and my celebrity value to some extent in order to help raise money for the space program. If he exploited my interest in space, I didn't mind it then, and I still don't, when the result is one that I'm in support of, too. Apart from that, was interesting how curious Von Braun was about the work that I was doing with Tom in aikido. How was it possible, he asked, to handle violence without resorting to violence yourself? The answer was in being responsible before the fact, making sure that the environment you were living in wasn't one in which violence *could* come forward. I think the answer gave him pause. When he died, his wife sent me one of his telescopes to mark our brief friendship. Out of my acquaintance with Von Braun came a real commitment on my part to the space program, and in my eyes, the issue of manned space flight became an environmental priority.

In a similar vein, the work I did with Tom led me to reexamine what I knew about nutrition. Consequently, questions about nutrition became questions about hunger, and the specter of a hungry planet became, for me at any rate, a defining crisis of the environment. I pretended to no profound understanding of the problem of hunger in the world; I had no technical expertise. But I kept asking myself why hunger is allowed to exist. The question gnawed at me, left over from when Annie and I had visited Mexico City for the RCA convention just as I was starting out in recording. Annie and I had seen such terrible poverty all around the city, and I don't remember ever seeing impoverished circumstances of the kind we saw there, even in Japan after World War II. Or maybe it *was* like that in postwar Japan, but I was too young to recognize it. In Mexico City I recognized its face. It belonged to the peasants who came on their knees to petition their god for some small consideration. It was in the faces of people who had been dispossessed, just like my father's family, and to some extent my mother's, had been in the Thirties.

The old church, in the center of the city, where these peasants worshipped was very beautiful and opulent. At the gate, peasants would prostrate themselves and crawl forward, up the steps and into the sanctuary, praying as they went. Those who were too old to crawl got pulled along on little squares of rug. The contrast between this place of wealth and these people of hunger was hard to reconcile. How could the two exist side by side?

The statistics were an obscenity: forty thousand deaths a day in the world due to starvation, twenty-four thousand of them children under the age of five. This, on a planet that produces enough to feed twice its population, and is technically capable of doing twice that.

Dick Gregory had a lot to do with my increasing awareness of the problem with hunger. I'd known Dick since my Mitchell Trio days, when we did shows together, and I loved his work. He did topical stuff, talked about what was going on in the world, and I liked being associated with that. I tried to do it in my own shows.

Dick had acquired a kind of a stigma in the business because of the lingering fear that he was still the angry black man he had shown himself to be onstage at the crest of the civil rights movement. When he started a series of fasts, he seemed a bit crazed. First Dick had fasted for health reasons, because he had become corpulent, but then he fasted to draw attention to hunger in the world. For someone with his moral commitments, it was a natural progression, and I admired him for it.

Just after "Country Roads" was released, I was doing a show in St. Louis, which is where Dick is from, and he asked if he could open for me. I arranged things so he could. It was a great show—he was great, I was great—and we did it again, a few months later, at the Greek Theater in Los Angeles. During our week in L.A. we'd ride to work together down Sunset Boulevard and talk about numerology, about nutrition, and inevitably about hungry people, who we seemed to be seeing more and more of every day as we went along. My reading of it all was that the world was getting more and more out of balance.

One night soon after the L.A. show, I joined Dick, Shirley MacLaine, and Harry Chapin on a network talk show for a discussion about what made hunger persist in the world and what could be done to eliminate it. Was there the political will to take this on? Or was hunger simply endemic? Harry, whom I had met on the folk music circuit, was even more of an activist on this front than Dick was. To hammer home the message, Harry had organized World Hunger Year, a charity for which he did half his concerts.

Where it came to grass-roots political action, mine was clearly the voice of the novice. I had neither Harry's intensity nor Dick's perseverance, but I continued to raise questions for myself about hunger and its persistence, and I began to see hunger as a truly environmental issue.

Meanwhile, the aura of global citizen—citizen writ large—settled around me; I cultivated it while it cultivated me. For my model, I took Will Rogers and started taking myself into areas I'd glimpsed only from a distance. During the presidential campaign in 1976, I was a big supporter of Jimmy Carter—I responded to his humility—although in retrospect, I can see that Mo Udall's ideas were closer to my heart. Though part of the glamour of being a star was in making that kind of stand, and I liked it when candidates sought me out, my brief appearances on the '76 campaign trail were slightly demeaning. What they asked me to do and how they did it seemed exploitive and shallow. Still, I did perform a service, and it gave me the chance to do something meaningful.

Now it was later in the game, after things had really taken off for me, and Werner Erhard revived my interest in the paradox of a hungry planet. He came on one of the "Tonight Show"s that I was hosting and we went over the interesting question: If literally thousands of people in hundreds of organizations around the world in this century alone have spent millions and maybe billions to feed people, why does hunger persist? A few weeks later at an EST board meeting, the president of the EST Foundation, Bob Fuller, showed a documentary film by a West Coast filmmaker named Keith Bloom called *The Hungry Planet.* The film left us all disturbed and determined to form a forceful body that would eliminate this problem once and for all. It is hard to believe how dulled the world's consciousness had become on the subject. On the spot, I volunteered to take the film to Washington and get it into the hands of legislators. I thought I could work through Wendell Anderson, the U.S. senator from Minnesota who was serving in the seat left vacant by Hubert Humphrey's death. Wendell was a fan and a friend. He'd been our sponsor in Zak's adoption, and when he was elected governor of Minnesota, I sang at his inaugural. In effect, my taking the film to Wendell was the start of the Hunger Project, and my song "I Want to Live" was the anthem I wrote for it:

There are children raised in sorrow on a scorched and
  barren plain
There are children raised beneath the golden sun
There are children of the water, children of the sand
And they cry out through the universe their voices
  raised as one
I want to live, I want to grow
I want to see, I want to know

I want to share what I can give
I want to be, I want to live
Have you gazed out on the ocean, seen the breaching
  of a whale
Have you watched the dolphins frolic in the foam
Have you heard the song the humpback hears five
  hundred miles away
Telling tales of ancient history of passages and home
For the worker and the warrior, the lover and the liar
For the native and the wanderer in kind
For the maker and the user and the mother and her
  son
I am looking for my family and all of you are mine
We are standing all together face to face and arm in
  arm
We are standing on the threshold of a dream
No more hunger, no more killing
  no more wasting life away
It is simply an idea
  and I know its time has come

Descending on Washington in a whirlwind lobbying effort, Keith, Bob, and I met first with Wendell and a couple of formidable Senate colleagues, including John Glenn, John Warner, and Pat Leahy, then with Burt Lance, the Georgia banker and politician who was head of OMB and one of President Carter's confidants, and finally with Chip Carter, the President's son. Each meeting was a step forward in the decision-making process, and it was all a priceless lesson in American civics. Yes, Chip was looking for something to take on, and yes, the President was interested in this issue. Very quickly the President's

Commission on World and Domestic Hunger was formed, and Harry Chapin and I were named as members. Actually, I wasn't really sure that I wanted to serve on the commission, but Werner Erhard and Joan Holmes, who was also part of the EST advisory board, felt it was important that I participate, and that was the final little push I needed. The commission had some very distinguished members, including Senator Bob Dole; Jean Mayer, who was the president of Tufts University; and D. W. Brooks, who at the time had been an agricultural adviser to every President since FDR. We met for two years and I attended meetings regularly.

Harry's untimely death came just before the commission's report was published. It should have been his memorial, but I think he would have been disappointed by the report's conclusions, which were drawn up by the commission's staff; I know I was. It added next to nothing to what had been stated before the commission's work began, and I thought we had done more than just a creditable job trying to bring the voice of moral urgency to a new level. If what we reported on after two years' worth of meetings meant anything—two years during which it became clear that as far as hunger went, we seemed to still be living in biblical times—wasn't it time for policy to get beyond its posturing and make something happen?

On the other hand, the Hunger Project itself continued—it still does—not so much to distribute food, but to keep broadening the terms of the debate, and to keep bringing individuals and organizations together so that the resolve to end hunger in our time carries on. The Hunger Project continued, Windstar kept evolving, and my involvement with space broadened.

And then, even before the hunger commission had wound down, I was off on the wind again, drawn this time into a project to develop a television documentary about Alaska's wilderness. Annie didn't want me to do it. She thought I was being frivolous to give so much of my time to it. By then we had separated and come back together again not once but twice, and we had psychic wounds to heal. Moreover, Hal and Milt thought I needed to be spending my time on my music.

But the wanderlust was strong; it still is. I didn't see that it mattered where I was if I was doing what I needed to do for my own personal growth, and anyhow, what I was doing I couldn't *not* do. I needed those experiences more than I needed Annie's understanding and more than I feared her anger. And in this arc of time, she became unforgiving.

I'd always wanted to go to Alaska. Alaska epitomized for me what it must have been like in the wilderness of the American West before we began to misuse it. Everything that I was hearing about wilderness seemed to have to do with Alaska—man living with nature, not against it; working to survive. Neither the music I was doing nor much of what I took in in general during this period influenced my inner sense of space more fundamentally than seeing Alaska with my own eyes.

I had the feeling that enormous changes were taking place there, changes that didn't make sense to me if we were to take the planet's needs seriously, changes that were going to cut across the paths of all our lives. With the building of the pipeline from Barrow, Alaska as I saw it in 1979 was being drawn into a vortex of development. It was being pressed into service to meet the energy needs of the Lower 48, which I thought, and still do think, is dead wrong as public policy.

If Columbus could be said to have discovered America, I

wanted to do likewise and *discover* Alaska—not to plunder it, but to pay homage to what was there and take a stand against the changes that threatened it. We'd bring a film crew in and document Alaska's ecology in terms that made sense to me. I'd turn reporter. The ABC network took an interest in the project, and even Jerry Weintraub, no friend of the Earth, liked the idea: He pronounced it a bankable project.

Environmentalism was a dirty word in Washington at that point, and I could feel my old shrill self waking to the challenge. Up until then I really hadn't thought of myself as an environmentalist, though I had recognized the need to stand up to the developers and protect the wilderness from shortsighted exploitation. We needed wilderness more than wilderness needed us. In other words, there was more to gain from not exploiting this precious resource than from doing so. The stream of experiences that had taken me to the Rockies and allowed me to begin to know and understand myself was starting to move me to higher ground. I was beginning to figure out what I could do with what I'd learned and with whom I was.

After ABC committed to the show, they brought in John Wilcox to produce it. John, who also lives in the Rockies and is a man whose sensibilities make him a master of what he does, started by finding us transportation with two bush pilots—Tony Oney and his partner, Hoppy Harrower—who, when they die, will go immediately to Alaska's Valhalla. Tony and Hoppy were dentists from Oklahoma who decades earlier had found their American dream while working as hunters and guides north of the Arctic Circle. People like Tony and Hoppy, when and if they agree to help on a project like this, give themselves completely to it, and if the work is meaningful, their commitment never really ends. I am the same way. We're a bunch of people who've known one another for lifetimes.

I can't do justice here to how exciting it was to fly in with Tony and Hoppy, and a third pilot, Ace Dodson, another Alaskan legend, who came along to help us bring in all our gear. My sense of Alaska would have been a lot different, no doubt, had I not first seen the place through their eyes. I was like a kid discovering the world for the first time, and that feeling repeated itself every day.

One night at a whaling festival on the Bering Strait, at Point Hope, which is one of the westernmost places in the United States, one of the young bucks who didn't care for our presence cut the tires on the airplanes. In Alaska you get killed for less than that, and no court would convict your killers. We were up there in the middle of a lot of antagonistic forces and had to watch our backs.

Besides performing at the festival, I tried to show my good country manners by eating raw whale meat with the boys, which earned me, if not friendship, at least acceptance. I even submitted to being tossed in the air from a tarp of skins, the kind of game we might have played at old family reunions with the Deutschendorfs. When they brought out the rope for tug-of-war, I knew I was home. The Inuit got a big laugh out of my enthusiasm.

The Inuit used the whale kill to reenact an ancient sense of community, but sadly it was clear not just that that sense of community was breaking down, but that the loss was truly demoralizing. In traditional circumstances, the captain of the crew that caught the whale had an obligation to be the village benefactor: First his crew, then everybody else got a share of the catch.

In the traditional culture, the presumption was that only those who had paid their dues—meaning those wise in the ways of the culture—got to be captain. You became captain when you could afford a boat, afford the equipment, afford to feed a crew for the weeks it takes to be out in the straits trying to get a whale, and, most important, when you understood the tradition and culture around the whole whaling experience and could pass that on to the people who worked with you. In the traditional world only the elders got to that stage.

What was happening, though, was that some of the young bucks were going off to work in the oil fields, making a lot of money, then coming back with vaunted notions of what money entitled them to. They were returning with high-powered guns and boats, and going out on the ice to kill whales, but with no thought of bringing them in. It was just wanton rage (but also, I think, rage about real cultural losses they were feeling, even if they couldn't find the words to say so). Two hundred years of history in the Lower 48 were being repeated in Alaska in a matter of a decade, and not only in regard to the land and its resources, but also the spiritual and cultural needs of its people. In fact, with time, that rage has grown, and it continues to grow, as it has in the Lower 48 and all over the world.

We found signs of that rage on the American side of deep Alaska, too. Guided by Red Dodge, another legend of the territory, we traveled by raft out of Kukaklek Lake on the Alagaak River to a place that hadn't yet seen the predatory nature of industrial man.

Red had been a pilot for Western Airlines and had spent his entire life in Alaska; he knew my dad from the work he did in aviation and through me they became friends. I'd started out my exploration of Alaska on an idealistic impulse but under his tutelage—his growly voice insinuating itself into my ears and through them into my brain—ended up with an intense addiction. (Now I need only to hear the growl of a voice on the phone and automatically I conjure him up.)

McCarthy, our last stop, was a little town like any other, if you can imagine a small community of less than fifty sitting dwarf-like at the foot of a glacier, except it has this wild streak of industrial violence in its history that also just sits there, brooding in the night. Kennicott Copper opened a mine there in the nineteenth century and made a good living from it for seventy-five years. But when a campaign was organized to start a union among its work force, Kennicott saw fit to shut down the mine and walked away. Not much more than an abandoned hamlet remained, with about twenty-seven inhabitants, and they all seemed to spit nails when they talked.

On our first night there, they pulled a hoax that I'm sure they still talk about. We were in the town's main emporium, planning how the next day's shooting would go, when suddenly we heard gunshots, and Cary Linley, one of our crew, came running in white as a sheet, shouting, "My God, they shot him! They just shot him!" He was pointing to the back room, where the local pool players were assembled. "Shot who?" we asked in alarm, and rushed back there. But the only victims we found were ourselves. The locals enjoyed spooking us, and they had a good laugh at how well they'd done it this time. Over the next couple of days it became a volatile situation. One night, one of the jokesters turned edgy, feeling one of us had gotten too interested in his girlfriend. The next day we finished up and got out of there, maybe none too soon. Not that long afterward, McCarthy made it into the national news. A local had gone berserk and shot up the place, killing twelve people. The slaughter of innocents is probably a fate that is written into the destiny of places where dreams begin to dry up.

♦   ♦   ♦

If McCarthy represented one of the direst moments of that trip, the purest was probably earlier that summer when, flying the leg from Nome to Anchorage, Tony let me take control of his plane. Whether he did this out of friendship or because he was testing me, rookie that I was, I can't say, but I appreciated being given the opportunity to try out my skills. I'd started flying just a year or two before. Below us, as we went along, the landscape was literally strewn with plane wrecks, each of which obviously had a story behind it. In Tony's telling, each wreck seemed to have turned on blind fate. Why was he telling me all this? And then we came to Rainy Pass: Rainy Pass was the litmus test.

When you flew Rainy Pass, Tony said, God was your copilot. Tony knew seasoned pilots who had ended up going down flying through Rainy Pass. It had canyons that went off into dead ends. To fly it was to risk everything. Even to recall that flight, I automatically catch my breath. But I flew it, and did it without maps; just flew it by instinct. For that I earned Tony's admiration. In turn, the space I was making filled out like a sail.

The film we produced didn't get the television audience I'd hoped for—and never again would I make so lavish a documentary production of a *truth* I was defending (not yet, anyway)—but it plunked me, and through me Windstar, down into the middle of an argument that still goes on, and in which Windstar and I still participate. Through the film we were able to encourage many staff people from the various wilderness preservation organizations to come together in support of the Alaskan Lands Bill, which set aside more land for national parks and wilderness than had previously been set aside in the history of the United States, and quite probably in the world. For that alone, I feel our effort was a success of no small measure.

The powerful mining and timber interests, and the businesses aligned with them against the bill, must have thought we had a bit to do with changing things. They took unkindly to having to give ground like that, since in their minds it was their ground to exploit, and they started to say so in a very public way. After we premiered our work in Alaska that winter, I was invited to return as the Grand Marshall of the Fur Rendezvous Parade the following May. But Old Red Dodge, Tony, and Ace called one day to very diplomatically dissuade me from accepting. They thought that some of the people threatening me were less than masterful in hitting what they aimed their guns at. They were worried that innocent bystanders—like themselves—might get shot instead. Not only did I forego the honors of parade master and stay away from Alaska for a few years after that phone call, but when I did go back there again, I did it very quietly. Red, Tony, and Ace were men whose judgment in these matters was worth listening to.

So my space grew and grew, and it was indeed mine for the making. In fact, during this period, I even found a space that Dad and I could occupy peacefully. Or maybe I should just say we found a *kind* of peace. The kind that passeth all understanding.

There are still conversations that we didn't have before he died, but some things were settled, and one of them was the business of flight itself. It was flight not only in the aviation sense, but in the sense, too, that while I always loved him very much, in many ways I'd fled his presence—which when I was growing up sometimes overwhelmed me.

When we lived in Texas, it would bother him when I went off for the night to play with a band. For him, it was a waste of time.

He had no sympathy for what I was trying to accomplish in music. For that matter, I don't think he could sympathize with whatever Ron was trying to do with his life. His powers of sympathy and empathy ran in a narrow channel to what he knew growing up himself. It was a mark against me that I was a musician and not talented in other things. He had some real fears about that for me, which he wasn't able to express without turning belligerent.

I remember one time—I was fifteen and not yet a driver—when he made me change the tires on the Mercury before I could go off to band practice and then chewed me out unmercifully for not doing it right. "You've got to pay attention, boy" is how Dad liked to put it. In my rush to finish, I didn't notice the bevel on the side of the bolts that held the wheels on and ended up screwing them in backward. He wasn't cruel about it intentionally, but he was certainly patronizing. It hurt when he said, "How stupid can you be?"

After several such encounters with Dad, I came away feeling, What's the use? And feeling as if nothing I did was ever good enough. Finally, I felt that it made no sense to put myself in such situations, and consequently, we never talked. I knew objectively that he was a man capable of great acts of consideration and compassion for his fellow man, but I never saw myself as the focus of that.

Of course, Dad's feelings about my musical career changed when he saw I was making a go of it. He was proud of me and happy about my success. If nothing else, it allayed his fears about my being able to pay my bills, a worry that he had about my brother as well. In fact, he was tortured by not seeing Ron doing as well. He had a punishing sense of having failed as a father because of it, or at least he was struggling to reconcile himself with his conscience before he died. One of the last letters that he wrote to me—angrily saying everything but what he wanted me to do about it—was on this subject.

For my part, when things were on the rise for me, I wanted to include him and my mother. I'd bring them out to concerts or TV shows I did, so that they could see how well I was doing. But that didn't mean that we talked more, or that we were closer.

Then he and I started to fly together and that put us on a different stage. If we didn't come to it on the most equal of terms, we at least came to it on terms that both of us could understand. He was the expert, and a great instructor; I was the student, with everything to learn. What is a teacher without a student? What's a student without a teacher? Out of flying and out of the opportunity for both of us to be serving each other, to be taking advantage of each other, we found our way to a relationship between father and son that seemed to work for the first time.

Originally, I'd given up the idea of flying after I got out of high school. My vision was less than perfect—that's the reason for the granny glasses—and I had been told that the military wouldn't have me as a pilot because of it. The vague idea I had of following in Dad's footsteps had to be scratched.

Then one night in a chartered jet, flying back to Minneapolis from a concert in Dayton, the pilot let me go up front, and thirty-five thousand feet up on a gloriously clear night, I got drawn back to that fantasy. Here we were in a real spaceship, a red glow playing over all the instrument dials. Over there was Gary, Indiana, and farther east was South Bend. Ahead of us was Chicago, laid out like jewels on velvet. Off to the right you could see the whole finger of Lake Michigan, and to the left somewhere there, the Chicago River. I could almost pick out the building where Annie and I had lived.

There was O'Hare. And then coming up fast, Milwaukee, and then Madison. It was a spectacular display, and my responses told me that flying was something I had in my blood. A few weeks later I started taking lessons at the airport in Aspen, and after seven hours of lessons, I soloed.

When I called home to talk about what I was doing, Dad was thrilled. Suddenly, after all the silences between us, we were plugged into the same current. "We have to get you a plane," he announced. He was proud and proprietary. And when he heard that the insurance policy for the Cessna I ended up buying required that I have fifty hours of duel time in the plane before I could solo in it, he wouldn't hear of my doing it with anyone but him.

There were pilots around the world who held Dad in very high regard, but that had always been outside of my experience of him. I had had very little to do with the man they knew. When he went off to work in the morning, he didn't bring his kids with him ever. But in flying with him, we stepped outside the constraining circle of father and son.

There was a story Dad liked to tell about a guy he was giving jet instruction to. It's a story that meant a lot to me in many circumstances then and later. This fellow was a big hotshot corporate pilot who didn't think he needed to take guff from anybody, including Dad. He hadn't flown a jet before, much less a Lear, which was Dad's specialty, but he'd flown every twin there was and he'd flown in the service. He was certain he could fly the jet, and that was the wrong attitude to have with Dad; Ron and I could have told him that.

The first day out, Dad proceeded very quietly to just beat this guy to a pulp. Until he opened himself to learning—to being taught, Dad said—there was nothing anyone could say to him that would have gotten through. At one point, in frustration, the fellow said, "How deep does this hole get?" Up to that point he could do nothing right in that plane. And Dad said, "Well, you may have just reached bottom. Maybe now I can teach you something."

When Dad was teaching me, I knew he had a lifetime of experience to back it up and that he was trying to impart as much of it to me as I could take in. If he'd start speaking sharply to me in the cockpit, I knew it was because I was trying to kill us both. When he'd yell, I took it in stride. I knew if I could stay open to what he was doing and how he was doing it, I'd learn a lot. But I must say, however thrilling, it *was* a harrowing experience.

Dad's credo was: Make the plane do what you want it to do. And he did some things in airplanes that not only nobody else has ever done, but nobody would ever want to do. Things that took an enormous amount of courage, and confidence, and understanding. "Make the airplane do what you want it to do." I took this as an all-purpose metaphor.

Later, when I bought a Lear myself, Dad's tutoring continued, only the experience of instruction was even more harrowing than before. I remember one flight that we made to Pueblo, Colorado, where he was throwing everything at me. I'd have to lose an engine on takeoff. I'd have to lose an engine on landing. I flew on instruments. For forty-five minutes, he had me flying around out there in this high-performance airplane as if my life was on the line, which I suppose it was.

Finally he let me land. I taxied off the runway, and then started to come back on it again, prepared to continue with this endlessly challenging routine. It was then that he said, "I've got it; take a break." But I didn't want a break: I was ready to break his ass, or try, because I was so angry at that point. "I'm okay," I insisted, still clutching the controls. "Relax," he said, resting a hand on my shoulder. I could feel my rib cage, full of withheld breathing, finally relax. My shirt was soaking wet and my body was worn to a frazzle.

Then I noticed the look of glee on his face. He was sitting there, a beaming giant, knowing very well how hard I was trying to keep myself centered. He probably had felt much the same after wrestling Grandpa Deutschendorf to the ground to prove his manhood that time when he was home on his first Army furlough. I wouldn't be surprised if my grandfather's face had shown that same look of glee.

The one space that I went looking for and couldn't find was the one I shared with Annie. We probably both kept trying to find the space; in our hearts we never expected things to end. We just didn't do a good job communicating. We'd been attempting to excavate through all the built-up layers of mistrust and misunderstanding, through all the denials our Midwest upbringing had taught us to make, through all the walls we'd erected to keep from seeing what the other was about, but in the end it proved impossible.

And the truth of it is, I didn't have much patience for a lot of Annie's friends when I came off the road. Aspen has circles and circles of friends, and our energies—Annie's and mine—were running off in opposite directions. She started getting into transactional analysis, which I tried for myself but found wanting, and I didn't know how to say that. I just didn't know how to say that or anything like it without making it seem like confrontation, without sounding patronizing or condescending. There are a number of things I could have said much sooner to Annie than I did that would have given us the opportunity to fix the relationship. I should have known better, but I didn't. I should have been courageous enough to tell the truth, but I wasn't.

SEASONS OF THE HEART

*I*ak's memory of the late Seventies might be better than mine, and he was only six when it ended. But there is one thing I remember as well as he, a memory that puts the decade in the right frame for me. Speaking of me, he told a reporter, "He was always on the move, and I always thought that's what he did—concerts and things—and that he had to do it. . . . He just came and went. . . ."

Came in and went out.

Doing music always involved movement, and a lot of it was tied up with the imagery of running away. Running away to where? Running away to start over again; running to make a new and different impression. Running to get away from the contradictions that were uncomfortable and unconfrontable back home. In fact, someone once wrote about me that I was a pastoral escapist, which misses the heart of the matter, I think.

But it's true that I loved the going and the getting there, and the going on again, and the getting free. Going to Australia in the late Seventies was the epitome of that kind of flight. It was far away and very different, and it was brimming over with romantic possibilities. The late 1970s were like that too. Beginning with 1977, I sensed a great *veering* in relationships on all fronts: my music, the band, Jerry, Annie, even the sense I had of myself as a human being. The changes began then and continued with increasing complication, through the next four or five years. It was as if I was flying along and then the plane flipped.

Above all else, things changed regarding the sense I had of myself as human being as opposed to human doing, though it took a while for all of it to bubble up and mean something to me. Much of it was too subtle to read; things just happened, complications for the better *and* for the worse. But from 1977 on, the moral terrain I was exploring began to take unanticipated turns. I was still climbing a mountain, only now I started climbing down, and the way down, as the *I Ching* teaches, isn't the same as the way up. Nor, the wise man knows, is climbing a mountain preparation for what's on the other side.

Most momentously, and joyfully, Annie and I adopted a second child, Anna Kate; we got word about it just before my thirty-third birthday. (Anna Kate is now a young woman, in fact, and a performer herself—a dancer. Now it's *her* performances that leave *me* in awe, just as mine used to leave her.) We had started the process of adoption late that fall, gotten sidetracked for various and sundry reasons, and then around the Christmas holidays worked to make it happen finally. I'd just returned from a trip to Japan, my first there since a forgotten part of my childhood, and I remember being in thrall still to what I had experienced there when we met with the director of the agency: I was trying to strike the positive note. Earlier, in the preliminary stages of the arrangements we were making with the agency, the director had called to ask about stories he had heard that

Annie and I were separating again. We had convinced him the stories were ungrounded—we had even convinced ourselves of that; only cynics would have said otherwise—and I was trying to stay convincing. In Japan, I'd been taken in hand by an American friend who was a real connoisseur of Japanese cultural practices and in a week I'd been exposed to more of Japanese life than the average tourist there gets to see in a lifetime: I couldn't say too much in praise of what I had experienced.

In any case, as with Zak's adoption, we had asked the agency only that the child found for us be one who could live with us in the mountains: otherwise we sought no special considerations, except that it be a girl. But as I have said elsewhere, and remain convinced of, the element of the divine is never absent from these exchanges. The night we were told about Anna Kate, Annie and I were in L.A., where I was making the film *Oh God!*, and we'd gone to see a remake of *A Star Is Born,* with Barbra Streisand. We were real movie buffs, but for some reason we both felt restless in the theater, and left before the film was over—the first time we'd ever done so. We couldn't figure out what the problem was. But when we got back to the hotel, there was a message from the adoption agency; the director had been trying to get in touch with us. He'd found a child for us. She was a Japanese-American girl; Anna Kate had just been born.

Of course, in truth, despite all our good intentions, everything was conspiring against our marriage, including ourselves. I naively thought that sheer willing it could make anything happen, including marriage. I have learned otherwise, especially about marriage. And I had no notion of what was involved psychologically in being a parent. I was of the school of thought that love conquered all. Bringing Anna Kate home filled our house with that love. We had two small children and I couldn't have been more proud. If I'd had a choice, I would have stayed home and watched them grow, as Annie did, but the music business got very busy for me then: bookings in big halls, concerts in the round, full and enthusiastic audiences. The recognition I received in those places was just irresistible to me; it drew me out of myself. Even in Tokyo, where the sound of spoken English in the concert hall was still exotic, everyone who came to our sold-out shows knew the words to "Sunshine on My Shoulders" and heartily sang along. (Contrast this with my attempt to sing the song in Japanese: a moment of uncertainty when I finished, and then a little burst of polite laughter.)

I expanded the band—to seven instrumentalists—acquired additional backup singers, and overall I began an expansionary phase in my music. Even as the songs slipped a bit on the charts, I kept it up. I was really at the height of my performing career—with the band, without the band, with only strings. I always tried to vary the format.

Bands, I should interject here, are like nothing else in life. If you're not part of that culture, it may be hard to grasp the special bond. Maybe a record producer understands some of it, but you don't really understand what happens among a band unless you've been a part of one. I'm tempted to make a comparison with a sports team. There's the same strong bonding, the same group aggression. It isn't necessarily a male thing, but it comes under the category of being macho. Where singer-songwriters are concerned, the bonding takes the form of breathing together. And when the music you're making is about your life, and the whole length and breadth of your soul, the people who are out there with you in front of an audience—breathing with you while you are putting your life on the line—are like none other.

For the record, the historical record, the first John Denver band was Mike Taylor on acoustic guitar, Dick Kniss on bass, and me doing vocals and guitar; our first gig was the one with Bill and Taffy Danoff at the Cellar Door in Washington during the winter of 1970–71, when we introduced "Country Roads." The little guitar lick that sets up that song, which people recognize very quickly, was our band expressing a personality. Very little changed for a long time, except maybe the sound got bigger. Around 1974, I replaced Mike with Steve "Pokey" Weisberg, who also played the Dobro, and in 1975 I added a fourth member, John Sommers, who played mandolin, fiddle, banjo, and bluegrass guitar; Pokey and John were two musicians who, like me, had migrated to Aspen. It was that constellation, along with some terrific studio musicians, that carried me through some big years touring and recording.

Then in 1977 everything involving the band changed. Early in the year I must have had a sudden intuition that affected my tolerance for idiosyncrasy and I parted ways with Pokey, mostly over a rift in our temperaments. He was called Pokey because he was slow and always late, and in the studio he always wanted to do the song again after we thought we'd laid it to rest. There are a lot of musicians like that. You're in the studio, and you're trying to save money, and you get it down, and this guy will start to listen for something that maybe nobody else knows about; he doesn't even know if he can get it, but he wants to try one more time. Pokey was the king of those guys. I just reached a point where I didn't want to work with him anymore.

That winter, while getting ready to go into the studio to do the *I Want to Live* album, and thinking about the band I wanted to take for the tour of Australia, I realized I wanted the music to take yet another step, and that Dick wouldn't fit into that. John

Sommers was the only one of the band I asked to stay on. An ex-Navy flyer, he and I were close friends.

Unfortunately, our second day in the studio, John came to me to report that the musicians I'd hired—including James Burton and Glen D. Hardin, former Elvis Presley band members—intimidated him; they were that good. Anyway, he said, he'd never wanted to play in a big band and he was leaving. I was a little stunned, and let down, because at that point he was the only guy in the band I was friendly with. I was counting on his presence when we toured. The new musicians intimidated me, too. I'd long been intimidated by the musicians whom Milt Okun found to play with me in recording sessions; they were all that good. What I found intimidating was being unable to tell them what I wanted them to play. I know I heard the other parts—guitar, bass, some kind of percussion—but I couldn't say what worked and what didn't, and I would just take what they gave me, it was all such incredible stuff. So I could sympathize with John's panic.

In fact, I didn't stop thinking I could bring John out of it, that my growth would be a catalyst for his. After he left, we were playing huge concerts everywhere, and once in the fall of 1978, I asked him to sit in for a couple of shows; we were playing at the Summit in Houston. He really enjoyed it. It was probably the best time he'd ever had on the stage. But when he came off stage the second night, he had this grandiose fantasy that he was not only good enough to stay with the band, he was good enough to be its leader. When I disabused him of the idea, he went berserk, throwing his guitar case out of the window of his hotel room—or was it a suitcase?

When I heard about that the next morning, I prepared for the worst, which would have been his coming out onstage in the middle of the show and making a fuss. But instead, twenty minutes before curtains, he came to my dressing room and ranted about me personally, and about my music. The police were there, standing outside my door, along with Jerry Weintraub and a music critic from the *Los Angeles Times* who had flown in to do a review of the show. But I felt that there was no alternative but to keep the door locked and let him get it off his chest; that's how dumb I was.

In the end, it worked out. After a half-hour, the storm passed, and I went out and did a show as if nothing had happened. But that little confrontation left its residue of psychic strain, of which there was no small amount during this hectic period. In fact, for a time I was having nightmares about a week or two before we'd go out on the road. Mostly they were recurring fantasies about those initial moments of getting out there onstage and finding my guitar not there, or finding it there but without strings, or hearing myself being introduced while I was still in the shower. By the late 1970s, we were touring scores of cities every couple of months, here, there, and everywhere. On one itinerary from that period I find that we performed in sixty-three cities between mid-September and mid-December. I'd barely get home and would have to turn around and go back out again.

It had always been the case that my concerts were better received than my recordings. In fact, I've never been particularly happy with my singing on records. Now the concerts were better than ever and we became very glamorous, popular figures indeed. Even grist for the scandal mills. One year, a *faux pas* of mine at a press conference earned tabloid headlines around the world practically before I had a chance to leave the room, so hot were we and our simple doings.

We had been laying low in Sydney for a couple of days, recovering from jet lag. There were a lot of people on this tour, counting the band, the crew, and everyone else. We had planned it like a military operation, so that there'd be no hassles. Australia was already coming down heavy on visiting musicians. Frank Sinatra had just canceled a tour there because of the way the press was carrying on. Someone had scored some grass for us that was fantastic. As far as I can remember, everybody tried it. Now it was time to leave on the first leg of the tour and I held the customary tour-opening press conference.

I knew of Australia's reputation for tabloid journalism at its most vile, but when I walked into the room where the press conference was to be held, I was unprepared for the chaos, or the characters trying to outdo one another in being disrespectful, not only of me but of themselves. Nobody had warned me about what to expect. There was one guy with strips of tape all over his face from where he'd nicked himself shaving; he looked sort of like Alfalfa from Our Gang with his hair all slicked back, and in the midst of this media frenzy, he asked, "Do you smoke hash?" And flippantly I answered, "Every chance I get." It was the wrong thing to say. It stopped everyone in the room. The next day tabloid headlines around the world read, JOHN DENVER SMOKES HASH! or words to that effect. I might as well have given away the secret to the atomic bomb. I thought that Sal Bonafede, Jerry's deputy on the tour, who was in charge of public relations, would die right there. It also dawned on me that the guy who we had seen around our hotel at all hours of the day and night and who we couldn't fit into a context must have been a cop assigned to tail us. In a state of paranoia I flushed all the grass down the john in the hotel room, for which I don't think anyone ever forgave me—even to this day.

As if that weren't enough, the next day I got ticketed in Melbourne for driving a motorcycle without a helmet, and there were headlines again. Then in Perth, the day after that, I was photographed driving a motorcycle the wrong way down a one-way street—more gonzo publicity. By that time it was hard to avoid the conclusion that I was being picked on. I was a bit rattled.

In fact, when we came back to Australia the following year, I created a terrible flap one day out of my anxiety about keeping a good face on things. It was a getaway day; everyone had gone off to the airport ahead of me while I stayed behind to appear on television. I'd been named Entertainer of the Year by the Country Music Association (Entertainer of the Year and Song of the Year, actually), and they had fixed up a satellite feed in the building where we'd performed the night before so that I could beam into the proceedings at the Grand Ole Opry house in Nashville. As usual everything ran long, and when I didn't show up at the gate by departure time, K.O. and Barney Wyckoff, who was working as his assistant, took off to look for me in the terminal. When I did arrive, and my limo was waved through the gate so it could take me directly to the plane, K.O. and Barney were nowhere to be found and I was afraid to push our luck. We were flying on a commercial flight and they flew by the book and on schedule. I didn't want to attract attention at that moment by delaying the flight.

It was like a Keystone Cops comedy situation. The only problem was, by the time K.O. and Barney caught up with us late that night, in Adelaide, their sense of humor had worn thin. I had sent Sal to the airport to meet their plane with a limo, and he had taken a bouquet of flowers, but K.O. and Barney weren't placated. Instead of coming back to the hotel in the limo, they hopped into a cab and worked off their insulted feelings in an all-night binge. Unfortunately for them, my dad was along on that tour and caught them coming back. He chewed them out, up one side and down the other. When I met with them the next morning, I had to soothe doubly ruffled sensibilities.

That was about as much in the way of scandal as our tours produced, but it was the kind of turbulence the press enjoyed working up into stories. There was very little in this period that I hated more than dealing with this aspect of the press. On the other hand, as things evolved for me as an environmental activist, I found at least some of the press interested in that aspect of my life, too. On our European tours, for example, reporters wanted to know where I stood on nuclear energy and not just what was happening with me and Annie.

Windstar, in its original conception, was in part going to be something like what the pyramids were: a demonstration of what we know scientifically and technologically that is in harmony with nature. We were looking at the use of energy in the world. Nuclear power was the subject of much debate at this time, and one year there were initiatives on the ballot in Oregon and California about establishing nuclear power plants, which I worked to defeat. Buckminster Fuller, of whom I considered myself a disciple, said nuclear power is great, but it has one qualifying factor in relationship to human beings: It needs to be approximately 92 million miles away, and then it is still dangerous. Of course, he was speaking about the sun.

In developing Windstar, Tom Crum and I focused on renewable forms of energy: the wind and the sun. Even before I thought of the sun as energy, I connected to it pragmatically: the sun as the source of life on this planet. "Sunshine on My Shoulders" was about this, not about pastoral escapism. The sun gives its light and energy to everyone without judgment. And the wind passes over us all through this thin layer of atmosphere that we live in all together. I wanted to know how the Earth, something so essentially fragile, nevertheless managed to go on. How did it manage its wobble in the midst of a void?

In 1976 I bought a thousand acres of land in Snowmass, Colorado, for Windstar, and the place that I had dreamed about since my salad days began to materialize. Hal Thau, Tom Crum, and I made up the first board of directors, and Tom operated it. We staffed it, worked out an organization, designed a program. In effect it was a school—and for me, heady stuff to participate in. We were going to construct a complex of high-tech buildings where we'd have conferences and year-round workshops. People would come to learn about the environment so that they could take what they learned back out into the world. Workshops and conferences would focus on the environment and be built around the connections between mind, body, and spirit.

While I was doing that, I developed a closeness with a man named Stewart Mace and his family. Stewart was starting a small farm project down in the Huerfano Valley in southeastern Colorado, near Pueblo, and I wanted to support that work, too; I helped him buy some land. I thought somewhere down the line that my efforts were going to come back to me, not in the form of money, but in terms of knowledge. It was going to balance what we were doing at Windstar.

For a while there, too, I thought I might turn my land into a working ranch, although that idea was abandoned when Windstar was established. In all of this planning, I had the sense, in terms of the environment, that heavy-duty problems lay ahead of us. And along with this, I shared the belief that we were going to have to learn to survive in nature, that it was important to build in a way that was harmonious with nature—in a way that would sustain us when it all started falling apart.

This was also the period when I was giving an enormous amount of time and energy to both the Hunger Project and to the Presidential Commission on World and Domestic Hunger. I was going twice a month to meetings in Washington, attending other commission meetings around the country, and sometimes going off on my own to make speeches about the commission's work. Busy as I was, pressured as I was, I was fully invested.

It wasn't just that I felt that I was doing something that was going to have a real, profound impact on the world. I also liked being around people who were committed to making a positive difference in the world, people who were doing something that had value far outside their own lives. The participation took me very close to who I am and what I wanted to be, and I was proud of having gotten myself there and for having been to some degree a catalyst. As Buckminster Fuller was saying, humanity's greatest challenge was to educate ourselves so that new spontaneous behaviors spring forth that will ensure the continuance of the human species as opposed to its extinction. And that is certainly how I saw my commitment; how I'd seen it all my life, in fact, although I'd never put it that way.

Supporting all that activity became expensive. It would reach the point where I needed to take home more than $2 million a year in order to do it. It would become an enormous treadmill that kept going faster and faster. But at that point who took seriously anything said on the side of prudence? In 1978, I had six albums on the charts, and the money was flowing.

It wasn't just my own success, by the way, that was flourishing. During this period, everyone connected to John Denver in a business sense enjoyed success, too. Just as my enterprises

On tour in Amsterdam, 1975.

With Tony Bennett.

John and Hal Thau backstage at the Grand Ole Opry, 1987.

Milt Okun, John, and Hal Thau, 1979.

Visiting Africa with the Hunger Project, October 1984.

ABOVE: *With Hume Cronyn and Jessica Tandy during the filming of* Foxfire.

RIGHT: *John in 1980.*

In 1983, the Air Force let John and another pilot take up an F-80.

Fishing in Alaska.

Cassie and three-month-old Jesse Belle.

John with his beautiful children: Anna Kate, Jesse Belle, and Zak.

were launched, theirs were as well. From A to Z, all and sundry who were working for me got a shot at what they wanted to make for themselves, not the least of whom was Jerry Weintraub, whose ambition really came to the fore during this period. As I reached my zenith as a performer, Jerry was creating clout for himself throughout the entertainment industry. And therein lies a tale.

Jerry was still making things happen for me, but out of every situation he was making the best for himself, too. A good example of this is how, on the basis of the first feature film I did, he launched himself as a movie producer. It was David Geffen's brainstorm to cast me in the role of an innocent to whom God appears, in the film *Oh, God!*; he went to Jerry with the idea. But when the film became a big box-office draw, Jerry claimed credit for masterminding the whole thing. More than that, he talked me into taking a percentage of the film's earnings in lieu of a salary, and into going fifty-fifty with him on that percentage, instead of our usual eighty-twenty arrangement which was more customary between client and manager; plus he got a billing as the film's producer, although what he did as producer escapes me. Okay, even if I thought fifty-fifty was more to his advantage than the situation warranted, my main consideration was eventually being able to build on that work, so I went along with the arrangement. In fact, one day in his office, Jerry showed me a statement he had drawn up and signed at the bottom with a flourish. He felt that since he had a career in movies now and that I'd been an integral part of making that happen for him, and since he got 20 percent of everything I did, I was going to get a percentage of what he did in the movies. Far out, wonderful, I remember saying. I was so terribly naive; I just trusted him. If he was going to work harder than you could imagine anybody doing, and be brilliant in pulling off some of these things, then I was happy to let him do it. But subsequently only one possibility for a movie role emerged, and I turned it down. No other role materialized. "I'm reading scripts, kid," he'd say when I asked about it. He *was* reading scripts—and letting it be known that any film John Denver participated in had to include him in an executive capacity.

He promoted his interests in the concert business the same way, trading on my popularity and then parlaying it into further advantages. I'd need to be a magician to map out how he did it, how it was conjured up from small change, this outfit called Concerts West that Jerry brought in to promote my concerts after I became popular. He then took over Concerts West and used it to get Elvis Presley to go out on the road, to get one of Frank Sinatra's tours, you name it. The legend is that Elvis's manager, Colonel Tom Parker, came to Jerry and said, "Jerry, I like you. I've heard a lot of good things about you."

This was in the mid-1970s, and the "good things," if the truth be told, was the concert business we were doing. Concerts West was built around my show. It was my and K.O.'s experience doing shows that gave our concerts their professionalism, standards that I'd learned in my years with the Mitchell Trio, and that K.O. and I knew from when we started out in the touring business. This involved setting things up and taking care of all the details so that everything was the way it should be when you showed up in a place for your concerts. O'Connor and I wrote the book on this stuff—stuff that people all over the world do now, and that we taught them how to do.

"Jerry," the Colonel said, "bring me a million dollars tomorrow"—or maybe it was $100,000—"and I'll give you Elvis's tour." And Jerry, of course, got the tour. He raised the money overnight. Jerry worshipped the ground Colonel Parker walked on. And when he had all these things lined up—the Denver tour, the Presley tour, the Sinatra tour, the Moody Blues tour, and more—he went to all the major venues around the country and said, "If you want Denver, if you want Elvis, if you want the Moody Blues, you've got to work with Concerts West." He sewed up the market so tightly that a band couldn't go into these places unless Concerts West got a piece of the action.

Of course, it worked to my advantage that Jerry controlled these venues. Disc jockeys who were influential in the business weren't always inclined to play my records; I was marginal to their interests in rock 'n' roll. Jerry forced their hand by threatening to withhold tickets to concerts that they wanted to attend. But because Jerry was a principal of Concerts West, he had himself a real sweet deal, getting a percentage for managing me and a percentage for promoting the concerts.

It was also the case in television work. I was Jerry's first television star. Because of my success, he had the clout to get spots for other recording artists. And when he did, he put his interests first, irrespective of any conflicts of loyalty. He was a genius at obscuring what he was doing, offering a variety of chimeras as distractions, and I went along with it.

For example, when we formed a production company to do my television specials and I agreed to split fifty-fifty with him, my understanding was that he was going to have a lot of other artists doing television and those shows would also fall under our production company. But nothing like that happened; my trust was totally misplaced, the promises didn't materialize, and conflicts with Jerry's agenda began to crop up more and more.

♦ ♦ ♦

Meanwhile, starting in 1977, Annie was launching her own enterprise. It wasn't a business, this enterprise, it was her own self, her own individuality, apart from me. Her own circle of friends, her own interests, her own inclinations. I'd come off the road, sometimes from abroad, wanting nothing more in the world than to sit at home for a few days, and it would be as if I were an interloper. She had her life, she had a routine, she had a schedule, and everything that went on in the house was geared to that. I tried to be there, but there was no place for me to be, except with the children. About each other, to each other, there was very little to say. When I tried to tell her what was going on with me, she'd put on a face, the kind that EST would teach you to wear to fend off verbal assaults; it says, "I'm listening, but it doesn't touch me." The least pretext, it seemed, would set off an argument. After a few of these episodes, I couldn't wait to get out on the road again.

My idea of heaven at that point was boarding an airplane with my band and crew, who were my best friends, after having sung my way through a two-and-a-half-hour concert, and finding a hot meal waiting, an open bar, a bottle of champagne, and a couple of stewardesses to serve it all. What could be more soothing, more civilizing, to the savage beast within? By the time we got to our next hotel, I'd have a pretty good buzz on. If the bar was open, we'd go there and try to get lucky. Yet behind the bravado I would long and ache for coming home. Running away only exacerbated the situation.

Whatever my flights were doing to Annie—and I really had no notion of it from her side, as I might now—it became excruciatingly depressing to me each time I went away and came back only to find myself still at square one. My anger about it grew increasingly unwieldy. Once during this period, while cutting a

Christmas album in London with Jim Henson's Muppets, I got so frustrated with Annie over the phone, so lost and demoralized about what was going on with our relationship, that I thought I'd kill myself. For a moment I couldn't figure out a more appropriate response to how cold and condemning she sounded. The recording dates were moving along and, feeling good about the music but missing everybody at home, I called her. But there was nothing but shit coming over the phone, which, being guilt-ridden as I was, I took all so seriously. Hemmed in by the good middle-class thoughts I was brought up on, I feared that I was going to be stuck in this agony for the rest of my life, which was diametrically opposed to what I was as a human being! When Annie hung up, my sense of despair and betrayal got the better of me. I grabbed my guitar and headed out to the balcony, ten stories above Grosvenor Square. I was going to jump with the guitar.

But then I think I felt the air tremble; the Concorde was landing. I noticed that it was a beautiful day. I took a moment to look down to the street and inhaled a deep breath of air. I came back in. What was this madness for? Why was I letting myself be consumed by it? I sat down, and holding on to myself the only way I knew how, I wrote a song called "In My Heart." It was meant as a gift, but I don't think Annie ever unpacked it.

I don't know why we still live together;
We're so far apart so much of the time.
I don't know why this beautiful weather
Is breaking my spirit and tearing my mind all apart.
Are you so lonely? Are you so sad?
Have you lost your purpose, the faith that you had?
If life is a question I don't understand,

If time is the reason, then nobody can.
In my heart, it is just an illusion; it's not even real.
It's much more than you think, much more than you feel.
My ears are still ringing, there's nothing to say.
Why look to the ocean to wash me away?
There goes my best friend, there goes my last dime;
If love is the answer, I'm wasting my time.

This burden of feeling got heavier and heavier. Annie had for-given me my transgressions, but not really. At least, it felt a little abrasive to me, this forgiveness, this space that was left for us to work things out. But by 1980 I was beginning to feel that things were going to take a dive, and I needed Annie; I needed to feel that she was a part of what I was doing. So I tried as best I could to be ameliorative, to create some common ground. I made a commitment to renovate the house and agreed that she'd be in charge. But being in charge had a different valence for her than it did for me, and she became so hard about it. I put her on the board of Windstar; I put her analyst on the board, too. But she was hard and oppositional there as well. What was there to enjoy about the transformation wrought by her newfound authority? She wanted me to come out from behind my facade and resolve things. Fine, but I could do no better than write these songs. That was the way I cared, and showed that I cared. Annie han-dled it differently; most women do. But then, for that matter, most men are like me. Men find it harder than women to ex-press intimacy by sitting around talking about it. I know it's all changing; I began changing, too. But back then, we argued.

We argued, for example, about macrobiotics, to give an idea of the banality of our disagreements. I wanted to quit eating hotel food, and junk food in general, on the road. I knew it wasn't good for me, and when Ron Lemire showed up, I knew I could get some help with this. Ron was a physical therapist, a macrobiotic cook, a Golden Gloves boxer, a hippie, and a rebel without a cause. (It was Ron who would guide me through the powerful experience of fasting on Lake Powell, which I described in Chapter 3.) So I hired him as my security guy and cook and went off on tour again—two weeks on the road and two weeks home through the spring and summer.

After a few days on Ron's food, I was full of energy. My voice was clear, I was sleeping well at night, my vitality was up. Then when I'd come home and eat Annie's cooking again—full of rich sauces and so forth—I'd become lethargic, find it hard to wake up, feel heavy and full of aches. After a couple of these extraordinary swings in physiology, I found it something worth discussing, but Annie didn't want to hear about it. In fact, she took my suggestion that she try cooking like Ron as unkind. When I suggested at a Windstar board meeting that Michio Kushi be invited to speak about macrobiotics, she flat-out opposed it, and so did her analyst; the culture wars had come home.

By the time I went off to Los Angeles to work with Milt on another new album and its demands got the better of me, I knew I was in dire straits. The frustration I was feeling just spilled over. I'd been to the Oakland ashram to see one of my spiritual teachers Swami Muktananda, whom I felt was really there for me, and I think that was the catalyst for recognizing a whole range of things that had been gnawing at me, a great grief that had been all tied up. There was dissension in the band and I couldn't deal with it; I couldn't deal with the pressure to get things done.

The immediate problem was that I wasn't that good a musician yet; I could still get excited while playing a song and speed up. Then Hal Blaine, being maternal and the kind of drummer who had worked with musicians who weren't really musicians, would follow me instead of the band—when I sped up, he sped up. The band wanted him to sit on the beat and groove. It was two different philosophies and I needed to be the one who resolved it: to be or not to be. Plus Milt needed me to write another love song for the album; I don't think he knew what was going on with me, but I felt that I needed out. I called the studio and uncharacteristically begged off for the day. Inside my head it felt like a man having a nervous breakdown.

I got in my car, and with Annie's brother, Ben, who was helping out working as my personal assistant, I drove up the coast as far as Big Sur. I felt so much turmoil, and I started to let it come out. Driving back, I started thinking about all the ways I've experienced love—not that I was feeling very loved right then, or that I had a love in my life anymore, but it was good to remember.

I started remembering love and certain expressions of love, and I tried to describe that. I tried to describe all the ways that people think of love, and how love is really all of those things, and these beautiful lines came pouring out of me:

Perhaps love is like a resting place
A shelter from the storm
It exists to give you comfort
It is there to keep you warm
And in those times of trouble
When you are most alone
The memory of love will bring you home
Perhaps love is like a window
Perhaps an open door
It invites you to come closer

It wants to show you more
And even if you lose yourself
And don't know what to do
The memory of love will see you
    through

Oh, love to some is like a cloud
To some as strong as steel
For some a way of living
For some a way to feel
And some say love is holding on
And some say letting go
And some say love is everything
And some say they don't know
Perhaps love is like the ocean
Full of conflict, full of change
Like a fire when it's cold outside
Or thunder when it rains
If I should live forever
And all my dreams come true
My memories of love will be of you

And not for the first time, the new song and the act of creating it brought me out of my funk. My sense of humor returned. I saw, fleetingly maybe, that life can't be all great, but that discovering this knowledge is a part of living. So what if life is painful and then you die. The sun was shining. Put your consciousness down, underfoot, I told myself; be relaxed, breathe, notice all the rest, fool that you are. Ben and I drove back to L.A. and I took "Perhaps Love" to Milt, and then I finished recording the album. Milt thought, as always, that all's well that ends well.

But RCA rejected the album: They didn't think it was up to the mark, given the way they were investing in me. They were giving me $1 million advances at that point, and they had new management, whose interests were geared more to other music than the kind I was making. Country music, for example. And Jerry unaccountably went along with them; not only did he not raise a fuss, but he took their side. In effect, he fired Milt Okun as producer and had me go to Nashville to do a different album with a producer of country music. I did it, but it wasn't a happy experience. It was only Milt's encouragement that kept me at it. The hardest part of it was having to swallow the news that "Perhaps Love," along with a lot of other songs of mine, somehow wasn't right for this record.

Milt had been hurt by the firing, but had dismissed it from his mind; still, no love was lost between Jerry and him. Columbia Records had hired Milt to produce the first recording of Plácido Domingo singing contemporary material, including "Annie's Song," in which I was going to accompany him on guitar, and he was already working on it. When Milt heard that "Perhaps Love" wasn't being used on my new album, he took the song to Plácido and Plácido agreed to record it himself—with me singing along. Had RCA chosen to issue "Perhaps Love" as a co-release with Columbia at that point, as Milt suggested, it would have been a big deal. As soon as it was released, the duet was given a lot of airplay. But RCA declined, according to Jerry, saying they were committed solely to the country album that had been produced in Nashville. Later I found out that what had happened was just one more instance of Jerry's self-aggrandizement. If Milt wanted a co-release, Jerry had told him, then Milt would have to deliver him Plácido's management contract. And so on *absurdum infinitum*. I didn't believe that story when I heard it, but I believe it now.

Somewhere in this drove of dismal events, having resolved nothing regarding my marriage, I moved into the guest house. It was only one hundred yards away, and the move was self-imposed, but still I felt as if I'd been banished into the wilderness. I was heartbroken and not thinking logically anymore. I let myself get into a really bad way, unable to communicate with anyone about all of this. All I could think about were various forms of escape, and one place I often escaped to was the local tavern, where I would drink, sorry and solitary. Or when the spirit moved me in a more uplifted direction, I'd take off for the ski resorts in Switzerland or to the Hawaiian Islands to explore underwater photography. After the time spent in L.A. to make the failed album, and after a fall tour that included a disastrous falling-out with Kris O'Connor in Germany, I came back home and tried to get into the spirit of a family Christmas, but it was living a lie—a sad task rather than a celebration. Then in February 1981 Annie and I started another long separation, this one lasting six months. When I came back in July, having wandered around China for a month, and then Tibet, things were better for a while. Through that summer the gloom seemed to lighten. There were times when we could go beyond what had pulled us apart and actually live like husband and wife. Then it became all antagonism again—what agony. I felt angry not only with Annie, but with her analyst. At one point, rationally or not, I had a sneaking feeling that he wanted to be the person who gave Windstar its direction; he and Annie apparently had their own agenda for the environment.

Enough guilt. I needed to end the charade. I needed Annie to get to that point, too. This time I decided I'd stay put, not run away. If we were going to split apart, I needed Annie to see the reasons for it for herself. One time she was around when I was practicing a new song I'd written, "Seasons of the Heart," and she said from her cold, hard, sarcastic place—this wonderful woman, you wouldn't believe it—"Are you trying to tell me something?" Was that Annie dissembling or was she being obtuse? Now that it wasn't only me making the decision about coming or going, I could see she had her own fears, things she couldn't say. There is so much about a person you never know. I said nothing, or I lied. And I didn't play the song for her anymore.

Of course we have our differences, you shouldn't be surprised.
It's as natural as changes in the seasons and the skies.
Sometimes we grow together, sometimes we drift apart.
A wiser man than I might know the seasons of the heart.

And I'm walking here beside you in the early evening chill.
A thing we've always loved to do, I know we always will.
We have so much in common, so many things we share
That I can't believe my heart, when it implies that you're not
    there.

Love is why I came here in the first place.
Love is now the reason I must go.
Love is all I ever hoped to find here.
Love is still the only dream I know.

So I don't know how to tell you, it's difficult to say.
I never in my wildest dreams imagined it this way.
But sometimes I just don't know you, there's a stranger in our
    home.
When I'm lying right beside you is when I'm most alone.

And I think my heart is broken, there's an emptiness inside.
So many things I've longed for have so often been denied.
Still I wouldn't try to change you, there's no one that's to blame.
It's just some things that mean so much and we just don't feel
    the same.

Love is why I came here in the first place.
Love is now the reason I must go.
Love is all I ever hoped to find here.
Love is still the only dream I know.
True love is still the only dream I know.

That fall in New York, while recording another album, I was swept away by an affair that was more than just hello and good-bye. Everything in a woman that I hadn't had for such a long period of time was, all of a sudden, there for me. It wasn't that she was everything I wanted in a woman, or that I was every-thing she wanted, but I was shown sides of a woman I hadn't seen before, sides that, in my mind, Annie didn't have. That was a big realization. I'm sure Annie was getting something from the people around her that she wasn't getting from me, but I real-ized I, too, wanted more for myself. That realization only hard-ened what was already a hard spot. It wasn't worth the time or the energy anymore to try to make things different.

Ironically, Annie's Christmas present to me that year was a new wedding ring—a beautiful silver ring, two bands entwined, one rough-surfaced and one smooth. In November we had gone boating with some friends, and I'd lost my original wedding ring while diving. We'd looked for it but hadn't found it. Annie had made a sarcastic comment, but then at Christmas she gave me this new wedding ring, and I couldn't wear it.

◆   ◆   ◆

Then, without warning, Dad died.

He had left the Air Force during the Vietnam War. He'd had an argument with the brass about what constituted proper training for pilots who were going to fly a new generation of jets, which he knew how to fly better than anyone. Finding themselves in a bind over manpower, the Air Force wanted to compromise on training time, and Dad stood up against it, for which he was court-martialed. He was very courageous to speak out as he did. Though eventually the Air Force rescinded the court-martial, Dad stayed retired, at least from the military. At first he found work piloting air freight out of Columbus, Ohio. He tried to adjust to having his glory days behind him, but that must have been harder than he let on. When I told him I wanted to buy a jet plane and learn to fly it, he happily took on the business of getting me a good one, taking care of it, and finding and training the pilots who would fly it for me when he was gone. And he came to work for me as chief of Windstar Aviation. That doesn't mean we talked about things that were there between us, but we enjoyed working side by side. If he could no longer enjoy his own glory days, he could at least share in mine. Everyone enjoyed his being along.

In fact, he probably had as intimate a relationship with the pilots he trained for me as he had with anyone in the second half of his life. Although it wasn't like him to show much emotion, I think he expressed a lot in his relationship with these guys that didn't come out anywhere else.

Then we were visited by one of those tricks life plays on you when you least expect it. While he was training them, he started to be a little more conscious about health and exercise, and he quit drinking. "Quit" is an understatement; he was very strong-willed about it, as with everything he did. When he had a cataract removed from one of his eyes, he wouldn't let the doctors deaden the nerves when they operated. He sat there and held the eye open for them. Strong and straight. He'd set his mind on doing something, and it was going to get done. So it was with his rejection of drinking.

About the time Dad quit drinking, I was getting into macrobiotics and told him about it. In fact, I started working on him by getting him and my mother to do the EST training, which they finally agreed to but which was quite a struggle for them. There were some exercises in the EST training that had to do with putting oneself in touch with the more intuitive and psychic sides of one's nature, and this blew Dad away. For some of this, you have to be in a certain frame of mind, or place of looking, and it stopped making sense to him after a while. Some of the things he was learning he had never thought about before. He had never been in touch with any kind of meditation. It was interesting to watch him try.

Then he got interested in macrobiotics. He'd always been a meat-and-potatoes man, but he must have seen or felt the change in me when I changed my own diet. He even took it upon himself to go to one of Michio Kushi's seminars in Boulder. Examining him, Michio found Dad's body riddled with toxins.

So, he stopped drinking and started to pay attention to health and exercise, and all the toxins started coming out. But then he came down with pneumonia in Tulsa, while he and Mom were visiting my mother's family. He got well and then he got sick again and went into the hospital in Denver. When I visited, I was stunned. I'd never seen him look so drawn and old. Lying there, he was kind of angry: "Shit," he said, "one of the things I really enjoyed in my life was drinking. I quit drinking and I have to go through this? I'd rather drink." And he started again.

In the spring of 1982 he came out to Lake Tahoe to attend one of my shows. The week before, he'd put me through my paces in the Lear over at Grand Junction, where you do all the stuff you do in a Learjet, plus a couple of things you're not supposed to. He was such a great pilot, and he wanted me to be just as good. I didn't think I had done a very good show that night in Tahoe, and he came into my dressing room and said he thought I'd been great. He laughed and he was happy, and he and Mom went home that way. But right after he got home, he had a massive heart attack, and nothing could be done to alleviate the damage. He died a day later, on the Ides of March, a month shy of his sixty-second birthday. He was buried in the military cemetery in Denver. A lot of people came. A formation of planes, with one missing, flew overhead. It was pretty moving.

A few months later, on our wedding anniversary, Annie finally said she wanted a divorce. My spring tour that year had ended on June 7. On June 8 I joined Jimmy Buffett and Judy Collins onstage in Denver at a mobilization for peace that Windstar helped organize, part of a series of such demonstrations across the country. June 9 was Annie's and my fifteenth anniversary.

The first gloom of the Reagan years settled around me. After the promise of *I Want to Live,* I now had to face the pain of starting over.

HOLD ON TIGHTLY,
LET GO LIGHTLY

Lost in a boat on the ocean
Lost in a ship out at sea
Lost in the dark of misfortune
Where is a light I can see.
Where is the highway to heaven
Where is the love we all need
Where is the peace that we long for
Where is the man who is free

Here in the heart there is freedom
Here in the heart there is peace
Here in the heart is the answer
To questions much deeper than these

You've got to hold on tightly
Let go lightly
It's only surrender, it's all in the game
If you just hold on tightly

Let go lightly
There's always forgiveness and no one to blame

apricorns have a hard time coping when they're young. To help themselves, they develop a kind of armor. When they get older, they outgrow the shell they made, but keep some of it in habits of mind; they are creatures of history. On the other hand, as Capricorns grow older, their younger selves often come through, as if time were turned around and going in a different direction. In other words, as we get older, we get younger. Or so the sages say. It seems ironic to me now to think that all the facing up I had to do in the early Eighties, all the uprooting that my life endured then, was about this shedding of armor, and the particular histories that this armor clothed.

In some ways it was easy to let go of Dad; not that I floated through it, but I dealt with it in large part by doing the talking for Mom. She couldn't talk, she was crying so hard; neither could Ron. So I was the one who said good-bye, even while so much remained unsaid; in my solitary moments I still work it over in my head. I told Dad that we were going to let him go—unhook him from the machine that was keeping his body alive—and that we loved him: *Go in peace.* I knew he was already brain-dead, but Ron and I needed Mom to see it, and saying it helped her and it helped me. Still, I was full of regrets. Regret, the Buddhists say, is as common to man as air is to birds. We regret the love we didn't give, and we resent the love we didn't get.

In letting go of marriage to Annie I experienced some of the same helpless inevitability. While not a death, the loss was similar. First there was the numbing reality of formal separation; then a series of aftershocks, which had me lashing out at hurts

I still felt being inflicted; and then, finally, emotional surrender to it.

One incident serves as illustration: the worst such moment of wanting some nameless revenge. I was staying for a few days up in Wood's Lake, where we had a family getaway, about an hour and a half outside of Aspen. The kids had come with their nanny to stay for a while, so I knew Annie would be back home alone. I'd been obsessing about slights I'd felt, real and imagined. On my way to Woods Lake, I had gone by the house to get some camping gear and discovered that Annie had cut down a stand of shrub oaks without even talking to me about it; it broke my heart. When I built the house, the view past those trees was as much a part of it as the walls and windows. Words can't communicate the violation I felt. Then I fixated on the house, from which I was now excluded. With mayhem in mind, I hatched a plot.

The next morning, about eight A.M., on my way to the Aspen airport, I showed up at the house. I didn't have the key anymore, so I rang the doorbell. Annie came and opened the door and, to her surprise, I strode in with my power saw. She thought—she told me later—I had come to kill her.

In the kitchen I laid the power saw down on the table, and in a voice you'd use to order groceries, I asked Annie once again to explain why she had committed this atrocity on the trees. Almost immediately she started turning away, as if I was some fool, and I grabbed her. That part was unpremeditated. Before I knew it, I had her up on the kitchen counter and my hands were around her throat. And I stopped. I had *almost* lost control, but I didn't.

I apologized for the display of brutishness; I hadn't come to hurt her, I said. What I had come to do was leave behind a message. And that's when I got the power saw going.

Annie had turned into quite a socialite in Aspen. She was the hostess of many famous dinner parties, to which I was never invited, being on the road as I was. But I thought her guests should know my work, even if they didn't know me.

First I cut off a corner of the kitchen table and then I cut up the dining table. When people came for dinner henceforth, I said, they'd be reminded of my patronage. I might not get any acknowledgment for it, but at least they'd think about it.

Then in the same manner I descended on the bedroom, where during the remodeling of the house Annie had installed a bed and headboard made out of this grayish-purplish wood that I couldn't stand. *Whrrrr.* I sawed the headboard all the way across until the sheets got entangled and the saw jammed. In adolescent triumph, I announced that I had done what I had come for, then I left the house and drove off.

Later I cringed. What if the story got out? And I cringed, too, in self-realization; I hadn't thought myself capable of that kind of violence. But otherwise I felt purged; I'd never been so hurt or angry in my life. And after a while, with diminishing effects, the aftershocks somehow just got integrated into everyday life. With time, as I said, Annie and I even reestablished our friendship.

When the ties that bound Jerry and me finally snapped, in 1984, it was more melodramatic than tragic, but when you're in the situation, the banality of it isn't apparent. Late in the summer that year, Jerry obtained a role for me in a projected TV movie of the week. He had an idea about how to make the TV movie work off the country album I had done in Nashville. It was going to be called "The Cowboy and the Lady," after one of the songs I'd recorded, written by Bobby Goldsboro. Using the song, he said, was key to the whole thing. I went along with it, enthusiastic for the chance to do some acting. I even found an actress, a ballet dancer in Houston, for the female lead. Because it would conflict with the film's shooting schedule, Jerry had me scrap a solo tour organized in Europe for that fall.

Then suddenly it transpired that the movie wasn't going to be shot during the period in question; it had been put off for four months. Jerry hadn't been able to get the people he wanted; or so he said. The meaner truth, as I learned later, was that the movie schedule was put back because Jerry hadn't had time to follow through on some necessary meetings; he was engaged elsewhere, making a different film. He'd left me totally at loose ends.

So now I was trying to call Jerry every day and he was never in the office, always at some other number. And I was slowly unraveling. Without hearing from him, I went off to London, to the one booking I'd been able to keep when all my plans were shuffled around, and I could barely keep my anxieties from swamping me. I remember that concert, in Albert Hall, as one of the most painful nights I've ever had working on a stage. I'd spent most of the day in tears of frustration. When my call finally got through to Jerry, it was only to confirm what I had feared: I'd been displaced in the order of things by *The Karate Kid,* the film Jerry was doing. I suppose I should have been philosophical about it, but I felt utterly abandoned.

Some English friends came around to cheer me up and even brought along a psychic who promised to "read" the future—but I was in such pain that I couldn't talk. All I could manage was a walk in a park outside of London, where my mind filled with dismal thoughts. I did the concert that evening, but in a state of wretchedness. In the night, my angel visited me and we wrestled until dawn. It felt as if everything was falling down around me, and I didn't know how to stop it.

The next day I flew up to Edinburgh, rented a car, and then I drove around Scotland for four days, doing some real soul-searching. It was just the tonic I needed. My mood lifted as I made my way into the highlands. The Scottish fall was beautiful, and the Scots themselves were wonderful. They wouldn't let me pay for a room or buy a meal—or even a *wee Scotch,* for that matter. Every innkeeper seemed to know me: I was "John, my lad!" wherever I went. The gentleness alone healed the hurt I was feeling. I'd bring out the guitar, sing a few songs. At the end of four days, I'd convinced myself that I couldn't work with Jerry Weintraub anymore, although I still resisted going through this change.

The curious thing is how abruptly Jerry let himself lose his temper when I told him I wanted out. After all, he was a man who never let anyone see him come emotionally undone. When I landed at the Van Nuys airport that next Monday morning, he had a car meet me, and he was all solicitous and unctuous on the car phone. "Hi ya, kid. When are you coming to see me? Can't wait to see you. I'll be here waiting." But when I walked into his office and said I didn't want to work with him anymore, I thought he was going to fight me. To call what followed a tirade would be charitable. I can concede that, in the surprise of the confrontation, Jerry might have felt that it was me betraying him; we had such different assumptions about what we were meant to be doing together. The expletives he bombarded me with were shocking. At one point, before he threw me out of his office, he called me a Nazi, which was an accurate measure of Jerry's hysteria at that moment. And all this from a man who liked to say I was his best friend.

"Don't worry about it, kid," Jerry would say when I'd bend my principles to support something he wanted of me. And of course every time you bend your principles—whether because you don't want to worry about it, or because you're afraid to stand up for fear of what you might lose—you sell your soul to the devil. You can do it in one big shot, but more often, it's those little insidious things that happen over time and keep going on and on. This time there was no space for bending.

Out of respect for my friendship with Jerry's wife, I called Jane to tell her what happened, but for my troubles, I got the cold shoulder. Jane already knew what had happened, and in fact Jerry called right back and warned me not to try calling her again. I think then I went to bed rather than deal with the turmoil and anger I felt. It would be a year before we spoke again, and then it was only briefly over the phone. Out of the blue, he called one day, probably on the spur of the moment, to apologize for his vulgarities. But by then my anger had solidified and there was nothing more to talk about.

Initially Jerry had threatened a legal suit to enforce our contract—it still had three and a half years to run—but he never followed up on it. The silence that followed that last brief phone conversation has gone on for a decade, during which time Jerry became first a Hollywood mogul and then the company bearing his name went bankrupt.

What I did to myself professionally after cutting that tie is something I continually turn over in my head, but not in my heart. Certainly I bled, but it was also the beginning of my really taking responsibility for myself as a man. For a while I let two friends manage me—the aforementioned Barney Wyckoff, who now runs an art gallery in Aspen, and Don Coder, who had gone on road trips with us—and it got way out of hand: a dull echo of the Weintraub fiasco. It seems that all too often in the entertainment business when people come to work for you they suddenly feel empowered to take you over, lock, stock and barrel. Finally I had to part company with Barney and Don and they wound up suing me. Eventually we settled, but what was most painful about that situation was that I let it happen. Someone said that the first time a thing like this happens in your life it is a tragedy; the second time it's more like comedy.

An even more serious dilemma for me was splitting with RCA Records. In these other instances, it was me letting go; this time it was me being let go. In the pre-Reagan years, before rip-off artists had gained ascendancy in the higher reaches of the industry, a relationship that spanned twenty-five albums would have been nurtured for its ongoing possibilities. The Reagan era rendered such niceties imprudent. After first turning down the *Perhaps Love* album, and then sending me off to Nashville to do an "ersatz" country album (*Some Days are Diamonds*), RCA Records not only made nothing of the fact that this Country Music Entertainer of the Year recipient was recording in Nashville for the first time, they never promoted the album.

Was it a willful policy of benign neglect or merely RCA Records' disarray? It's hard to say. In the years that I was with them, they had always been the worst-run company in the business. Their management wanted to merely repeat what had worked the year before; they never really knew what they were about musically, and they never were sensitive to the possibilities. By the early Eighties, when RCA was first gobbled up by General Electric and then gobbled up a second time when General Electric sold RCA Records to BMG, they had become an organization of pure opportunists.

No one who worked there knew what was going to come of all

these changes, and everyone was reduced to hustling for themselves—looking out for their jobs, but not their artists. Nobody who was connected to my success was there anymore, and consequently no one was remotely interested in me. By the spring of 1986, RCA Records not only lacked interest in promoting my albums, they were no longer interested in releasing them. To get my last album with RCA released, I had to fight them on it.

The recording business, right about then, became all gloss, just like the country. Reagan's men were spending millions on things like Star Wars, and various covert actions, which we will probably be paying for for the rest of our lives; but everything looked good. And everybody wanted to buy into looking good. It didn't matter if you were good or if you felt good. It didn't matter if you were being educated or not, so long as you looked good and could talk "good." The show became the thing, which is what the Reagan years epitomized. In fact, the spectacle of the Olympics in L.A. almost overshadowed the games themselves. Likewise, you could hardly have a hit record anymore unless you could dance to it, which I might wish I could do, but as I was no Michael Jackson, that didn't seem to be an option. Songs like "Sunshine on My Shoulders" lost their place in that market. The whole mood of the country shifted. We still did great shows, but I didn't have the hit record out there anymore, so I just about disappeared from the radio. When I was at the top, I'd let Jerry flaunt it over the media; for access to me, he demanded and received favors. Now I was going to pay for such hubris.

Culturally the mid-Eighties were a peculiar time. The world was opening for exploration in a way that hadn't been possible for a long time, and I let myself get drawn into it. Here was the perfect opportunity for me to travel. Instead of getting hung up in someone's else's bad dream of what my present musical output was supposed to be about, I'd go out and make some possible futures happen, not so much with respect to my career, but instead to deepen my understanding of humanity. *If not me, who then will lead?* used to be one of the questions I wrestled with in church fellowship. *If not me, who then?* In the wilderness, when you find yourself without a compass and you start to feel lost, you look for moss on a tree to tell you which way north is, you look for a stream to see which way the water is running, you wait for the stars to be visible to see which way they move across the sky. With not much more than those aids as moral compass, I decided to set off in some new directions.

For one thing, I made my first trip to Africa: a fact-finding mission for the Carter administration, traveling with a delegation from the Hunger Project. As a followup to *The Hungry Planet,* we wanted to do a film that focused less on the starving children and more on what there was in Africa that could be built upon. I think of the chief we met in one small village. His people were going to have no crop that year. The lake was dry. The women who had been left behind were picking grass. The chief said: *When the rains come—god willing—we will know what to do. The future is ours.* He had that kind of hope. He had a real vision of the future. What he needed from the West was a helping hand, not false charity.

Of starving babies, we saw and heard plenty. When we started out, in fact, I was full of misgivings that I would come up short of what was needed to deal with it in my conscience. I had taken a stand that hunger in the world could be eliminated by the year 2000 and I was afraid that going to Africa and seeing the heart of hunger, seeing the real thing, would dampen my enthusiasm and lessen my commitment. I thought the reality might be so overwhelming that I'd lose my conviction that it can be ended. But instead, what I saw made me all the more resolute. (Later in the Eighties, it broke my heart to not be included in the Live Aid, Band Aid, and We Are the World concerts; even in being a helping hand one couldn't avoid political divisiveness.)

I was sleeping overnight in a village in Burkina Faso, when a dust storm woke me. I couldn't get back to sleep—I kept hearing this strange noise. Finally, at about five in the morning, I heard a beautiful sound—the sound of roosters crowing. But that strange noise kept interrupting it. Then suddenly I realized it was the sound of babies crying from the pain of malnutrition, and I knew those babies were probably going to die. There was probably a mother and a father there with them who could do nothing to save them. In those hours of wakefulness, instead of overwhelming me, Africa imprinted itself on my imagination:

African sunrise, shine on a brand new day
African sunrise, shine on a brand new way
Give us the beautiful morning,
Show us forever beginning to stand on our own
African sunrise, smile on my African home.

In this hour of quiet concentration,
The stillness of the dawning calms my mind
I face the day with heartfelt exaltation,
The life is both a promise and a sign
In the darkness we have lost the son of our sister
Though the beauty of his spirit lingers still
This was a child of love, a child of laughter
Who cannot understand the way that I feel?

Is it not the sun that gives the season?
Is it not the sun that brings the rain?
Our throats are choked with dust,
But we're still singing
Our song will not be silenced by the pain.
All around the village, I can hear the roosters crowing
There was a time it was like music to my ears
Now all I can hear is the sound of hungry babies crying
I pray for rain to wash away their tears.

African sunrise, light of the brand new day
African sunrise, light of the brand new way
With one who will be our brother,
And one who will be our partner
To teach us to know
African sunrise, light of my African home
African sunrise, light of my African home

Around this time, too, I made my first visit to the Soviet Union. The *glasnost* movement hadn't yet surfaced. Our cultural ties with the Soviets had been formally severed in 1980 in response to the Soviet invasion of Afghanistan. I thought that, given my celebrity as a singer and songwriter, I might be able to do something to further the cause of East/West understanding.

I'd grown up in a military family, where it was better to be dead than red, and I had defined my adolescent rebellion by choosing the opposite stance, but now seemed like a good time to try to see the human face behind all the propaganda. The Russians say that the first swallow of spring won't make the weather for the whole season, but it can mark the turn toward a warmer climate. I tried to be that swallow. Maybe that was hubris, too.

In the absence of cultural ties, the diplomatic overtures that had to be made to arrange my tour were more cumbersome than usual. It took the better part of a year, using all the goodwill available, and then some. But with the help of Jim Hickman of the Esalen Institute and Don Kendall of Pepsico, among others, I stayed with it and by 1985, with *glasnost*'s mood spreading, a tour began to take shape. In the fall of that year, doing advance work for the tour, I visited Leningrad and I was humbled:

Here lies the people Leningrad,
Here are its citizens, men, women and children,
With them the Red Army soldiers, who gave their lives
Defending you, Leningrad . . .

Their noble names we cannot list here,
So many beneath the eternal protection of granite here lie.
But you who hearken to these stones should know,
No one is forgotten, nothing is forgotten.

These were words I found engraved in granite on a statue at the memorial cemetery of Piskaryovka, a cemetery commemorating the Russians who lost their lives in World War II. The Soviet Union lost more than 20 million people in the war. An entire generation is missing, people my parents' age. In Piskaryovka Cemetery, 470,000 people are buried who died during the nine-hundred-day siege of Leningrad. They are in mass graves that simply denote the dead by the years in which they died: 1941, 1942, 1943, 1944—the years of the siege.

At the entrance to the cemetery is a small hexagonal building, inside of which are black-and-white pictures taken during the siege of Leningrad. One of them shows a sled loaded with bodies. Beside it, on the registration journal, it says, "On February 15, 1942, 8,452 bodies were delivered to the cemetery. On February 20, 1942, 10,043 bodies were delivered to the cemetery." There are no names of people, only of hospitals and city districts, along with the total number of bodies.

Enclosed in a small wooden case with a glass top is the diary of eleven-year-old Tanya Savicheva. There are seven pages from her diary. The first page says, "Vheyna died on December 28th at 12:30 in the morning, 1941." Vheyna was her older sister. The second and subsequent pages read, "Grannie died on January 25th at 3:00 in the afternoon, 1942. Lyoka [her brother] died on March 17th at 5:00 in the morning, 1942. Uncle Vasya died on May 10th at 4:00 in the afternoon, 1942. Mama on May 13th at 7:30 in the morning, 1942." Tanya could not say "died" about her mother. "The Savichevas are dead, they are 11 dead, there is only Tanya left." Shortly after writing this, Tanya herself died of malnutrition. It was too late to save her.

Families wandered through the cemetery to pay their respects. On the jacket lapels of the old men were medals from the war. An old woman sitting off to the side under a tree, flowers in hand, wept beside a grave that read, simply, "1941" or "1942" or "1943." And music played constantly.

On that day that I visited Piskaryovka Cemetery, I started writing the lyrics that became "Let Us Begin (What Are We Making Weapons For?)":

> *I am the son of a grassland farmer*
> *Western Oklahoma 1943*
> *I always felt grateful to live in the land of the free*
> *I gave up my father to South Korea*

The mind of my brother to Vietnam
Now there's a banker who says I must give up my land
There are four generations of blood in this topsoil
Four generations of love on this farm
Before I give up I would gladly give up my right arm

What are we making weapons for
Why keep on feeding the war machine
We take it right out of the mouths of our babies
Take it away from the hands of the poor
Tell me, what are we making weapons for

I had a son and my son was a soldier
He was so like my father, he was so much like me
To be a good comrade was the best that he dreamed he
   could be
He gave up his future to revolution
His life to a battle that just can't be won
For this is not living, to live at the point of a gun
I remember the nine hundred days of Leningrad
The sound of the dying, the cut of the cold
I remember the moments I prayed I would never grow old

CHORUS

For the first time in my life I feel like a prisoner
A slave to the ways of the powers that be
And I fear for my children, as I fear for the future I see
Tell me how can it be we're still fighting each other
What does it take for a people to learn
If our song is not sung as a chorus, we surely will burn

CHORUS

Have we forgotten
All the lives that were given
All the vows that were taken
Saying never again
Now for the first time
This could be the last time
If peace is our vision
Let us begin.

The following spring, 1986, marked the first time an American artist was invited to give public performances in the Soviet Union since the cultural exchange agreement had been abrogated. In Leningrad, Tallinn, and Moscow, I got to hear my audiences sing "Annie's Song" in English and they got to hear me sing it in Russian. Despite the language barriers, we seemed to communicate well enough.

In both Moscow and Leningrad I got to meet my Soviet counterparts. Out of those meetings grew my later collaboration with the great Russian singer Alexander Gradsky. We sang "Let Us Begin" together on a global video hookup, he in Russian while standing on Soviet soil, me in English while standing on American soil. It was guaranteed to make you a believer, if you were lucky enough to hear us. Few were.

My official hosts were the Union of Composers, and Pepsico sponsored the tour; RCA, with whom I was still under contract at the time, wouldn't participate. Alexander Churlin, one of the cultural deputies in the Soviet Foreign Department, was especially lyrical when he toasted our enterprise. Noting the difficulties that we had overcome in order to get there, he said giving concerts was necessary, and he quoted a nineteenth-century philosopher: "When music plays, canons keep quiet." Ah, if only that were still true. But at least we carried on as if it were, and that's important, too. That's what you have to do when you're about to step into the abyss.

Afterward, when I was back in the States, I was given an audience with Secretary of State George Shultz: *See here, young man, what are you up to?* I was practicing citizen diplomacy and he needed to check me out. I don't know that commercially I will ever get to profit from that early opening in the Cold War as others have who came later; in fact, the trip lightened my pockets by about half a million dollars. Still, *if not me, then who?* That question continues to motivate me. The possibility that my concerts had been a catalyst for the one thing that Gorbachev and Reagan agreed on at their first summit, namely to reestablish cultural exchange between our two countries, was in my terms *far out.*

In Beijing, where I went after Moscow, I met up with Hal and together we tried to negotiate a worldwide TV special via satellite. Unfortunately, when it came to capitalist enterprise and the modern marketplace, the directors of the Chinese television network had a narrow perspective and we couldn't agree on terms. Although they had invited us to do this, they expected a payment of one million dollars. We wanted the venture to be a partnership: fifty-fifty. On the other hand, they threw some lovely banquets for us. One night in their honor we gave a banquet fit for a king and they loved it.

They took us around to look at possible sites for the show and we negotiated. We thought at first that we'd tape it from the Great Wall, but when we thought about it again, it seemed too impractical, and beyond the wall's enormity, what more was there? How about the Forbidden City? we asked. We could set up a stage in one of the courtyards. We were told it was out of the question.

How many people were we talking about? they wanted to know. Thousands, we told them. They stirred uneasily, contemplating so many people gathering in one place. I suggested Tiananmen Square, thinking of a crowd of 500,000. It was about that time that the negotiations were called off.

On the last night of our visit I gave the American community in Beijing, which included many Chinese friends, an impromptu concert and the songs I chose to share—about the yearnings of the heart, the pleasures of home, and the dream of freedom—underscored the mood: It felt like home. We left China empty-handed, but we left behind lots of goodwill, and in subsequent years we would build on it.

In Japan—by the mid-1980s, I was in their bloodstream—I was paid the ultimate tribute of imitation by a popular singer, Kosetsu Minami, who became known as the Japanese John Denver. He's no longer that, but when he started singing, he wore little round glasses like I did, played acoustic guitar, and sang in a kind of country idiom Japanese-style. More crucially, he was also an environmentalist. One of the great things he's done every year for the last ten years is organize concerts for peace at Nagasaki and Hiroshima, on August 6. When in 1985 the Japanese saw signs that Lake Biwa, a huge, beautiful freshwater lake in Shiga Prefecture, was starting to die, Kosetsu and I teamed up to headline a promotional concert for a conference on the pollution of bodies of freshwater in the world.

That summer, incidentally, insurgencies erupted in all parts of the world, late-twentieth-century wars for freedom that are with us still, in one form or another: South Africa, Eastern Europe,

Central America, Haiti, the Philippines. With them came this heightened sense of environmental disaster waiting to happen, or happening already. Were there ever wars in which the environment wasn't blighted?

During this time, my own urgent moral consciousness about Planet Earth found voice, too. In it, mixed into my own thought, I could hear Buckminster Fuller's moral vocabulary and Jacques Cousteau's, David Brower's, and Amory Lovins', and that of a dozen others who are real stewards of the Earth. My performance tours thereafter were conceived less as ends in themselves and more as an ongoing effort to celebrate the Earth as home. That seemed focus enough. Where I was already deeply committed, I grew even more deeply so. There was nothing I could take for granted anymore about the processes of renewal as they affect life on the planet.

I've always had a martyr complex—it's come to the fore whenever I've been rebuffed or struggled for my independence. That summer of 1986, in Berlin, I was suddenly convinced that my martyrdom was at hand, that I was at risk for standing up for my beliefs. I can't think of anything more telling about my state of mind at that point.

Everybody else had canceled their tours of Europe. That summer, hijackings of an airliner and a cruise ship had made all of Europe very wary. Americans and other nationals were told to lie low. Berlin was not the place for an American to be, especially out in front of an audience. I can't really say what made me decide to brave it, but the night before the concert, I had this harrowing dream in which I saw myself assassinated. I said nothing about it to anyone, but I was terrified. I reminded our security guy, who was conscientious as it was, to stay alert.

The concert was outdoors. It was a beautiful evening in Berlin, and a wonderful, enthusiastic audience had gathered. On one level, I could have stood up there and sung all night, but I wasn't worth a damn because I was so afraid, and I was listening to everything that was going on around me. At one point there were three guys down front, all of them wearing suits of the same color, who suddenly bolted from where they were standing, walked quickly up some stairs, and disappeared. I couldn't stop wondering what that was about, and nobody I asked knew either. What a relief it was when the concert ended. It hurt to realize how badly I wanted to get off that stage. Afterward I went back to my hotel with this young Australian singer I was falling in love with and had myself a good cry in her arms. The truly amazing thing out of that whole night was that she was there.

During this fourth decade of my life, this belated passage I was trying to effect from late adolescence to the beginnings of my adulthood, the only other *changes* wrought in my psyche with anywhere near the same charge of excitement that falling in love again produced, were those connected to getting to know Buckminster Fuller beyond the superficial graces, and through that relationship seeing Windstar's possibilities taken to another, higher level. From the late Seventies to the early Eighties, my visibility as a celebrity attracted a lot of mentors, but Bucky's mentoring bit into my vital core. His unique way of looking at the world and of seeing its care as perhaps man's highest calling gave me a framework for thinking about all the causes for environmental action that I was anxious to support. However, he made his real contribution to the formation of my thinking through the sheer example of his life. He demonstrated not only to me but to a whole generation of us outside of formal institutions of study and learning what one person could accomplish standing on the minimal grounds of his own moral authority. I say this not to minimize any of the other work in the environmental community that was influencing us then, but at Windstar Bucky was first among equals, and he gave what we were doing there a solidity that we badly needed when he sailed into our orbit, or better yet when we sailed into his.

I met him first through the EST Foundation sometime in 1977. Werner invited him to speak at one of the foundation's conferences.

About a year later, coming home from a speech I'd given in the Midwest on behalf of the President's Commission on World and Domestic Hunger, I stopped off in Denver to attend a conference on the environment with Tom Crum and met up with Bucky again. He was there to talk about his new book, *Critical Path,* and, in one of these mysterious confluences that life is always providing, I wound up onstage as Bucky's prop. If I didn't know enough to ask him challenging questions, at least I understood the spirit of what he was saying, and that seemed to mean something to him. Instead of talking out to the audience, of whom he had only a dim visual sense because of his poor eyesight, he had my face up close to bounce his ideas off. In exchange for the raptness of my attention, he gave me the fullness of his thought, and I was flattered. And what you listen to with care becomes part of you.

Afterward Tom and I took Bucky to a café in downtown Denver and regaled him with all the plans we had for Windstar. In the brief time since our first meeting, Windstar had become a physical entity, and we had all sorts of programs ready to lift off. A lesser spirit might have been chased away by our enthusiasms. With Bucky it all registered meaningfully. He saw us as part of his human family and became very interested in what we were doing. Although nearly eighty-five, a grandfatherly figure, nearing the end of his life, he still had all the vitality and sense of wonder—all of the juices—of a child. At the end of our conversation, to our amazement and delight, he spontaneously decided to abort his busy schedule and come back with us to Aspen. Without so much as a *by your leave,* he just jumped on the plane with us like a Sixties Ken Kesey merry prankster. In Aspen, we rounded up the Windstar crew and Bucky led us through a seminar on the principles of his synergetics. The airy-fairy projection of a place up in the mountains where people would come to develop a critical consciousness in regard to the Earth suddenly found its life.

He was so taken by the whole setup in Snowmass and by our ingenuous response to his ideas that he immediately offered himself as an advisor, and we in turn spontaneously invited him to join our board of directors, which we were just then forming. There were very few times in his adult life when he allowed his ideas to be identified with an institution, and this was one of them. He said "this is what I want in my life, too." His interest in Windstar was neither intellectual nor technological. Rather he was trying to pass on something that was a foundation of his knowledge and wisdom and searching to those who he thought could carry it on. I felt somehow that he saw in what I was doing in the world an extension of his own work and wanted me to keep doing it. I took that as a trust. His generosity in joining along with what we were doing made us feel bolder than we might have otherwise as we started out on so urgent an undertaking. At least, we felt that what we were doing was urgent and he lent us his corroboration.

Trying to mirror Bucky's broad humanity, our first prospectus spoke in magisterial terms of "recognizing that the planet Earth is a living, breathing organism whose vitality, beauty, and growth depend on its ability to exist as a unified and harmonious whole." Our aim was to communicate that perspective "so that all humanity might resonate more deeply with the natural forces of our universe." In our statement of purposes, we declared Marshall McLuhan's Global Village at hand: "The citizen of central Kansas learns about Islamic law and slaughter of seals; the Maori watches contrails webbing the sky and checks the time on a digital watch." As think tank and school we were going to foster the concept of harmony individually, collectively, and environmentally. The prospectus quoted the writer George Leonard: "The most serious obstacle to our getting on with the necessary business of transforming our life-style and our society is the unwillingness or the inability to say clearly and publicly that we've come to the end of one way of life and to the beginning of another." With the example of Bucky's long engagement with the planet's well-being in mind, we stated that we *must* learn to live lightly on the planet. We must make a conscious choice.

Under Bucky's tutelage we re-envisioned Windstar less as a model of environmental concern than as a state of consciousness. As Bucky said, we're information gatherers, pragmatists pulling together what's available to create whatever Spaceship Earth needs to move where the universe is moving. We have no special status on which to declare our immortality. We're evolving; what we evolve to depends on how well we follow the principles of the universe. If we don't do that well, we'll be eliminated, just like the dinosaurs.

The last evolution in consciousness, Bucky reminded us, was consolidated with the Copernican understanding that Earth wasn't the center of the universe. Now, as Bucky would say, with his whole self resonating with the integrity of a seeker who has arrived at his destination, we are at the next stage of consciousness, which is the recognition that we are one. Our singularities are drawn from the same common humanity; we breathe together. That needn't deny our national feelings, or our ethnic heritage: our culture. Those things give us reasons to appreciate our singularity, even as we recognize our oneness. It is such complexity and diversity that we need to defend. This was the spirit of what Bucky wanted us to know, before he died in 1983.

FOR YOU

Just the words of a love song
Just the beat of my heart
Just the pledge of my life, my love, for you

Why should falling in love *again* have come as such a surprise? What could be more natural, like the beat of a heart. Cassandra was my heart's desire. She was heartache waiting to happen. She was a girl in a white dress, alone in her own space, once upon a time.

It was the spring of 1986, and I had gone to Australia to work hard. I was really trying to get things going, both in recording and in all the other business aspects of my life. Windstar, through feckless management, had run up a substantial debt, which I was beginning to sense the seriousness of, and I wanted to get out in front of that. Plus I felt the environmental struggle was at a critical juncture, and I wanted to be active in that, too.

I was also struggling to grow up. Or at least to grow into the voice I found myself carrying around in the world. Some of my contemporaries in the music business, who had also been anointed superstars in the Seventies, had by then either lost their minds or themselves. I thought I was holding up my end fairly well, considering the vicissitudes that sometimes made it seem as if I was pushing against a rock.

It had been a while since I'd been to Australia. I'd had a lot of luck there, my popularity was still pretty high, and I felt a mutual affection for the Australians—I still do. It turned out to be a big, enjoyable tour, the biggest I'd ever done there, and there was lots of hoopla, including gruesome headlines. The tabloids had taken a perverse interest in what Annie and I had gone through, which was par for the course, and I suppose I took a perverse interest in their concern. Likewise, I took it as a welcome home of sorts.

Did I think I was going to meet someone here?

Was I looking to fall in love?

Australia is a country full of beautiful women, but getting into a romantic relationship with one of them was the farthest thing from my mind.

We had done most of the tour, and coming up were the last of the Sydney concerts. Sydney Harbour is one of the wonders of the world, and I was looking forward to taking a boat out between shows. There is nothing like being adrift on the ocean when you are feeling at sea yourself.

As part of the media hype, I'd been booked to participate in the TV broadcast of the Loggies, the Australian Grammys, Emmys, and Oscars combined, where I would sing a few songs and present the award for Show of the Year. So I called my promoter, Kevin Jacobson, and asked if there was somebody I could take. He and his colleagues thought it over and came up with the name Rowena Wallace. Rowena had been the previous year's Entertainer of the Year and was going to present that award to her successor.

So that was fine. Rowena had been married, I was told, but

now she was single. And more to the point, she was involved in activism through a religious organization that dealt with the hungry. One of the guys in Kevin's office said she was quite attractive and we arranged to have this date.

Then it all got complicated and weird, as if a magician standing offstage had started pulling rabbits out of a hat. Or am I the only gullible one in the crowd? On the night I was due to arrive in Sydney, RCA Records in Australia was going to host a dinner party for me, the band, and the crew at a restaurant in King's Cross, the center of Sydney nightlife. We were going to invite a bunch of girls. So I flew into Sydney on the appointed day, and I called Rowena to make plans for our Loggie appearance. We agreed to have lunch together the next day to discuss it. But then she called back and said she really wanted to meet that night, and she was quite insistent. She was coming into town, anyway, and didn't have anything to do; couldn't she come by the hotel for a drink? What was this, a come-on? Capricorns understand better than most people how unsettling moments like these can be. But being gracious, I agreed to work it out.

At about nine P.M., as arranged, I excused myself from the RCA dinner and walked over to my hotel. The lounge was empty, so I looked in the bar, and there, seated at one end, in a white dress, was a young girl with long blond hair who just stopped me cold.

Of course, I wasn't there looking for this, I reminded myself, and I certainly couldn't go talk to her and invite her back to the dinner, no matter how she might attract me; I wasn't even going to let the thought die slowly. But just then something distracting happened: A woman came into the bar, and when I looked back, this apparition of whiteness had vanished, as if in a puff of smoke. I looked around and she was nowhere to be seen.

So in this bemused state I ordered a beer and waited, and in a few minutes Rowena Wallace came in. We chatted for about an hour. She acted a bit odd, I thought, but I tried to ignore it. She was actually very nice. Of course, she probably thought I was odd myself, going on as I do. In the middle of it, the girl in white reappeared and walked across the lobby. She wasn't just beautiful, but strikingly so. Her face, I couldn't help noticing, was a cross between Julie Christie's and Jacqueline Bisset's, two actresses I worshipped from afar, the way you do when you're a red-blooded American boy going to the movies on Saturday night. After saying good night to Rowena, I went back to my dinner even more bemused, if not mystified.

But at that point I was prepared to let it remain a mystery. Even when a telegram arrived from "the girl in white—I saw you in the bar," with a phone number to call, signed "Cassandra Delaney," I was still going to let it go. I'd been receiving unsolicited flowers and phone numbers for five years, and I wasn't going to make a move. She was persistent, though; the next day a letter arrived with her promotional material, including a photograph that reminded me of how beautiful she was. She was a singer, twenty-six years old, and she was asking if she could sing with me while I was in Australia.

Though I didn't respond to that request—singing together just wasn't in the cards—I had Doug Belcher, my road manager at the time, invite her to a concert and to a boat party afterward, and she came with her mother, although no one believed Lorraine *could* be her mother, she seemed so young herself.

All kinds of people were on the boat that night and I was in a weird frame of mind. I probably didn't say more than a few words to Cassie and her mother all night. In fact, I spent most of the time stoned out of my head, sitting on the prow of the boat drinking beer and enjoying the Sydney skyline, thinking about where I was in my life. Every once in a while, I'd rouse myself to wander around, making small talk as befits the thoughtful host, but my mood was a strange one. Once we were out on the water, I didn't feel connected anywhere on the boat. I was just lost in all kinds of thought, and was getting more and more drunk. When the party broke up, I gave Cassie and her mother a lift home, and that should have been it.

But lo and behold, there she was again the next night at a postconcert party for RCA. Doug had invited her. Seeing my apparent lack of interest, he thought he'd hit on her himself. And that morning I had beat myself up about being rude to this beautiful girl, so I was pleasantly surprised to see her and determined to make amends. It evolved into an evening of serious distractions, but at some point when I saw Cassandra slip away, I slipped away after her and we finally got to talk. The party broke up, then we ended up walking down by the harbor, and we talked so long that we saw the dawn come up.

And so it began. An innocent flirtation.

She wouldn't come back to my hotel with me, and I was taking off in a few hours to finish the tour, but we agreed to get together when I got back to Sydney. My bemusement had taken a turn. Even though for the most part it was clear I was flying in the face of chance, what was there to lose? Who said, "If you give your heart freely, you get an extra space in heaven"? Everything that happened afterward, and for the rest of the summer, seemed to fall into place as if by design.

When I got back to Sydney, the paper I'd scribbled her phone number on was gone. And there were a million Delaneys in the phone book, none of them Cassandra. What was a guy to do? I'd be gone tomorrow. But a page in the phone book had been folded back at the Delaney *L*'s, and when I ran my eye down the column, Cassie's mother's name, Lorraine, bounced back out at me. I called Cassie at home, we had dinner, we went to a Sting concert. That night she told me she was in a relationship with a man, which had been going on for two years, but still she came back to the hotel with me. I flipped. The next morning a couple of friends and I went to Hamilton Island to do some diving off the Great Barrier Reef for a few days and Cassie came along. She just threw some things in a bag and was ready, just like in the movies.

She was a breath of spring air: bright, funny, irreverent. We dove, we walked on the beach in the mist, we played with the porpoises, and then when the few days were up, she agreed when I asked, inspired as much by the possibility of her saying yes as by the certainty of her saying no, whether she'd come back to the States with me.

Still, I wasn't sure she'd actually come through. Back in Sydney, she dropped out of sight for a few days. I didn't talk with her again until we were about to leave, and there she was at the plane.

It was a strange few days, going back and forth across her city and obliquely coming into contact with facets of Cassie's past, but not with Cassie. One day, over the phone, Cassie's mother wondered aloud if I knew what I was doing, and I couldn't say that I did. So I was in sort of a state of suspended belief until that moment I saw her at the airport ready to fly. She had brought her boyfriend Andrew along, and I had no alternative but to go off with him for a beer while he plied me with stories that put Cassandra in the worst possible light. He asked me not to take her with me, and I simply demurred. It was her call, not mine. Had I ever been so cavalier?

Even then it was strange that our affair was able to go further because she had no visa. She shouldn't have been let on the plane, much less allowed to enter the U.S. Eventually the airline was fined for letting her board, but that didn't happen until later that fall. At the Sydney airport, Kevin Jacobson helped her board without being questioned; he had had lots of practice shepherding rock 'n' roll bands through Customs. In L.A., where we landed, an immigration agent essentially let her through on the strength of knowing who I was. He called Washington and they okayed the necessary paperwork. Things like that just didn't happen every day. And so we continued to move like that, by the skin of our teeth, through the rest of the spring and all summer long.

A week after arriving home from Australia, I left for a European tour, and Cassie came with me; she stayed the whole time, from Blackpool to Rome. It had been a long time since I had had anybody to come home to like that. It was a fantasy come true, especially in Berlin, the night I let my fears escape and get the better of me. Here I'd just made love to several thousand people in a sense, given my heart and soul, and had come away from it feeling frightened. And there was someone to hold me. I could let it go. I could be a fearful child again, a man full of uncertainties.

Not that Cassandra saw that incident in Berlin the same way I did. Or that we agreed that in falling in love, you stay there. After those first six weeks on the road, we could have each gone our own way easily enough and not seen each other again. In the meandering way that life unfolds, you might meet your soul mates, but you don't necessarily marry them. I was just happy to have it go on for as long as it would.

Even when I finished my European dates and she came back

to Aspen with me for the rest of that summer, we weren't making any bets. I had my baggage to deal with, and she had hers. Hers, I realize in retrospect, was considerable, but I don't know that I was even capable of making those distinctions then.

Once that summer when she was off on her own, I picked up the rumor that she had been involved with somebody down in Santa Fe. There was a pretty good case against her, but I didn't want to believe it; I wanted to believe the story she ended up telling me. There had already been more treachery in my life than I could bear. If it took self-deception to get through this patch, I was willing to endure it. And it wasn't my place to prevent her from doing what she liked. For two-and-a-half years, the relationship went through many such trials and tribulations.

The thing that I loved about Cassandra was that, through thick and thin, she came on the road with me, not just that once, but time after time. And she was good on the road; she sort of grew up there and knew what it was all about. She kept me centered just by being there. I know she was being on her very best behavior because she was after something: first to marry me, and beyond that to further her career. She never said as much, but that was okay; I was supporting that, too. Only our fantasies were going in different directions.

Mine operated more or less as a set of idealistic propositions. There may be a better way of explaining it than that, but that's how I framed it. By taking Cassandra along with me, I was doing a good thing; I was making her my protégée. I was going to help her with a career that she was obviously interested in pursuing, show her places under the best possible circumstances, introduce her to the States. I'd share what I knew of the business, and not only with Cassie, but with her mother, too. Lorraine Delaney was really a very good country singer, and I thought she would have done well in Nashville, all things being equal.

In fact, I got involved with Cassie's whole family as my romance with her evolved. It was a family that was all tied up with things that were painful and disheartening, and, being a do-gooder, I saw myself as its rescuer, its healer, just as I wanted to rescue and heal the world. In retrospect, I think I had to go through this experience with them to realize, a bit late in life maybe, that there were limits to what you could do for another person.

When I call Cassie my protégée, I realize it's a term that might be misconstrued; I pictured her alongside me, not under me or under my control. A lot of men find women and try to mold them into who they want, and a lot of women even want that themselves. Whatever it took, I wanted our relationship to be open and supportive. I didn't want us to behave out of our expectations of each another, because I knew that would start pulling us apart. There are times when you have to be true to yourself, rather than true to the other, in order to keep the relationship healthy.

Of course, if that happened, I didn't necessarily want to know about it if Cassandra had such an experience, or to tell her about it if I did. Were those just mutual games of deceit? I thought they were ground rules. How could I have had it so wrong? And that misunderstanding said as much about me and my limitations as it did about her and where she was coming from.

When I saw Cassandra acting in a way that struck me as immature, I told myself that I was twenty years older and wrote it off to the fact that Cassie was young, and even younger in her self-identity. For example, the circle of friends she ran around with in Aspen really strained credulity; they were the flightiest, most irresponsible women in town. Cassie was brighter, wittier, and prettier than the whole lot of them, but she wouldn't step beyond them because they were hers to dominate. Still I rationalized it all. About some things I wasn't all that mature myself, nor am I yet.

Once I took Cassandra to meet Gurumayi Chidvilasananda at Swami Muktananda's ashram in upstate New York, and Gurumayi was equally taken with her vivaciousness. Gurumayi, Muktananda's successor, had been a friend of mine since the days when she was still Muktananda's young disciple. After Muktananda died, I never hesitated to seek reassurance from Gurumayi when my sense of things wasn't clear to me. Cassandra and she were more or less contemporaries, and it reassured me to see them enjoy each other's company; Gurumayi seemed like a young girl again in Cassie's presence. But I was misreading the situation, and later Gurumayi told me of the troubling feelings she'd had about Cassie, which she didn't feel it appropriate to express then.

And then, in the late summer of 1988, the magician offstage pulled yet one more rabbit out of his hat. Despite my medical history, Cassie and I had had lots of fantasies about having a family. She was sure it could happen, and she convinced me. Out of curiosity, I even went to see the doctor who had diagnosed my condition earlier, and found there were new solutions for my problem. He said if I wanted, I could try them. The odds weren't that much better than before, but there were some new things to consider. Scientists had become more adept at taking sperm samples and fertilizing eggs with them.

I even started a regime with another of my doctors who practiced homeopathic medicine in Aspen. It involved my taking pills of genital tissue, along with a series of injections that I gave myself in the leg for six weeks; I had to use an extraordinarily long needle for this, and it was of the hardest things I've had to do in my life. Still, there was no change in my sperm count or the sperm's mobility, and I went off on tour again, with the matter of my fertility unresolved.

We were playing again in Sydney, when Doug Belcher told me of a healer he had gone to in Melbourne, a woman who had experience healing cancer and other equally incredible trans-formations. She practiced a process called reiki. He thought the session he'd had with her had been extraordinary and suggested I try it. Doug was a spiritually oriented person who had had out-of-body experiences, and my curiosity was aroused. The next day I was in Melbourne.

The healer laid me down, rested her hands on my shoulders, and every once in a while asked a question. And there was always something in me to respond. They were seemingly sim-ple questions: What was on my mind? Why was I there? What was I looking for? As I said, seemingly simple stuff, but it loos-ened something in me. Something began to flow.

We got onto the subject of one's birthright, and what came out of that for me was the deep conviction that, having been given life to experience, it was one's birthright to take it in freely, as much as the air we breathed, the water we drank; to experience the joy of life, and to be loved. One ought not to have to fight for those things or to doubt one's right to them. They were there, if you allowed yourself to experience them, if you surrendered yourself to them, if you let go and let in. Letting go and letting in were notions I had turned over in my mind for some time. Now somehow they made sense in a way they hadn't before. When I came out of the session, I had a buzz like I was about to take off.

When I told Cassie about the experience, she arranged a

session for herself, and the healer came up to Sydney the next day. Cassie had the same strong, positive response as I did. What Cassie focused on, in response to the laying on of hands and the questioning, was her desire to bear my child. And the healer, who normally was reticent about these things, told her, according to Cassie, that she thought Cassie was going to have a child. When I heard this, of course, I was interested, but I wasn't going to hold my breath. The nomad has a saying: Trust in God, but tie up your camel. If it happened, it would be a miracle.

We went on through the summer and finished the tour, and on August 12, Cassie and I got married. She came home and I went off to the Soviet Union on a personal mission, trying to arrange my participation in a flight into space with Soviet cosmonauts. When I flew back, to perform in Seattle that weekend, I called Cassie to say hello—she was in Los Angeles with her mother and a friend who was heading back to Australia—her voice was filled with excitement. She had noticed her breasts getting bigger and had done a home pregnancy test, and the results had been positive.

The next day I went down to Los Angeles to see for myself, and she was right—her breasts had gotten larger. We went back to Aspen immediately and went to our doctor, who also performed a pregnancy test, and again the results came back positive. Sometime during the first week of our marriage, the doctor estimated, Cassie had conceived. To say I was flabbergasted would be the least of it.

That fall it was a struggle getting through my work obligations. But then, finally, December came, and all the way through to the spring I stayed close to home. I can't remember a time when the mundane matters of everyday life absorbed me so totally. Among other things Cassandra and I went to birthing classes together. We initially thought of having the birth at home, but in the end opted for the Valley Hospital, where Annie and I had donated a pediatric wing in honor of Zak and Anna Kate. We had a midwife to oversee things and Cassie's mother was going to be on hand for general, all-purpose support. When labor began, I was to be Cassie's breathing coach. And if things worked out—if I held up under the circumstances—I was going to deliver the baby.

If music is possibility given form, then Jesse Belle's birth was pure music. In fact, during early labor, part of me was still detached, as if I were there as a privileged spectator, having an aesthetic experience watching Cassie and her mother, who were wonderful to see together in that situation. Her mother was a great comfort and Cassie was just remarkable in response. I tried to set the rhythm for the breathing.

But then Cassie moved to a second stage of labor before I realized it. I had her breathing one way while her physiological reactions were going another way and she wasn't able to handle it. Feeling nervous, I called the midwife and urged her to come, and then I sort of held Cassie off from having any drugs. When the midwife got there, she immediately moved Cassie onto this other level of breathing. Cassie focused on her and on her mother, who was there holding her, and she just went on from there.

The labor continued for eight hours. Then all at once, or so it seemed, the midwife turned to me and asked, "Do you want to deliver the baby?" I didn't have time to think about it, I just got the gloves on and I got down at the foot of the delivery table. The baby's head was about to emerge. I'd never seen a live birth. All I knew was what I had heard, and the technical descriptions of how it happened didn't compute in my mind. Didn't click. Now here we were and I could feel the baby moving; I could hear its heartbeat, see it there about to be born. It was a real miracle.

Until the very end, we didn't know if it was a boy or a girl. We had purposely chosen not to know. We had groups of friends on one side predicting a boy and saying they'd been right every time, and groups of friends on the other side, equally certain, predicting a girl. We didn't want to know. And we didn't really care one way or the other.

Cassandra pushed and a little crown appeared. There was hair and you could see that, but that's all you could see: It still wasn't "the baby." So the midwife went into action, urging Cassie to push one more time, and all of a sudden the baby's head popped out. I was aghast. Then the midwife turned the baby's head in order to get a shoulder out, and for a second I panicked: "Don't! You're pulling its head off!" The midwife had to reassure me: "No, I just want to get the shoulder out." When she got the baby to where she wanted it to be, she told me, "Turn the head the other way and get the other shoulder out." Which is what I did, and pop, out came the baby into my arms.

Before I realized what was happening, the midwife was saying, "It's a girl!" and handed me my daughter; at that point I was a puddle of tears. And I barely regained control of myself when the midwife thrust a pair of scissors into my hand and asked me to cut the baby's umbilical cord. I couldn't believe it, even when I did it.

Finally, I put the baby on Cassie's bosom. I thought I could start to step back from it a bit and take pleasure in seeing mother and child in repose, but it was too soon. The midwife had to attend to Cassie and handed the baby back to me. This time, I went over to a corner and sat down, baby Jesse Belle in my arms. How was it, I wondered, that for centuries men could absent themselves from this whole process? It was beyond me how they could accept not being allowed to participate in this incredible voyage. At that moment, I couldn't conceive that there was anywhere else to be. Just then Jesse Belle opened up the biggest blue eyes you've ever seen—they still are—and we just looked at each other. Then I sang to her and talked to her and, finally finding release, I cried all over her.

For a little while Cassandra and I reconstituted paradise. Jesse Belle's birth and all the excitement around it gave us a little cushion before the world closed in on us again, and while it lasted we did all the things you do in paradise. But then paradise was lost. Or am I dreaming that paradise was ever a possibility?

Cassie and I had never discussed how we'd live *after* Jesse's birth, and on this subject my consciousness had only one file; Cassandra's had none. I simply assumed that what we had once agreed on—being the free spirits we proposed to be—needed reconsidering until Jesse Belle had at least grown into herself. Cassie, on the other hand, saw no reason to change the ground rules; family obligation meant something entirely different to her than it did to me. She wanted to do things to prove herself, which at that point meant taking on minor film roles in Australia, and she wanted my unconditional support for it.

We were pulled apart more and more, disagreements resurfaced, and there were some things she had no interest even in talking out. I doubt that she recognized a role for fathers; not that I was offering myself as an exemplary model, but I was asking to be considered. And I think that's where I was most self-deluded.

At one point, trying to visualize how to meet Cassandra halfway and make the marriage work, I thought that leaving Aspen would solve something. Cassie complained that Starwood had ghosts from my first marriage, and that they were more than she could abide. This couldn't help but remind me of the grief I had endured when Annie and I were splitting up and I had had to face the thought of giving up our home to her.

The problem then had been that very few of my assets were liquid, and selling the house was one of the solutions proposed. I hadn't really stopped to think what that meant to me; we were simply moving chess pieces around in our minds. And then one night Hal had called me backstage in Dublin to tell me Annie was in turmoil about where the money for the divorce settlement would come from and wanted to put the place on the market!

I called her to see what the hell was going on and had a fight with her on the phone across the Atlantic Ocean in which nothing was resolved: *Look, you're going to get your money, and if you don't want the house, I want it!* If she needed money all she had to do was write a check; I hadn't cut her off from anything, as she was complaining. I'd been as much of a gentleman as I could be in such a situation.

And then I went out onstage and started singing. Every time the word *home* came up in a song that night I saw my home in Starwood, and realized that home was one place to me. As a child, I'd never had a home; I was an Air Force brat, and we moved all over. This piece of land in Colorado was my home; I couldn't let it go.

The audience was singing every song with me, very softly. And because it was so cold in this barn we were in—everybody had on their down jackets—when they sang the frost came off their breath. With each phrase, little clouds of vapor formed above their heads and floated stageward. I could have sung for them all night. Irish audiences don't hold back when they sing. And their singing with me would have gotten me out of my funk. But because I was so enmeshed in this thing about home I did my perfunctory one encore, went offstage, and called Hal. I woke him out of a dead sleep. *I want the house. I don't care what it costs for the divorce, I want the house.* He said: *Go back to sleep, you won't have to lose the house; we'll find another way.*

I had gone through so much and finally had kept my home the first time. But if it meant so much to Cassie now to leave it, and even to leave Aspen, I'd mobilize myself in that direction.

I had to go through the process of letting go. I had to articulate to myself that this was the place and the time from which I had to move on. And I had to know that I had the inner resolve to follow up on it. I'm not one who consciously prays, who sits down before a concert and says, "Father, who art in heaven, forgive me my trespasses." I don't do it that way. I have great respect for that and I also have a longing for it, but that's not who I am, as far as I can tell. Instead I'm one who goes forth in quest; I'm a seeker.

And so, looking for enlightenment, I flew to Maui and began a curious journey, inland as much as inward. I started out by playing golf and hanging out with some construction workers who were working on sites in the area. And then on impulse, as much as by instinct, I think, I started moving around trying to find a golf course that wasn't in the wind. Some people don't like the bitter cold, some people don't like hot weather. I can deal with either. The one thing that I've always had the most problem with is a constant wind, and in Hawaii, the wind was constant.

As the days progressed, I was meeting more and more different kinds of people, and it was all moving in a certain direction: not just north or south, or east or west, but further and further away from where I'd come, where everything was ensnared with heartrending complication. Somewhere in this flow I met Dennis Marini.

Dennis may be the most interesting person I've met in my life (he may also be the most innocuous). He was born in New Jersey, but his hero, or at least his favorite story, was Tarzan— everything about Tarzan. I myself am a Tarzan freak, too. I had always wanted to live in the jungle with the animals, and there wasn't a tree I couldn't climb. But I had never got to be Tarzan, whereas Dennis had. When I met Dennis on Maui, we took to each other instantly, and he invited me to spend a few days at his place in Kipahulu.

You can't get farther away from civilization in Hawaii than in Kipahulu, which stands on the southernmost tip of Maui near the Kaupo Gap at the base of Haleakala. Where the mountain spills out in the Kaupo Gap is a dense rain forest. When it rains, the flow coming down can be dangerous.

On the day I was driving down there, I had the first test of my quest. I was on this isolated beat-up road that you're not even supposed to be on with a rental car, and the sun was straight above me. What had started out as a calm day on this side of the island suddenly turned fiercely gusty. The channel between Maui and the big island of Hawaii runs very deep, and the ocean can really move through it. I could see squalls a quarter mile in diameter moving out over the water, and, in the distance, the island of Hawaii. I stopped the car and got out to photograph it, and the wind hit me, knocking me to the ground.

By this point, I'd had enough of the wind. I got up and walked out to the edge of the cliff, and said, "Okay, give me your best shot," and leaned out, letting the wind hold me up. And the wind just washed me clean. It swept away all the foulness that had built up on me, spiritually and physically, from the push-and-pull of my life. I could feel the energy in the air, and myself being replenished. When I got to Dennis's place that evening, I was ready to walk in Tarzan's path.

Dennis even looks like Tarzan. He's not a big, bulky guy; in fact he's really lean and lithe—but strong. He lived in a little house, with a gazebo for a bedroom, and an incredible beach below. Not a sandy beach, but round stones pressed together and tough to walk on. Dennis had come there with a sleeping bag in the Seventies, after serving with the Navy in Vietnam. Now all kinds of people showed up at his doorstep, including me, and probably all of them had the same fantasy of going native.

In the morning, after we had our coffee and papaya, and tuned in to what there was to hear and see and smell all around us, we set off for the natural pools. Running and jogging along, I could feel dormant states of mind, as well as all the little muscles, springing to life.

Just beyond the ruins of a Hawaiian village from the last century, we arrived at the entrance to the Haleakala National Park, where the Seven Sacred Pools are located. There are actually hundreds of pools and waterfalls between Hana and Kipahulu—all of them sacred, in my opinion—and Dennis knew every one of them. The test was to see how far up this body of living water—*from the clouds to you in an hour or two*—I could go before I begged off.

Mastery meant not only being able to navigate the current in the pool, and quickly learning where all the toe holds and traps were, but remembering to monitor what was happening up on the mountain as well. It had been raining all night, so the pools were really pumping. The danger was that the water level would rise too fast and catch you unaware and too tired to respond decisively. If you lost track of what was happening for even fifteen minutes, it could be fatal.

Watching Dennis, I learned all the moves to make and followed along. You'd jump in, swim under the waterfall, then find your footing on some underwater ledge so that you could stand under the waterfall and let it beat down on you. That is such a fantastic feeling. In tandem we progressed from pool to pool through the afternoon, but the current had been strong all day, and I finally became exhausted. I watched Dennis go into a pool where the water was really pumping hard and I started swimming after him, but halfway there I realized I couldn't do it. I had to beg off. It was the first time in my life that I came face to face with something I couldn't complete. Dennis, good teacher that he was, didn't try to persuade me otherwise. I'd sort of known how out of shape I was, but coming face to face with the physical reality like that was disappointing. I needed another good night's sleep, I told myself.

We had another night out under the stars. Dennis cooked dinner. We talked about all the things we cared about. We watched the Southern Cross rise in the night sky. In the morning, refreshed and confident, I followed Dennis as he retraced our path to the pools. I was already anticipating the feel of the waterfalls on my back. But to my chagrin the first place where we jumped in had a stronger current under the surface of the water than I realized and I found myself being pulled down into a vortex, drowning. Dennis had to grab me before I went under and pull me back to the other side of the waterfall. It was just an instant of disarray, but it was near deadly and it took me half an hour to pull myself together again. So much for my long-lived sense of feeling physically omnipotent. Being Tarzan was more difficult than I thought.

That experience of nature, as radical an immersion as it might have been, is what I needed to center myself again. There was a letting go; but more, there was renewal. I failed Dennis's test, but gained a world. In fact, when I later returned to Kipahulu, I'd regained my form and passed Dennis's trials handily, if not with Tarzan-like abandon. But my first test, my immersion in the power of nature, showed me that I'd lost touch with the deeper springs of life. Being reminded of them was a step in the right direction. I had forgotten what it was I was singing about, and being reminded of it gave me something new to hold on to.

THE WANDERING
SOUL:
IN TRANSITION

There is a longing deep within the wandering soul
It's like the half that understands it once was whole
Like the two who only dream of being one
Like the moon whose only light is in the sun

A t fifty, a man ought to at least have begun figuring out how to use what he knows; I may be just at that point. He ought to know who his gods are, if he has any, and what's in his heart. He ought to know something about the qualities of the place where he lives—climate, geography, history, as well as the character of its sands and flowers, and the condition of knowledge within its borders. And he ought to be able to nurture who and what's around him, and in turn be nurtured by them. We learn in the presence of other generations. The old need to teach the young and the young need to teach the old.

Michio Kushi once said, "When we have grown blind to wholeness and can no longer see every process as a balanced cycle, when we can't remember a clear dream of the future, we resort to expediency. Through fear we have changed the surface of the earth, striving to ensure a good harvest; the cause of fear is lack of faith."

Faith is a kind of knowing; it is different from hope. My faith is that life is purposeful; of that I'm sure. There is a god, there is intelligence, there is consciousness. And behind all of this, there is incredible compassion. Life didn't just happen. Relationships don't just happen. We're not an accident in the midst of a lifeless universe. I've not yet found a way to express my faith within the form of religious observance, but I know that my faith is what I stand on, what I'm going for.

Although I'm no less distressed about the Earth's needs than when I was younger, I see more clearly now what I can do about it, and I see that it needs doing as I live my life, daily, reverently. This isn't the reverence of "holier than thou," it's the reverence that says, "Do thyself no harm, for we are all here together." Not you *or* me, but you and me.

I still go on the road to do concerts. I'm still going to Hawaii when I need out, and to Alaska when I need in. I'm still performing concerts for the Australians, and still trying to learn the right way to do them for the Chinese, not to mention points on the map in between.

When the world of the Pacific Rim gets to redefine itself on the basis of its commonalities and interdependencies, I'm going to be there with them, mixing my American virtues, such as they are, into the common pot, and redefining myself in turn.

I'm still full of energy for the territory ahead, but at the same time still homeward bound—those are the polar opposites between which my spirit wanders. Despite my known protestations to the contrary, I've learned that home is where the heart is, beyond categories.

I can't remember when life felt more divisive, or when there'd been such a depression in the market where possibilities are traded. I think that's the effect of the Reagan years. A recent page-one story in *The New York Times* was filled with the unctuous remarks of elected and corporate officials who feel we've "overspent on environmental issues," or that "the money spent was misplaced," or that "the problems weren't as great as we thought," or that "the problem affects rats and mice, but it's not clear how it affects humans." I'd argue with some of those notions, but the point is, more importantly, as a society we spent only superficially on the environment—and we were spending money on everything else. That's the real cynicism of the age.

The more thoughtful industrial societies, if one can characterize any as such, are beginning to see environmental issues from a global perspective, and that's to the good. Japan is a case in point. They have had an environmental ministry for a while, but it's always had more to do with maintaining appearances; the environmental minister didn't have any real clout. Now that's in the process of changing, as far as I can tell, because they see the environmental problems unfolding everywhere in the world.

The Chinese are going the same route. China has the worst environmental problems in the world right now because of the enormous growth and development that's taken place there in a very short time. Everything they do to support that growth has environmental repercussions around the world. At the policy level they couldn't care less, but despite claims to the contrary, they are affected by world opinion. They're trying to present themselves in world forums as responsible caretakers of their part of the planet. The problem there is finding a balance between what China needs economically and what we all need biogenetically.

For example, there is a massive dam-building program

planned for the three gorges on the Yangtze River to control the flooding that causes millions of dollars in damage every year. The floods hurt people and put them out of work; the dams will produce the hydroelectric power that China's industrial revolution will need when it's running at high speed—when everyone has their own refrigerators and television sets. It's a logical progression.

On the other hand, every one of those floods deposits rich silt over an enormous amount of land and helps it produce crops. By controlling the floods, you diminish the long-term productivity of the land. Moreover, there's a genetic effect that doesn't show up for a long period of time. How do you balance those competing concerns? If China were left to decide for itself, it would probably decline even to grapple with this issue, but it too doesn't want to be seen as less than responsive to global concerns.

The Chinese are sponsoring an enormous tree-planting program, but at the same time are still selling a tremendous amount of timber and forest land in the northeast section of their country. We'll soon see the shortage of woodlands becoming more serious in the former territories of the Soviet Union, too. Big projects are underfoot to farm the old growth forests of Siberia that nobody's ever touched. The same thing will be done there that has been done to the rain forests in North, South, and Central America.

In part all of this is happening because people go out and try to create a life for themselves. They see it as their right to be able to go out wherever they want and farm the land without regard for the local ecology. At the turn of the century we in the United States imposed ourselves that way on Latin America, defending the interests of large-scale agricultural investments and their "right" to ultimately destroy whole ways of life. But the soil that supported the rain forest doesn't support intensive monoculture farming.

The more cattle you run in, the more the land erodes.

When we have grown blind to wholeness and can no longer see every process as a balanced cycle, when we can't remember a clear dream of the future, we resort to expediency. Through fear we have changed the surface of the earth.

At any rate, we are less ignorant than we were. We have witnessed the continued and apparently inexorable impoverishment of most Africans, for example. Either we don't know what to do about this or, if we do know, we do nothing to reverse it. But we've isolated some of the physical and political causes: the destructive insistence on export crops; the hopeless imbalance deriving from terms of trade that move, more often than not, against the interests of the producers; the scourges of war and famine.

We are only now starting to consider the psychology of dispossession, to do more than merely report sadly on miseries and massacres, to perceive how these pathologies may be eliminated. More people are becoming aware of the *need* to understand the dispossessed. It is possible that we are getting beyond the stereotypes of "us or them."

It is also heartening to see more and more people trying to grow psychologically, trying to develop their self-understanding, and looking again at their relationship to the Earth. More of us are coming to see that you can't love yourself without loving the Earth. You can't be in a relationship with another unless you are in a relationship with your mother. When you poison the ocean, and you poison a cloud, and you poison the rain, and you poison the cells in your body, you poison your womb and you poison the child who was carried there. It's to increase the awareness of these problems that I've worked and that I still work, while I try to live my life, difficult as both sometimes seem.

My friend and sometime songwriting collaborator Joe Henry says that the only thing you can do in this life is nurture your own flame and keep it from going out. It's not your job, he says, to be taking that flame and spending it everywhere. People who need that light are going to come and get it if you're being true to yourself, keeping your candle bright. He tells me I'm spending too much time out there, trying to encourage change, when, he says, I should be staying at home taking care of myself. I say he contradicts himself by how much time and energy he spends writing and putting it out there and demanding that he get credit for what he writes. You cannot light someone else's lamp, Joe claims. I try to do just that. Silently we lock horns on this fine point and push against each other's hard places, neither of us giving ground. But sometimes I am almost persuaded. It's getting cold, a voice inside me says; and it's only going to get colder. At such times a big part of me surfaces that would rather go fishing, that would find it easier to close myself off from the difficulties around me. Maybe I'm not the person I thought I was. What's more important than my life and how I choose to live it, how I choose to give it?

For a long time, my greatest fear was that I'd do something that would negate the impact of my music in people's lives. I used to be afraid, for example, that people would find out I smoked marijuana, or that I'd used cocaine. I used to be afraid, too, that somebody would find out that I was unfaithful to my wife. I didn't want anyone to know that there was someplace where I was being dishonest with myself, and by extension with the world out there—where I could get caught, and risk having my music rejected because of it. I'm less inclined to worry about that now, but the thought still gives me pause. It still gives me my deepest pleasure to know that songs I've written reach out and touch people all over the world, about whose lives I know little but care very much.

Is the music my life? Certainly it is the music that has given rise to all of the other aspects of my life that are meaningful on a larger scale, but I don't think the music is my life. I think my life is something more than that.

I sort of know who "John Denver" is and a lot of me is in this guy—the investment of a lifetime, in fact. But that's only part of who I am, and that's become clear to me in the last couple of years. I've learned to step back from all the hoopla, to get back to myself. That means sitting down and finding out where I am and what resources I really do have available; it means being realistic about what I can't do, and how I want to spend the rest of my life. Doing this only deepens for me the sense that there's a whole lot here that I seem to have completely lost touch with, and about that I'm really sad. I'm a little afraid of facing up to it.

Just to have a peaceful, quiet evening at home, to sit by a fire and read a book like an ordinary person, is already asking a lot. My dilemma is epitomized by all the piles of stuff around the house—there's stuff everywhere, and I don't know what's important to me, so I keep it all. When it comes to matters of the mind, I've not been able to focus on any one thing for more than the length of a football game, and even then I find myself getting up to check on something over here, and doing something over there, and not getting anything done.

♦   ♦   ♦

Cassandra and I did stay in Aspen, and matters grew worse before they got better. Before our short-lived marriage ended in divorce, she managed to make a fool of me from one end of the valley to the other, although I must say there is a great tolerance in Aspen for the kind of fool I've been. Being a fool for love is one of the legitimate conditions to suffer from here. Most of the folks I know have either been there themselves or have close friends and relatives who have.

The day before I served Cassandra with court papers a shaman in Santa Fe named Sandy Ingerman helped me work through the vulnerability I was feeling. Shamans are our oldest priests—intermediaries between worlds. Mine was one who calls herself a soul-retriever.

I had read a fair bit about soul-retrieving in a book, *Healing Your Aloneness,* by a woman named Marjorie Paul. She sees soul-retrieving as part of a broader discussion. Her contention is that when things happen in your life that you can't integrate at the time—either because you can't accept it, or understand it, or participate in the experience—the part of you that's traumatized leaves. It goes out into the ether to a safer place, and waits there to be retrieved. In this context, the process of healing is about making that part of you more real to yourself. The idea is akin to one John Bradshaw espouses about getting in touch with the "inner child," except that Marjorie Paul makes the point that before you can get in touch, you must bond with your inner self. Sandy says you need to retrieve the part that's missing.

It's a curious process to undergo. I can't say what it requires in the way of active involvement to bring off, except perhaps to stretch out on the floor and relax alongside the shaman as she makes the shaman's journey. This shaman put herself in a trance, and "transported" herself to some inner realm, looking for my errant selves. *Is Henry John Deutschendorf Jr. out there? Is he ready to be retrieved? Would he like to come home?* In her trance, which might have lasted all of twenty minutes, the shaman I worked with found three parts of me that had been missing.

She found a part of me that had left at age three because my parents didn't *get me* when I needed them. They loved me, they were as good and true as parents could possibly be, better than most in a lot of ways, but Dad was focused on his career and Mom was all emotional and high-strung, and committed to being the perfect Air Force wife for my dad. In their preoccupations they didn't understand that I needed *rescuing.* Not only do I lack memories from that period, but when I look at the photographs taken of me then, I don't even recognize myself. No longer able to survive in that environment, I had by then already split, metaphorically speaking, into the two who dream of being one.

Another part of me that my shaman returned with came from when I was five, just before Ron was born. Therein lies the tale of all brothers but the lucky few. That's when I was finally abandoned and had to fend for myself, or so I felt. One day I'll have to come to terms with this; I haven't yet.

The third part was from when I was about seventeen and ran away from home. Coming to terms with the Henry John Deutschendorf Jr. of 1960, and then integrating him into this ongoing life of mine, is going to be a major lesson in living all on its own.

Lying beside my shaman, I could feel my whole body flush as she brought all of these Henry John Deutschendorf Juniors in from the cold. *Henry John Deutschendorf Jr., are you willing to be retrieved now?* They apparently were.

How was I to tell that this had happened? I asked in all innocence.

In the next few weeks, she said, pay attention to yourself and notice if you feel differently, and how you feel differently.

How will I feel? I asked.

You might feel more like yourself, she said.

In third, fourth, and fifth grades, Skipper Gherkey and George Nuttycomb and I used to ride our bicycles in a triangular formation. We called ourselves the Triangle Gang; later the Blue Jeans Gang. When we played cowboys and Indians, I felt extreme discomfort pretending to shoot them. Even in pretend, the violence it implied left me feeling lonelier than childhood normally does. My first escape, as I wrote earlier, was climbing trees. Up those trees, swaying back and forth, I was the first man on Earth, dreaming about a place in the mountains, a sanctuary for the good and the true. Looking back on it now, I see that's where I began to build my faith.

On her shaman's journey, Sandy said she saw the light that was present at my birth. I don't know what that image is supposed to signify, but I like it. I think of each of us as having that light. Though the light may become diminished in the process of living—it gets congealed, enmeshed, obscured—the interesting thing is that it stays turned on until you take your dying breath. And perhaps even after that: I believe that light is where we come from and where we go to.

For a while, in the midst of the divorce from Cassie, Zak moved in with me: two guys bacheloring it, father and son. I was glad for the shared moments of intimacy—maybe moments of intimacy are all you get, anyway. Although I know he still has a few miles to go, there's a sense of completion in seeing him grown up and moving out into the world. Of course, no life is all clear sailing, even one as privileged as his. Driving home one winter night, he fell asleep at the wheel and totaled a car his mother and I had just given him as a gift; thankfully, he walked away uninjured. But when I got angry about his carelessness, it hurt his pride and he went back to Annie's place. Fortunately, we've gotten beyond it now. As intent as I am on my own struggles, I feel it's a great gift to be close to him as he tries to define himself. I try to be there in the same way for Anna Kate, although it's harder to do. Our time together tends to be confined to school holidays, and sometimes other obligations crowd out the space that's there for us, and we have to make do. Annie berates me for it, but that's how it has to be sometimes. Fortunately, Anna Kate is more forgiving, and an incredible young person. When we're together she teaches me more about what it is to be a woman than any woman I've ever known. It's interesting to be able to see the child in each of them still operating, like light coming up from within.

Jesse Belle, still so young, is, of course, more light than matter. She, too, tends to intersect with my life on holidays. She lives in L.A. with her mother now, and goes to nursery school, where she is learning lots of stories and songs, and when we ski together in Aspen, she regales me with one or another:

In the meadow, we can build a snowman,
And pretend that he is person Brown . . .

" 'Parson,' Jesse, 'Parson Brown,' " I say, ever the serious soul.

"Okay, Dad," she says blithely, as only little girls can, in the midst of all the tumult that the adults around her have created.

When our lives line up and we manage to be in the same place at the same time, the four of us—Zachary, Anna Kate, Jesse Belle, and me—are like the Animal Family: creatures of different kinds, learning to love one another, open to one another's differences.

What's painful about the present is that, in the process of integrating it, all that is settled seems to come undone again. In trying to integrate this latest failure of a marriage, with its betrayals large and small, I have to pass through the chamber where my betrayals of Annie reside, and even through the one where Annie's betrayals of me are warehoused, and all the attendant angers and resentments that are stored there, before I can reach home. When Annie first started seeing other people after our divorce, I was surprised that it hurt as much as it did. I got over it, but I wasn't prepared to experience that kind of hurt a second time or to find it hurting worse. Why did I have such a hard time, in matters of personal difficulty, facing the truth? It took those endless sessions of court testimony to make it clear to me that you believe whatever you want to believe, you hear what you want to hear, you see what you want to see— particularly in marriage. I think it's a real part of what is going on for me now to get past that. I would like to get to where I'm living a smaller, simpler life, be clear about what's going on around me, and know when it's my emotions dictating my feelings, and not the tumult of the outside world. The question is where does "outside" begin?

Where do I go from here? I think I go in the direction of art. Not art songs, but songs that have artistic intention. Art serves as a catalyst for us to see ourselves. It might be the art of Michelangelo's *David,* which puts you in touch with your own spirituality, or it might be hearing a song like "Seasons of the Heart" and recognizing that you never really let go of that woman you divorced some years ago. They work on different levels, but they have the same intention.

One's art isn't for everybody, but in front of art you can't help what comes to the surface—and what comes to the surface is you, who you really are. If the work moves you to tears, that's who you really are. You can play games all you want, and put on any face you want, but when confronted with a work of art, you're going to confront yourself, and you're most likely going to show yourself. If anybody's watching, they get to see who you are. That's the kind of catalyst I want to be. And I don't mind it on those occasions when I push people's buttons. It comes with the territory. There aren't too many people who are noncommittal about what I do, as far as I can tell. I either get it right, or get it a hundred and eighty degrees wrong. Either you like my work or you feel it doesn't mean anything. But it seldom evokes nothing. (In at least that one respect I'm being the catalytic agent I've aspired to be. It's happened that way with my songs, as well as with a lot of people with whom I've worked.) And sometimes it gets to a place where I have to move on.

Given the way I look at things, and work on them, and move through them, and try to be in my own process, you can't stay around me and not grow also. And if you stay around me long enough, you're going to come up against something that had your name on it from the beginning of time. Which is probably what happens out in the universe, anyway.

In all of this looking beyond the present moment to the next, I'm as determined as ever not to sell myself short, and part of that insistence is about pushing back against those who want to make me into a "country singer," and all the assumptions that go with that.

A couple of years ago, when I cut a record in Nashville, I had some interesting conversations on this subject with record company executives, trying to promote some recording possibilities for my work. The standard refrain was: "I don't know how to get people to listen to those songs, as good as they are, unless I can get more of your songs on the radio. And in order to do that I have to be able to show people your commitment to country music."

Well, I refuse to make that commitment. I'm not trying to be a country singer. For that matter, I'm not trying to be a rock 'n' roll singer, or a folksinger, or a pop singer. I'm a singer, and I'm a songwriter. I try to write songs lyrically in a way that people anywhere in the world can relate to them.

I don't sit down every day to write songs, and I never have. It's not my job to go to the office five days a week and work on songs. That's not what I do. I'm not a natural writer. "Annie's Song," "Rocky Mountain High," "Country Roads," "Sunshine on My Shoulders," "Back Home Again," and "Leaving on a Jet Plane" were not songs that flowed from the pen between nine and five. They were my nature expressed. They were experiences musically stated. They were my emotions being brought up out of being there and seeing it. And being there and seeing it, you write the song so that you are true to it. Like the song whose lines preface this chapter.

I'd gone to visit friends in Santa Fe, two very special and spiritual people, Beth and Charles Miller. We were up on top of their lodge watching the sunset, and when the sun went down, the sky was this incredible color. That's a very moving time to me. (In fact, I often point that out to Jesse Belle at night during her visits with me: the color of the sky when the sun goes down, when it's all snow, when it's all blue, when it's purple.) At the lodge we were conjuring up all the emotional states that time of day evokes in people—the fears, the wonder, the air of excitement—and then recalling all the people who had gathered at the lodge with us at one time or another in the past, searchers all, of one kind or another, and remembering again all the stories that had brought them there. Back in Aspen, a few days before, I had been playing around with the first couple of lines of a new song, and the conversation that night in Santa Fe somehow worked its way back into the song stream. The next morning I went off on a hike, and midway to where I was headed, the song I was trying to write just came to me, fell from the sky:

In this magic hour of softening light
The moments in between the day and the night
The instant when all shadows disappear
The distance in between the love and the fear
There is a longing deep within the wandering soul
It's like the half that understands it once was whole
Like the two who only dream of being one
Like the moon whose only light is in the sun

There's a danger in forever looking outside
You start to believe that all your prayers have been denied
You forget the sound of your own name
Thus begins the suffering and the pain.

I wanted an answer, I wanted a way
I wanted to know just what to do and what to say
I wanted a reason, I wanted to know why

Can there ever be heaven right here on Earth
  and peace inside
Inside my heart, deep in my soul
Within each part and within the whole?

There's a promise in the journeys of the mind
You begin to believe there are roots you will find
And that someday you will remember who you are
The seed within a bright and shining star
It's like the flame that lives within the hungering heart
That only awaits the gift of love for it to start
Into a fire that burns forever.

In this magic hour between the dark and the dawn
In the space between the silence and the song
Suddenly the mystery is clearer
That love is only letting go of fear
Love is the answer, and love is the way
Love is knowing just what to do and what to say

And love is the reason, and love is the way
And love is heaven right here on Earth and deep inside
Inside your heart, deep in your soul
Within each part and in the whole
Love is the answer, love is the way
Love is knowing just what to do and what to say

My voice is stronger these days and I think my wisdom, as such, is deeper. I feel my life evolving, even if not into higher forms. Sometimes I think of myself—or rather find myself, and often while onstage—as an embodiment of Saint George, who has come to slay the dragon. Other days—like during the divorce proceedings with Cassandra—it is the dragon who has come to slay me.

The formal proceedings surrounding the divorce made for a long, drawn-out affair, and it was very painful. I knew I had had it easy when Annie and I broke up, despite the tensions and turmoil I described earlier; these proceedings made it clear how true that was. A team of accountants and lawyers from Beverly Hills did all they could to rake me over the coals and upset me. There were days when I would lose control of my feelings and you could hear it in my voice. I needed to stand up not only for myself in relation to Cassandra, but for our child as well. While Jesse Belle's and my right to be in each other's lives was being worked out, and before I had the moral understanding to sort it all through for myself, I had to walk through a fire of feelings.

One night in Michigan not that long ago, while heading north after a show, our little caravan of vehicles pulled off to the side of the road to look in the night sky for a promised midsummer meteor shower. Earlier that evening, the band and I had performed at a fairground and it had been one of those rare occasions, which I've spoken of before, when I went onstage angry and came off angry because of all sorts of confusions beyond my control. Fortunately, one of my close friends, Malcolm McDonald, a medicine man in every sense of the word, was along on the tour and kept me from coiling back into myself. That I could sing at all that night was a minor miracle, and totally attributable to Malcolm's powers. But the greater miracle was the meteor shower. We poured out of tour bus and car, passed the libations around, and stood in witness like our forebears. We explained the phenomenon to a visitor who was touring with us, who came from a big city in the East where they hardly see stars, much less meteor showers. It was activity in the universe, I said, that we didn't always get to see, but that always goes on. Out of the darkness we were being reminded of creation, and of mystery. Even as we stood there, an obscure bunch of musicians listening to the silence sing, little tendrils of light were leaking down out of the darkness onto the earth. Life operates like that, I realized. It fades in and fades out in endless cycles of time turning. You reach a threshold of understanding and then you see what there is to see. If you're lucky, you find a circle of people who are going to bring you through these cyclical journeys with ever-deepening insight. That's the journey one's life makes possible.

Ten thousand years ago, I'm told, no one's social circle—one's community of kindred spirits—was larger than twenty. Beyond the circle, one's moral understanding went off into uncharted territory.

In the late fall of 1993, on the night after the final hearing in my divorce from Cassandra, I apparently celebrated a bit too much and was stopped by the local constabulary as I drove home. I feel that I was perfectly in control of my faculties, but that's another story; I was cited. It meant losing my right to drive for a couple of months and doing a certain amount of community service. Just before Christmas, Arthur, who is my collaborator on this book, came to Starwood to work with me, and one snowy night I enlisted him as my driver so that I could make good on both counts of the penance I was doing. Finding the words to teach him how to operate a four-wheel-drive stick-shift down a

mountain with sharp turns and steep dips, the higher elevations
of which were glazed over with iced-over snow, was a real test
of my powers of communication. My dad was great at teaching
flying. There are others who are great at teaching golf. Still
others who are great schoolteachers. The ability to teach always
signified a moral capacity to me. I talked Arthur through the
maneuvers and he managed flawlessly. He drove me down to
the old-age home on the edge of Aspen to sing at Christmas
dinner, and then to a hotel in town, where I performed with the
local high school chorus. I figured if I could do that for Arthur,
who was terrified of driving off the mountain at one of the
slippery turns, then despite all the pricks of conscience I was
fending off, there was hope for me yet.

On the road these days, it gets a little funny. I'm not a young
buck anymore—not that I ever was precisely that—but mentally
life has changed; certain possibilities exist no more. A three-
week stint with only one day off every five days drives me up the
wall. There are always eight thousand things to decide about. It
wasn't this tough when I was with the Mitchell Trio, even when
I started running things.

I'm starting to feel like my own man again, which isn't to say
that I was ever anyone's man in any strict sense, but I think I've
always wanted so much to be liked that I would go out of my way
to please people. That's one reason why I did so many benefits.
I would agree to do them less out of an expression of my commitment to whatever cause than out of my inability to say no and
let someone down. I can handle that differently now.

I'd even handle playing football differently. Now that I've become a dedicated golfer, I have a different sense of what it is to

learn to play a game and of being in the game. Before I used to be obsessively worried about being hurt. In fact I was probably plain scared. Now as I get to know myself better, and find the courage to be who I am and not some other, I approach everything in my life differently. If you're afraid of who you are, you continually deny the expression of your experience. Now I would just enjoy playing football. And every once in a while, I'll catch myself wishing I could throw a football around with Dad. There was nothing more fun for him and me than throwing passes.

So what has all of this amounted to, these past fifty years, half of a century? On what farther shore have I landed? Or is it a journey back to myself that I'm engaged on?

I find myself thinking so often of the words to "On the Wings of a Dream," which I wrote shortly after my father died.

> *Yesterday I had a dream about dying*
> *About laying to rest and then flying*
> *How the moment at hand*
> *Is the only thing we really own*
> *And I lay in my bed and I wonder*
> *After all has been said and is done for*
> *Why is it thus we are here*
> *And so soon we are gone*
>
> *Is this life just a path*
> *To the place that we all have come from*
> *Does the heart know the way*
> *And if not can it ever be found*
> *In a smile or a tear*
> *Or a prayer or a sigh or a song*

And if so then I sing for my father
And in truth you must know I would rather
He were here by my side
We could fly on the wings of a dream
To a place where the spirit could find us
And joy and surrender would bind us
We are one anyway
Anyway we are more than we seem

There are those who will lead us
Protect us each step of the way
From beginning to end
For each moment forever each day
Such a gift has been given
It can never be taken away

Though the body in passing must leave us
There is one who remains to receive us
There are those in this life
Who are friends from our heavenly home
So I listen to the voices inside me
For I know they are there just to guide me
And my faith will proclaim it is so
We are never alone

From the life to the light
From the dark of the night to the dawn
He is so in my heart
He is here he could never be gone

Though the singer is silent
There still is the truth of the song

Yesterday I had a dream about dying
About laying to rest and then flying
How the moment at hand
Is the only thing we really own

And I lay in my bed and I wonder
After all has been said and is done for
Why is it thus we are here
And soon we are gone
Why is it thus we are here
And so soon we are gone

I'm not home yet, but I'm getting there.

DISCOGRAPHY

Rhymes and Reasons
Released October 1969

SIDE ONE:

1. The Love of Common People
2. Catch Another Butterfly
*3. Daydream
4. The Ballad of Spiro Agnew
*5. Circus
6. When I'm Sixty-Four
7. The Ballad of Richard Nixon
*8. Rhymes and Reasons

SIDE TWO:

1. Yellow Cat
*2. Leaving on a Jet Plane
3. (You Dun Stomped) On My Heart
4. My Old Man
5. I Wish I Knew How It Would Feel to Be Free
6. Today Is the First Day of the Rest of My Life

Take Me to Tomorrow
Released May 1970

SIDE ONE:

*1. Take Me To Tomorrow
*2. Isabel
*3. Follow Me
4. Forest Lawn
*5. Aspenglow
6. Amsterdam

SIDE TWO:

*1. Anthem Revelation
*2. Sticky Summer Weather

* Composed by John Denver

3. Carolina in My Mind
4. Jimmy Newman
5. Molly

Whose Garden Was This?
Released October 1970

SIDE ONE:

1. Tremble If You Must
*2. Sail Away Home
3. The Night They Drove Old Dixie Down
4. Mr. Bojangles
*5. I Wish I Could Have Been There

SIDE TWO:

1. Whose Garden Was This?
2. The Game is Over
3. Eleanor Rigby
4. Old Folks
5. Medley: Golden Septembers; *Sweet Sweet Life; Tremble If You Must
6. Jingle Bells (adapted by John Denver)

Poems, Prayers and Promises
Released May 1971: Certified Platinum by RIAA

SIDE ONE:

*1. Poems, Prayers and Promises
2. Let It Be
*3. My Sweet Lady
*4. Wooden Indian
5. Junk
6. Gospel Changes

SIDE TWO:

*1. Take Me Home, Country Roads (Gold Single)
*2. I Guess He'd Rather Be in Colorado
*3. Sunshine on My Shoulders
4. Around and Around
5. Fire and Rain
6. The Box

Aerie
Released February 1972; Certified Gold by RIAA

SIDE ONE:

*1. Starwood in Aspen
2. Everyday
3. Casey's Last Ride
4. City of New Orleans
5. Friends with You
*6. 60-second song for a bank—"May We Help You Today?"

SIDE TWO:

1. Blow up Your TV
*2. All of My Memories
3. She Won't Let Me Fly Away
4. Readjustment Blues
*5. The Eagle and the Hawk
*6. Tools

Rocky Mountain High
Released September 1972: Certified Platinum by RIAA

SIDE ONE:

*1. Rocky Mountain High
2. Mother Nature's Son
3. Paradise

*4. For Baby (For Bobbie)
5. Darcy Farrow
*6. Prisoners

SIDE TWO:
*1. Goodbye Again
*2. Season Suite: Summer, Fall, Winter, Late Winter, Early Spring, Spring

Farewell Andromeda

Released June 1973: Certified Gold by RIAA

SIDE ONE:
*1. I'd Rather Be a Cowboy
2. Berkeley Woman
3. Please, Daddy
4. Angels from Montgomery
5. River of Love

SIDE TWO:
*1. Rocky Mountain Suite (Cold Nights in Canada)
*2. Whiskey Basin Blues
3. Sweet Misery
*4. Zachary and Jennifer
5. We Don't Live Here No More
*6. Farewell Andromeda (Welcome to My Morning)

John Denver's Greatest Hits

Released November 1973: Certified Platinum by RIAA

SIDE ONE:
*1. Take Me Home, Country Roads
*2. Follow Me
*3. Starwood in Aspen
*4. For Baby (For Bobbie)
*5. Rhymes and Reasons
*6. Leaving on a Jet Plane

SIDE TWO:
*1. The Eagle and the Hawk
*2. Sunshine on My Shoulders
*3. Goodbye Again
*4. Poems, Prayers and Promises
*5. Rocky Mountain High

Back Home Again

Released 1974; Certified Platinum by RIAA

SIDE ONE:
*1. Back Home Again
2. On the Road
3. Grandma's Feather Bed
*4. Matthew
5. Thank God I'm a Country Boy
*6. The Music Is You

SIDE TWO:
*1. Annie's Song
2. It's Up to You
*3. Cool an' Green an' Shady
*4. Eclipse
*5. Sweet Surrender
*6. This Old Guitar

An Evening with John Denver

Released February 1975

SIDE A:
*1. The Music Is You
*2. Farewell Andromeda (Welcome to My Morning)
3. Mother Nature's Son
*4. Summer
5. Today
6. Saturday Night in Toledo, Ohio

SIDE B:
*1. Matthew
*2. Rocky Mountain Suite: (Cold Nights in Canada)
*3. Sweet Surrender
*4. Grandma's Feather Bed
*5. Annie's Song
*6. The Eagle and the Hawk

SIDE C:
*1. My Sweet Lady
*2. Annie's Other Song
3. Boy from the Country
*4. Rhymes and Reasons
5. Forest Lawn

SIDE D:
1. Pickin' the Sun Down
2. Thank God I'm a Country Boy
*3. Take Me Home, Country Roads
*4. Poems, Prayers and Promises
*5. Rocky Mountain High
6. This Old Guitar

Windsong

Released September 1975

SIDE A:
*1. Windsong
2. Cowboy's Delight
*3. Spirit
*4. Looking for Space
*5. Shipmates and Cheyenne
6. Late Nite Radio

SIDE B:
*1. Love Is Everywhere
*2. Two Shots
*3. I'm Sorry
*4. Fly Away
*5. Calypso
6. Song of Wyoming

Rocky Mountain Christmas

Released 1975

SIDE A:
*1. Aspenglow
2. The Christmas Song (Chestnuts Roasting on an Open Fire)
3. Rudolf the Red-Nosed Reindeer
4. Silver Bells
5. Please, Daddy (Don't Get Drunk This Christmas)
6. Christmas for Cowboys

SIDE B:
1. Away in a Manger
2. What Child Is This?
3. Coventry Carol
4. Oh Holy Night

5. Silent Night, Holy Night
*6. A Baby Just Like You

Spirit

Released August 1976

SIDE A:

*1. Come and Let Me Look in
    Your Eyes
2. Eli's Song
*3. Wrangell Mountain Song
*4. Hitchhiker
5. In a Grand Way
6. Polka Dots and
   Moonbeams

SIDE B:

*1. It Makes Me Giggle
2. Baby, You Look Good to
   Me Tonight
*3. Like a Sad Song
4. San Antonio Rose
*5. Pegasus
*6. The Wings that Fly Us
    Home

John Denver's Greatest Hits, Volume 2

Released March 1977

SIDE A:

*1. Annie's Song
*2. Farewell Andromeda
    (Welcome to My
    Morning)
*3. Fly Away
*4. Like a Sad Song
*5. Looking for Space
6. Thank God I'm a Country
   Boy

SIDE B:

1. Grandma's Feather Bed
*2. Back Home Again
*3. I'm Sorry
*4. My Sweet Lady
*5. Calypso
*6. This Old Guitar

I Want to Live

Released November 1977

SIDE A:

*1. How Can I Leave You
    Again
*2. Tradewinds
3. Bet On the Blues
*4. It Amazes Me
*5. To the Wild Country
6. Ripplin' Waters

SIDE B:

1. Thirsty Boots
2. Dearest Esmeralda
*3. Singing Skies and Dancing
    Waters
*4. I Want to Live
*5. Druthers

John Denver

Released January 1978

SIDE A:

*1. Downhill Stuff
2. Sweet Melinda
*3. What's on Your Mind
*4. Joseph and Joe
*5. Life Is So Good
6. Berkeley Woman

SIDE B:

1. Johnny B. Goode
*2. You're So Beautiful
3. Southwind
4. Garden Song
*5. Songs of . . .

A Christmas Together

Released October 1979:
John Denver and the Muppets

SIDE A:

1. Twelve Days of Christmas
2. Have Yourself a Merry
   Little Christmas
3. The Peace Carol
4. Christmas is Coming
*5. A Baby Just Like You
6. Deck the Halls
7. When the River Meets the
   Sea

SIDE B:

1. Little Saint Nick
2. Noel; Christmas Eve 1913
3. The Christmas Wish
4. Medley: *Alfie the
   Christmas Tree; Carol For
   a Christmas Tree; It's in
   Every One of Us
5. Silent Night, Holy Night
6. We Wish You a Merry
   Christmas

Autograph

Released February 1990

SIDE A:

*1. Dancing with the
    Mountains
2. The Mountain Song
3. How Mountain Girls Can
   Love
4. Song for the Life
5. The Ballad of St. Anne's
   Reel
*6. In My Heart

SIDE B:

*1. Wrangell Mountain Song
2. Whalebones and Crosses
*3. American Child
4. You Say that the Battle is
   Over
*5. Autograph

Some Days Are Diamonds

Released June 1981

SIDE A:

1. Some Days Are Diamonds
   (Some Days Are Stones)
2. Gravel on the Ground
3. San Francisco Mabel Joy
*4. Sleepin' Alone
5. Easy on Easy Street

SIDE B:

1. The Cowboy and the Lady
*2. Country Love
3. Till You Opened My Eyes
4. Wild Flowers in a Mason
   Jar
5. Boy from the Country

Seasons of the Heart

Released February 1982

SIDE A:

*1. Seasons of the Heart
*2. Opposite Tables
*3. Relatively Speaking
4. Dreams
5. Nothing But a Breeze
*6. What One Man Can Do

SIDE B:

*1. Shanghai Breezes
*2. Islands
*3. Heart to Heart
*4. Perhaps Love
*5. Children of the Universe

It's About Time

Released September 1983

SIDE A:

*1. Hold On Tightly
*2. Thought of You
*3. Somethin' About
*4. On the Wings of a Dream
*5. Flight

SIDE B:

*1. Falling Out of Love
*2. I Remember Romance
*3. Wild Montana Skies
*4. World Game
*5. It's About Time

Rocky Mountain Holiday

Released November 1983:
John Denver and The Muppets

SIDE A:

*1. Hey Old Pal
2. Grandma's Feather Bed
3. She'll Be Comin' Round the Mountain
4. Catch Another Butterfly
5. Down by the Old Mill Stream
*6. Durango Mountain Caballero
7. Gone Fishin'

SIDE B:

1. Medley: Tumbling Tumbleweeds; Happy Trails
*2. Poems, Prayers and Promises
3. Take 'em Away
4. Going Camping
5. Home on the Range
6. No One Like You

John Denver's Greatest Hits, Volume 3

Released November 1984

SIDE A:

*1. How Can I Leave You Again
2. Some Days Are Diamonds (Some Days Are Stones)
*3. Shanghai Breezes
*4. Seasons of the Heart
*5. Perhaps Love
*6. Love Again

SIDE B:

*1. Dancing with the Mountains
*2. Wild Montana Skies
*3. I Want to Live
*4. The Gold and Beyond
*5. Autograph

Dreamland Express

Released June 1985

SIDE A:

*1. Dreamland Express
2. Claudette
3. Gimme Your Love
4. Got My Heart Set on You
5. If Ever

SIDE B:

*1. The Harder They Fall
2. Don't Close Your Eyes Tonight
*3. A Wild Heart Looking for Home
4. I'm in the Mood to be Desired

*5. Trail of Tears
*6. African Sunrise

One World

Released June 1986

SIDE A:

*1. Love Is the Master
*2. Love Again
3. I Remember You
*4. Hey There, Mr. Lonely Heart
*5. Let Us Begin

SIDE B:

1. Along for the Ride ('56 T-Bird)
*2. I Can't Escape
*3. True Love Takes Time
*4. One World
*5. It's a Possibility
*6. Flying for Me

Higher Ground

Released September 1989 by Windstar Records

SIDE ONE:

*1. Higher Ground
2. Homegrown Tomatoes
*3. Whispering Jesse
*4. Never a Doubt
*5. Deal with the Ladies
*6. Sing Australia

SIDE TWO:

*1. A Country Girl in Paris
*2. For You
*3. All This Joy
*4. Falling Leaves (The Refugees)
*5. Bread and Roses
*6. Alaska and Me

Earth Songs

Released 1990 by Windstar Records

SIDE ONE:

*1. Windsong
*2. Rocky Mountain Suite (Cold Nights in Canada)

*3. Rocky Mountain High
*4. Sunshine on My Shoulders
*5. The Eagle and the Hawk
*6. Eclipse
7. The Flower that Shattered the Stone

SIDE TWO:

*1. Raven's Child
*2. Children of the Universe
*3. To the Wild Country
*4. American Child
*5. Calypso
*6. Islands
*7. Earth Day Every Day (Celebrate)

The Flower That Shattered the Stone

Released September 1990 by Windstar Records

SIDE ONE:

1. The Flower that Shattered the Stone
*2. Thanks to You
3. Postcard from Paris
4. High, Wide, and Handsome
*5. Eagles and Horses
6. A Little Further North

SIDE TWO:

*1. Raven's Child
*2. Ancient Rhymes

*3. The Gift You Are
4. I Watch You Sleeping
*5. Stonehaven Sunset
6. The Flower that Shattered the Stone (Reprise)

Christmas, Like a Lullaby

Released 1990 by Windstar Records

SIDE ONE:

*1. Christmas, Like a Lullaby
2. The First Noel
3. Away in a Manger
4. The Children of Bethlehem
5. Jingle Bells
6. White Christmas

SIDE TWO:

1. Marvelous Toy
2. Blue Christmas
3. Rudolph, the Red-Nosed Reindeer
4. Little Drummer Boy
5. Mary's Little Boy Child
6. The Christmas Song (Chestnuts Roasting on an Open Fire)
7. Have Yourself a Merry Little Christmas

Different Directions

Released September 1991 by Windstar Records

SIDE ONE:

1. Potter's Wheel
2. Ponies
*3. The Foxfire Suite: Spring is Alive; You Are . . . ; Whisper the Wind; Spring is Alive (Reprise)
4. Chained to the Wheel

SIDE TWO:

*1. Two Different Directions
2. Hold On to Me
3. The Chosen Ones
*4. Amazon (Let This Be a Voice)
5. Tenderly Calling

Collaborations:

"And So It Goes" with the Nitty Gritty Dirt Band, on *Will the Circle be Unbroken, Volume 2*

(Album of the Year, Country Music Award 1989)

"The Flower that Shattered the Stone" with Japanese recording artist Kosetsu Minami, 1990; Pony Canyon Records

CREDITS

INDEX

Made in the USA
Lexington, KY
19 October 2017